Teacher's Extended Edition

ATLAS
2

Learning-Centered Communication

David Nunan

with teacher's notes by Fran Byrnes

Heinle & Heinle Publishers
An International Thomson Publishing Company
Boston, MA 02116, U.S.A.

 The ITP logo is a trademark under license.

The publication of ATLAS was directed by the members of the Heinle & Heinle Global Innovations Publishing Team:

Elizabeth Holthaus, ESL Team Leader
David C. Lee, Editorial Director
John F. McHugh, Market Development Director
Lisa McLaughlin, Production Editor
Nancy Mann, Developmental Editor

Also participating in the publication of the program were:
Publisher: Stanley J. Galek
Assistant Editor: Kenneth Mattsson
Manufacturing Coordinator: Mary Beth Hennebury
Design and Production: Rollins Graphic Design and Production
Composition: Pre-Press Company

Copyright © 1995 by Heinle & Heinle Publishers

All rights reserved. No part of this publication may be reproduced or transmitted in any form or by any means, electronic or mechanical, including photocopying, recording, or any information storage and retrieval system, without permission in writing from the publisher.

Manufactured in the United States of America.

ISBN 0-8384-4094-0

Heinle & Heinle Publishers is an International Thomson Publishing Company

10 9 8 7 6 5 4 3

Preface

Atlas is a four-level ESL/EFL course for young adults and adults. Its learner-centered, task-based approach motivates learners and helps to create an active, communicative classroom.

Atlas develops the four language skills of listening, speaking, reading, and writing in a systematic and integrated fashion. Each level is designed to cover from 60 to 90 hours of classroom instruction. It can also be adapted for shorter or longer courses; suggestions for doing so are provided in the teacher's extended edition.

Each level of **Atlas** consists of the following components:

Student's Book The student's book contains 12 "core" units and 3 review units. Following the 15 units are "Communication Challenges," which provide extra communicative practice to conclude each unit. Grammar summaries for each unit appear at the end of the book, along with an irregular verb chart.

Teacher's Extended Edition The teacher's extended edition contains an introduction to the philosophy of the course, general guidelines for teaching with Atlas, detailed teaching suggestions for each unit, and extension activities. It also includes the tapescript and answer keys for the textbook and the workbook.

Teacher Tape The tapes contain spoken material for all of the listening activities in the student text.

Workbook The workbook provides practice and expansion of the vocabulary, structures, functions, and learning strategies in the student text.

Workbook Tape The workbook tape contains spoken material for all of the listening activities in the workbook.

Video The video, which contains lively, real-life material, provides reinforcement and expansion of the topics and functions found in the student text.

Assessment Package The assessment package will be available in 1995.

FEATURES	BENEFITS
Unit goals are explicitly stated at the beginning of each unit.	Awareness of goals helps students to focus their learning.
Listening and reading texts are derived from high-interest, authentic source material.	Naturalistic/realistic language prepares students for the language they will encounter outside the classroom.
Each unit is built around two task chains, sequences of tasks that are linked together in principled ways and in which succeeding tasks are built on those that come before.	Task chains enhance student interest and motivation by providing students with integrated learning experiences.
Units feature explicit focus on learning strategies.	Conscious development of a range of learning strategies helps students become more effective learners both in and out of class.
End-of-unit Self-Check section encourages students to record and reflect on what they have learned.	Developing personal records of achievement increases student confidence and motivation.

Table of Contents

Unit		Page	Topics	Language Focus Functions
1	**New People**	9	- physical description - personal information - greetings - introductions - occupations	- exchanging personal information - introducing yourself and others - giving physical descriptions
2	**Meet the Family**	17	- families - occupations - ages	- asking and telling about families - talking about what people do
3	**Old Friends**	25	- friends - personal qualities - occupations - relationships - social networks	- saying what someone is like - asking for information about other people
4	**Interesting People**	33	- descriptions - art - occupations - entertainment	- discussing occupations and people - talking about likes and dislikes - asking about and describing paintings
5	**Review**	41		
6	**A Place to Stay**	43	- accommodation - hotels - housing - furniture - prices	- asking for permission - making requests - talking about ability - talking about quantity
7	**In My Neighborhood**	51	- location - services - maps - activities	- talking about where things are located - saying what people are doing - discussing advantages and disadvantages - identifying problems and solutions

Language Focus Structures	Learning Strategies	Communication Challenges
- statements and yes/no questions with *to be* - *wh* questions: *what* and *where* + *to be* - subject pronouns - possessive adjectives	- classifying* - selective listening - inferencing - scanning - personalizing - practicing	- information gap: listening
- statements and yes/no questions with *do/does* - *wh* questions with *do/does*	- predicting* - scanning - selective listening - personalizing - practicing	- describing families
- present-tense questions with *do/does:* a review - *wh* questions: *who* + *do/does*	- selective listening - personalizing - brainstorming* - scanning - practicing	- information gap: reading postcards
- simple present with *like* - adjectives	- classifying - personalizing - brainstorming - selective listening* - scanning - practicing	- information gap: matching descriptions and photographs
- modal: *can* - How much? How many?	- personalizing* - scanning - selective listening - brainstorming	- information gap: listening, reading, and writing—finding the best place for Teresa to live
- prepositions: *on, next to, near* - present progressive for actions in progress	- classifying - cooperating - scanning* - selective listening	- information gap: finding where services are located

* The asterisked Learning Strategies are explicitly taught in the unit. The others are used passively.

Unit		Page	Topics	Language Focus Functions
8	New York, New York	59	- sightseeing - suggestions - plans - entertainment - location	- asking about and describing locations of places - making, accepting, and rejecting suggestions - giving reasons
9	Going Places	67	- climate - weather - temperature	- talking about the weather/climate - asking for and giving opinions and advice - saying how often something happens
10	Review	75		
11	Time Out	77	- hobbies - leisure - the past - entertainment - the weekend	- discussing hobbies and leisure activities - asking and talking about past events - describing a sequence of events
12	That's Entertainment	85	- entertainment - plans - opinions	- talking about entertainment plans - expressing opinions about entertainment
13	Healthy Living	93	- health - exercise - sports - diet - habits	- talking about past experiences - talking about how often things happen - describing sports - asking about habits

Table of Contents

Language Focus Structures	Learning Strategies	Communication Challenges
- making suggestions with *Why don't you . . . ?* - *there is/there are* and *one, any, some*	- memorizing conversational patterns* - classifying - selective listening - practicing - scanning - cooperating - personalizing	- listening and speaking: touring and tracing the route
- adverbs of frequency - modal: *should*	- scanning - cooperating* - selective listening - personalizing - inferencing - practicing	- information gap: reading about foreign cities
- simple past: statements and yes/no questions - simple past: connecting words and *wh* questions	- brainstorming - personalizing - selective listening - discovering* - practicing - cooperating	- information gap: talking about popular weekend activities
- present progressive for planned future - intensifiers: *too, fairly, pretty, very*	- brainstorming - personalizing - selective listening - practicing* - discovering	- making suggestions about entertainment and leisure activities
- present perfect and *Have you ever . . . ?* - time expressions and *How often . . . ?*	- personalizing - classifying - selective listening - inferencing - scanning - role-playing*	- role-playing: scenes at a health club

* The asterisked Learning Strategies are explicitly taught in the unit. The others are used passively.

Table of Contents

Unit		Page	Topics	Language Focus Functions
14	A Day in the Life	**101**	- lifestyles - comparisons - advice - obligations	- making comparisons - asking for and giving advice - expressing obligation
15	Review	**109**		

Communication Challenges	**111**
Grammar Summaries	**129**
Credits	**135**
Irregular Verb Chart	**136**

Student Tapescript	**137**
Atlas Workbook 2: Answers	**155**
Atlas Workbook 2: Tapescript	**167**

Language Focus Structures	Learning Strategies	Communication Challenges
- comparisons with adjectives - modals: *have to, should, could*	- brainstorming - selective listening - scanning - cooperating - skimming* - practicing	- information gap: talking about jobs

* The asterisked Learning Strategy is explicitly taught in the unit. The others are used passively.

Introduction

Atlas is a four-level ESL/EFL course for young adults and adults. Its learner-centered, task-based approach motivates learners and helps to create an active, communicative classroom.

Atlas represents an important step forward in language learning material. In **Atlas** topics, tasks, grammar, pronunciation, vocabulary, functions, notions, and learning-how-to-learn are all integrated. It is a complete teaching resource that can be used in a wide range of teaching situations. At the same time, it provides teachers with a unique opportunity to enhance and further develop their own classroom teaching skills.

Atlas can be used with existing curricula, courses, and methodologies. In addition, for those teachers who wish to explore new classroom approaches and techniques, this **Atlas** Teacher's Extended Edition offers a range of Optional activities and Variations on standard tasks, with explanations and comments.

Each book in the **Atlas** series is designed for a particular level of learner. Book 1 is for beginners, Book 2 is for high beginning learners or false beginners, Book 3 is for intermediate level learners, and Book 4 is for high intermediate learners. Each level of **Atlas** is designed to cover between 60–90 hours of classroom instruction.

In **Atlas**, students learn by using language creatively rather than by simply memorizing and reproducing it. Each unit is built on a task-based syllabus with a specific functional and grammatical focus and a relevant, contemporary, topical orientation. The topics, chosen to facilitate interesting and challenging communication, come from science and technology and popular culture as well as from everyday functional areas of communication.

This Book

Book 2 is for high beginning learners. Some students may have already completed Book 1 before they begin Book 2. However, this is not necessary; intermediate level students may begin with Book 2. Some of the themes and language points dealt with in Book 1 are reintroduced in more challenging ways in Book 2.

Course Components

Each level of this course consists of the following components:

- student's book
- teacher tape
- workbook
- workbook tape
- teacher's extended edition
- video
- assessment package

Approach

Atlas is unique in the following ways:

1. Atlas is learner-centered

Atlas focuses on helping learners to develop strategies that will help them learn. Developing strategies for learning a language is just as important as learning specific language items, and **Atlas** actively involves learners in the process of learning how to learn. It does this in a number of ways:

- goals and objectives are clearly explained to the learner;
- learners are involved in actively communicating with each other and with the teacher;
- as well as learning language, learners are taught about the learning process through a focus on learning strategies;
- learners are involved in making choices about their learning: choices about tasks, content, and the direction of the learning;
- learners are involved in monitoring their own progress;
- learners are encouraged to explore ways of learning that work for them;
- learners are given opportunities to predict, interpret, and make deductions from general to specific.

In addition, **Atlas** makes learning more meaningful by encouraging students to relate the material to their own knowledge and experience.

The following table shows the learning strategies that are presented in this course.

2. Atlas Uses a Task-Based Approach

Recent second language acquisition research shows that communicative interaction in the target language is very important for language

TASK TYPE	DEFINITION / EXAMPLE
CLASSIFYING	Putting things that are similar together in groups *Example: Study a list of proper names and classify them into male and female.*
PREDICTING	Predicting what is to come in the learning process *Example: Look at unit title and objectives and predict what will be learned.*
BRAINSTORMING	Thinking of as many new words and ideas as one can. *Example: Work in a group and think of as many occupations as you can.*
SELECTIVE LISTENING	Listening for key words and information without trying to understand every word. *Example: Listen to a conversation and decide where the people are.*
PERSONALIZING	Learners share their own opinions, feelings, and ideas about a subject. *Example: Read a letter from a person in trouble, and say what you would do.*
SCANNING	Looking quickly through a written text for specific information *Example: Look at the text and decide if it is a newspaper article, a letter, or an advertisement.*
CONVERSATIONAL PATTERNS	Using expressions to start conversations and keep them going *Example: Match formulaic expressions to situations.*
COOPERATING	Sharing ideas and learning with other students. *Example: Work in small groups to read a text and complete a table.*
DISCOVERING	Looking for patterns in language. *Example: Study a conversation and discover the rule for forming the simple past tense.*
PRACTICING	Doing controlled exercises to improve knowledge and skills. *Example: Listen to a conversation, and practice it with a partner.*
ROLE-PLAYING	Pretending to be somebody else and using the language for the situation you are in. *Example: You are a reporter. Use the information from the reading to interview the writer.*

development. **Atlas** uses communication and learning tasks as the central building blocks in the curriculum, and the tasks are linked to the overall goals and objectives of the course.

Each unit contains two "task chains," in which succeeding tasks draw on and exploit the tasks that have come before. The advantage of task chains is that new learning builds on what learners already know. This is an essential element in successful learning. In **Atlas,** each new task gives learners the chance to practice language they have learned in earlier tasks and to build on and extend this.

3. Atlas Uses Authentic Data

Another important feature of the **Atlas** series is the use of authentic and simulated data. By "authentic data" we mean any language (spoken or written) that has not been specifically produced for the purposes of language instruction. We have included authentic and simulated texts because specially written texts and dialogues do not, by themselves, adequately prepare learners for the kinds of language they will meet outside the language learning situation. **Atlas** provides learners with opportunities to work with authentic texts. The simulated texts and dialogues have been developed with reference to authentic texts and genuine communicative contexts and reflect these as closely as possible.

4. Atlas Takes a Communicative Approach to Teaching Grammar and Discourse

Atlas takes an organic approach to grammar rather than a linear one. A linear view of language acquisition assumes that learners learn one thing perfectly, before moving to the next—i.e. the learner masters item a, then item b, then item c, and so on. **Atlas** presents a different view of language acquisition. We have followed recent second language acquisition research which shows that learners acquire a number of features all at once, imperfectly. Learning is organic rather than linear, and language grows in the same way as a flower grows, and not step by step in the way that a wall is built.

Because grammar is critical in developing communicative skills, **Atlas** introduces grammar tasks within real communication contexts. The grammar tasks are also designed to involve the learners in actively thinking about how English works. Learners are not given grammar rules to memorize and apply, they are invited instead to use the examples and models in the material to recognize language patterns, and work out language rules for themselves.

5. Book Organization

The book is divided into fifteen units, each organized around a particular topic or theme, for example, Unit 1: New People, Unit 6: A Place to Stay, Unit 13: Healthy Living. Each unit includes a Warm-Up page with unit goals and introductory exercises, two Task Chains, two Language Focus pages, and a Self-Check page. Communication Challenge activities and grammar summaries for each unit are found at the back of the book. Units 5, 10, and 15 are review units that look back at the language covered in the previous four units.

6. General Teaching Strategies

Reading

Atlas presents a wide range of reading texts and includes tasks that involve different reading strategies.

Helping students to develop reading skills

Learners often feel that they must understand every word or their reading is not successful. This is not true. It is important to explain to students that there are many different ways of reading. How we read is determined by our purpose in reading. Sometimes we need to read texts very carefully and even slowly to make sure we have understood everything correctly. We read in detail like this when we read instructions for a new machine we want to use. But often we read just to get the main idea of the text, as in a magazine article or newspaper. This is called skimming. Or we read to find specific information and ignore the rest of the text. This is called scanning. We scan when we look up the TV program to find out what's on at 8 o'clock.

Atlas provides opportunities for students to skim and scan as well as to read for detailed information. In helping to develop reading strategies, you need to prepare them for what they are to read and why they are to read it. For example, are they to read for specific information? For details? For main ideas? They need to understand that the way we read something is determined by the kind of text it is—and by our purpose in reading it.

The goal of reading tasks is to help students understand some or all of the text. You can make comprehension easier for students if you prepare them for what they are going to read. Preparation tasks include brainstorming words and ideas linked to the text, discussing students' own experiences and knowledge, discussing possible contexts for the text, building up expectations of meaning, and so providing motivation to read. Learners are usually highly motivated to read each others' writing, and in **Atlas** there are many tasks where learners have the opportunity to do this.

Writing

Atlas presents a wide range of writing tasks that cover a variety of writing strategies.

Helping students to develop writing skills

Learners often feel stressed by writing tasks because they feel that they must write completely correct English at the first attempt. It is easier for students if the writing tasks are not individual tasks but are group or pair tasks, where two or more people work together to produce just one piece of writing. When the learners are producing their own written work, always allow time for them to write more than one draft. Let learners correct and revise, with your help, or by helping each other, so that the final draft is not the first draft. This enables students to learn from their own mistakes and relieves the pressure of producing a perfect piece of writing at the first attempt.

It is important to explain to students that, as with reading, there are many different ways of writing. How we write is determined by our reason for writing and by whom we are writing for. Sometimes we need to write rather formally, as in a business letter or job application, but often we write very informally or casually, as in notes, phone messages, or postcards, and this writing is much closer to spoken language.

You can make writing easier for students by always providing models of the kinds of texts you want the learners to produce. For example, if they are to write a postcard to a friend or a telephone message, or a business fax, show some examples of these, even if you have to produce these examples yourself. Talk about the features of the text, for example, whether the language is formal or friendly, or whether it has complete sentences or is abbreviated in places.

Listening

An important strategy in this course is selective listening. It is important to stress to students that, as with reading, it is not necessary to understand every word because at different times we listen in different ways and for different purposes. How we listen is determined by our reason for listening, by our knowledge of what we are listening to, and by what we are listening for. Sometimes we need to understand all, or almost all, of what we hear, but often we are only listening for part of what people are saying.

Helping students to develop listening skills You can make listening easier for students if you prepare them for what they are going to hear. Prediction tasks are a very important part of developing listening skills. Such tasks involve class discussion about what students are going to hear. This may involve predicting the topic or even predicting what people will actually say. Prediction tasks give students the chance to engage in a free exchange of ideas and so to listen to each other, but they also prepare students for what they will listen to. When we listen for something in particular, for example, to verify our own prediction, this raises our level of concentration and improves overall listening comprehension.

Many classroom listening tasks involve listening to recordings or videos, and **Atlas** provides these important resources. But do not let students ignore the fact that listening skills can also be developed whenever students listen to you or to each other—in class discussions and in pair or group work.

Listening and repeating is important for pronunciation and for grammatical awareness. Many tasks in **Atlas** engage students in repeating and practicing what they have heard.

Speaking

The speaking tasks in **Atlas** focus on a number of different speaking skills—discussions, interviews, surveys, role-plays, as well as practice and repeating tasks.

Each of the following activities focuses on speaking skills.

Left Margin model sentences and conversations set off in special type, have several purposes. They build confidence, they provide language models for some of the speaking tasks in the communication chains and challenges, and they give students an opportunity to improve their fluency and pronunciation.

Discussions The purpose of discussion tasks is to give students opportunities to practice talking about their own experiences, not necessarily for them to agree or disagree with the text or with each other. You may decide to set a time limit of only a few minutes for a discussion or allow it to continue for as long as students are interested and actively involved.

Discussions can be of two kinds. They can be very open, aimed at giving students the chance to air their views freely and to gain more confidence in speaking English. The focus is on the content of the discussion, that is, saying what one thinks and why, and exchanging ideas with others. Or they can be more controlled, focusing not only on what students think and say but also on how they say it, that is, giving attention to the use of correct language, both grammar and pronunciation.

Where possible, discussion tasks of either kind should give students opportunities to extend their thinking beyond what is familiar and known, so that they become aware of other ways of looking at the issue beyond what they already know and believe.

Pair work

Pair work tasks are designed to give learners a chance to exchange ideas and information, to compare thoughts and feelings about the learning, and to learn from each other. It is important that learners experience this important part of classroom learning and not feel that they can only learn from the teacher. Cooperating or sharing ideas with other students means learning together and is an important learning strategy. Many pair work tasks involve interviewing other individuals in the class, or carrying out surveys. The survey is a valuable task for practicing speaking, but, when doing surveys, many students concentrate on gathering information and do a minimum of talking. To make this a useful speaking exercise, mingle with the students during the activity and ensure that they ask the questions **in full** and **from memory**. They can refer to their survey form before asking each question, but they should ask the question without reading. Make sure the survey question is asked and answered orally. Do not allow the students to simply read and/or write on each other's papers. And make sure that students use the correct question forms.

Group work

One of the advantages of group learning is the opportunities it provides for learners to communicate with each other. Like pair work, group work is a way of giving learners a chance to express their thoughts freely and discuss the learning. Group work can be more focused if students are asked to concentrate on a specific question or issue. If class discussions are done in small groups rather than as a whole class more students have more opportunities to speak.

One important kind of group work is role-playing:

Role-plays involve pretending to be someone else and using language appropriate for a specific situation. Role-plays give opportunities for practicing language in a range of different contexts.

In all speaking tasks it is very important to give adequate time for learners to prepare for what they will have to say. Allow students time to practice the language structures or functions before they have to perform. Do not ask learners to use language before they have heard examples of what they are to say.

Class work

A number of the tasks in the course are designed as whole class activities. Brainstormng, often done as a whole class activity, is sharing as many thoughts and ideas as possible about a given topic. This is a good way for students to practice English, but it is also a good learning strategy because by hearing others' opinions, students can broaden their own views and learn about other ways of thinking.

Whole class activities make it possible to carry out more controlled discussion and are a most efficient way of giving all students information or instruction. Whole class activities are also particularly suitable for pre-task activities, to review previous learning, or to ascertain what learners already know.

Pronunciation

Pronunciation is an important part of communicative competence, and, like all language skills, it should be taught in context. Beyond a basic level, practicing discrete items of pronunciation such as minimal pair drill is not particularly effective for developing comprehensible pronunciation. However, it is important to provide students with contextualized pronunciation practice by focusing on pronunciation in the model dialogues that appear in most of the language focus sections of each unit. For these to be effective, it is important that you monitor and correct pronunciation, concentrating in particular on the stress, rhythm, and intonation.

Vocabulary

Increasing vocabulary is an important part of language learning, and each Unit in **Atlas** has a section where vocabulary is reviewed and extended. It is important for students to realize that all language learning involves encountering new vocabulary and that there are a number of strategies they can use when they come across words that they do not know.

Helping students to develop vocabulary skills

There are some important ways that learners can use to check how well they know a word. Here is a useful checklist.

1. Can you recognize the word when you hear it—what it sounds like?
2. Can you recognize the word when you see it—the spelling, what it looks like? This includes being able to distinguish it from similar words.
3. Can you recall its meaning?
4. Do you know more than one meaning for the word?
5. Do you know shades of meaning for the word when you find it in different contexts?
6. Do you know the grammatical patterns the word most often occurs in?
7. Do you know the limitations on using the word, according to function and situation?
8. Do you know which words are commonly found together with the word in English—what words it will collocate with?

Encourage your students to:

1. use their knowledge of language and the world to figure out meanings.
2. use the situation or context to make intelligent guesses about the meaning of new words.
3. use their own life experiences to help them work out the meaning of text and individual words.
4. use syntactic, semantic, and contextual clues to help them work out meanings of unknown words in a text.
5. use visual and other non-linguistic clues
6. use clues within words. Can they see other words or parts of a word within it? Prefix, suffix, root?
7. use information that has already gone before (in the conversation or in the text) to help construct meaning.
8. try to recall if they have heard/seen the word before. If so, where? In what context? Does it look like another word they know?
9. record vocabulary in a systematic way, a way that suits their own learning style and preferences.
10. use English-English dictionaries where possible rather than bilingual dictionaries.
11. use other learners and the teacher as a source of help.

Using dictionaries in class time should be avoided except when dealing with dictionary skills and strategies or where the task specifically requires it.

Review and Correction

There is a great deal of integration and recycling in the **Atlas** course. Learners have many opportunities to review and reprocess key language points in meaningful contexts. Many tasks allow for ongoing teacher correction while the students are working. Opportunities for teacher monitoring and correction are built into tasks in all the four skills—reading, writing, listening, and speaking. In addition, each unit has a self-checking section where learners can evaluate their progress, and there is a review unit after every four units.

Classroom management

Students learn in different ways, and to meet their different learning styles and strategies **Atlas** incorporates a range of different learning tasks, moving from individual work to pair and group work and back again from pair and group work to individual work to the whole class.

How Each Unit is Organized

> Unit Map
> Unit Goals
> Warm Up
> Task Chain 1
> Language Focus 1
> Task Chain 2
> Language Focus 2
> Self-Check
> Communication
>   Challenge
> Grammar Summary

Guidelines For Teaching A Unit

Unit Goals

The Unit Goals section gives teachers the chance to discuss learning goals with students. These goals provide learners with a sense of direction and progress in their learning. This is a very important part of learning, and the discussion at the beginning of each unit should include information about the topic and the kinds of tasks that students will work with in the unit. Each goal is followed by one or more sentences showing the goal in use.

Examples:

> In this unit, you will:
> **Exchange personal information**
> *"My name is Mike. What's your name?"*
> *"Where are you from?"*
> *"I'm from Tokyo."*
>
> **Describe yourself and other people**
> *"I'm twenty-three. I have dark hair."*
> *"Laura is fifty-five. She has green eyes."*
>
> **Introduce others**
> *"This is Yoko."*

You may choose to explain the grammar that students will practice in the unit.

Example:

> In this unit, you will:
> **Practice using the modal** *can*
> *"Can I smoke in here?"*
> *"Maria can speak five languages."*

You might also choose to talk about the kinds of texts that the students will work with in the Unit. If you choose to do this you should talk about both spoken and written texts.

Example:

> In this unit we will listen to friends talking together, read postcards from others, and write postcards to friends or family.
>
> In this unit you will listen to phone messages and read phone messages and faxes.

Warm-Up

The purpose of the warm-up section is to introduce students to some of the language patterns and vocabulary they will meet in the unit. It also provides an overview of the topics and content.

During the warm-up, and whenever possible in the unit, opportunities should be taken to relate the content of the unit to the students' own background knowledge and interests. This helps to motivate the students. Many warm-ups also contain model dialogues to provide students with initial fluency practice.

Task Chains

Each unit has two task chains, which are sequences of interrelated tasks.

The readings and listenings in the task chain present students with models of language and how it is used. Sometimes there are tasks that require students to use the language in the same way as it is used in the model.

In the Task Chains new learning builds on what learners already know. This is an essential part of successful learning. In **Atlas** each new task gives learners the chance to practice language they have learned in earlier tasks and to build on and extend this.

For example, in Unit 14, Task Chain 2, students are involved in asking for and giving advice. The chain evolves through the following tasks:

Task 1: Students read about advice columns in newspapers and predict what kind of advice they think that "Dear Deb" gives and what kind of people write to her.

Task 2: Students listen to four people talk about their problems. They identify the problems and the advice.

Task 3: Students match readers' letters with advice from a columnist in an advice column, and then discuss whether they agree with the advice.

Task 4: Students read another letter and discuss what advice to give.

Task 5: In pairs, students write their own letter to an advice column. They then exchange their letter with another pair and write an answer.

Some tasks in each unit are **optional.** These are an extra element to the primary task and you may choose not to do them if, for example, there is not time for more work at this point or if the task required learners to supply information or create language that has not been specifically dealt with in the unit.

There are also **Variation** Tasks in each Unit. These are alternative ways of doing the primary task, that is, you do the Variation task rather than the task as it is set out in the Student book. Teachers may choose not to do the Variation task, but those who do will need to explain to learners that this task is an alternate way of doing the learning activity and replaces the task in their book.

Variation tasks give teachers who wish to try new approaches or new teaching techniques a chance to do so and at the same time relate the new approach to the tasks in the student book, which represent techniques and methods that are more familiar.

You Choose

An important learning-how-to-learn feature in this course is teaching students to make choices. "You choose" gives opportunities for students to choose by presenting more than one task and having students select which of the tasks they want to do. At first these can be done as a whole class exercise until students become familiar with the concept and the practice of choosing for themselves.

Language Focus

The language focus sections analyse specific grammatical and functional points that have been presented in the preceding task chain, and include practice tasks for using the language in context. These sections allow you to strike a healthy balance between attention to form and function in language on the one hand and learner-centered communicative activities on the other.

Most language focus sections begin with a short dialogue or reading that reviews the language covered in the task chain. This allows students to refamiliarize themselves with the language to be practiced. Following the language model are several activities that range from controlled, cloze-type exercises to open-ended communicative tasks. You can choose to do the tasks in a different order than they are in the book. You may also omit exercises that you feel are not appropriate for your students.

The reason for placing each language focus after each task chain is that in this way learners are made familiar with the language in use before they begin to analyze it in detail and before they are required to use it themselves.

Alternative

Teachers sometimes prefer to present grammar before moving on to communicative tasks. This is a perfectly appropriate alternative. Or you may choose, just in certain units, to do the language focus work before involving learners in the communicative task chains.

Do You Know the Rule?

Occasionally you will find in this section a feature called "DO YOU KNOW THE RULE?" This feature is designed to help students to identify patterns in language and use these to figure out for themselves a language pattern or rule. Recognizing patterns and inducing rules is a more effective way of learning than simply memorizing rules.

Self-Check

The self-check sections are an important and integral part of the course. In this section learners are invited to review the unit. Self-monitoring and self-reflection are important aspects of learning how to learn and also help students to evaluate their progress.

Students first write down new words and structures they have learned. Some of these tasks can be done out of class and brought to the next lesson. If possible, students should do these tasks without looking back at the unit. Students then evaluate their progress. The self-evaluation tasks also serve to remind students of the goals of the unit. Finally, they are invited to reflect on ways in which they can improve their learning skills. They are helped in this by sample statements from other learners. As students progress through the book, the Self-Check becomes their own personalized learning journal.

Communication Challenge

At the end of each unit there is a reference to the unit's Communication Challenge with the page number(s) on which it will be found. The purpose of the Communication Challenge is to provide the learners with an opportunity to reinforce and practice language they have learned in the task chains. The Communication Challenge may be an information gap, a role-play, a guided discussion, or a problem-solving task.

Grammar Summaries

The grammar summaries, on pages 129 through 134, provide, for each unit, a quick review of the grammar taught in the unit. Consistent with the inductive approach to grammar in **Atlas,** they present examples, not rules, for the structures dealt with in the Language Focus sections of the unit. These can be especially valuable as reminders of what was taught in the unit and for additional practice. Call attention to them when you introduce the book to the students and when you assign the Self-Check pages at the end of each unit.

1 New People

Unit Goals

In this unit you will:

Exchange personal information

"My name is Mike. What's your name?"

"Where are you from?"

"I'm from Tokyo."

Describe yourself and other people

"I'm twenty-three. I have dark hair."

"Laura is fifty-five. She has green eyes."

Introduce others

"This is Yoko."

Warm-Up

1 Look at the picture. Where are these people? At school? At a party? At work? How do you know?

2 a  **Pair Work** Check [√] the words you both know.

☐ big ☐ old
☐ twenty ☐ tall
☐ elderly ☐ a beard
☐ eighteen ☐ dark eyes
☐ dark hair ☐ middle-aged
☐ a white beard ☐ blond hair
☐ short ☐ teenage
☐ young ☐ small
☐ twenty-three ☐ blue eyes

b Find words that describe the people in the picture. Write them down.

....

3 🎧 **Group Work** Listen. Then practice the conversation.

A: Hello. My name's Mike.
B: Pleased to meet you, Mike. I'm Yoko. This is Noriko.
C: Nice to meet you, Mike.
A: Nice to meet you, Noriko.

Work with another student. Introduce yourselves. Now introduce your partner to some other students.

New People 9

---

1 New People

📖 Student text page 9

Warm-Up

This section provides a context for the unit. It presents the language of introduction and words for describing yourself.

Unit Goals. Read aloud each goal and sample language. Ask students to circle those they can do in English. Ask a representative number of students for their responses. This way you can get an idea of the range in the group.

Learning Strategy. In each unit, students practice different learning strategies. Here, they are given explicit instruction and practice on one particular strategy—classifying.

1. Have the students work in pairs and make a list of the things in the picture that tell them where it was taken. **Variation.** Have students, working in pairs or small groups, make two lists: **i)** different reasons for having a party, and **ii)** what makes a good party and why. Groups then compare their ideas with other groups.

2. **(a)** Explain to students that the listed words are some of the key words they will need in the unit. In pairs have them check the words they know. Go through the list with the entire class. **Optional.** Have students look in the dictionary for words that neither of them knows. This could be assigned as homework and reviewed in the next lesson.

(b) Circulate as students choose words from the list. Answers will vary but should exclude, for example, *old, elderly, beard*.

3. 🎧 Have students listen to the conversation two or three times with books closed. Then, in groups of three, have students practice the conversation. Circulate and check pronunciation, particularly stress and intonation. In pairs, have students introduce one another and then introduce their partner to another pair.

New People 9

📖 Student text page 10–11

Task Chain 1: Giving personal information

Task 1. (a) Answer: airport. Students can tell because of name *Alitalia* and appearance of counter.

(b) 🎧 Have students listen and write the conversation number under each picture.
(Answers: top—2; center—1; bottom—3)

Optional. Ask students for the words/phrases that gave them the answers. **Optional.** Elicit what happened to Mike. (He left his bag in the restroom.)

Remind students that listening can be effective even when they don't understand every word. The first time they only have to listen for the answer words. **Optional.** If the tape is too fast, you can pause it at several points during the conversations.

Task 2. Have students check the words they know, and compare with others. **Optional.** Students fill out the form at the bottom of the page (name, address, etc.) with information that is true for them.

Task 3. 🎧 Play the tape one more time and have students fill out the form. You may play the tape several times. If the task seems too difficult, reproduce the form on the board or on an overhead and do it as a class activity. You can model the process by playing the first part of the tape and completing the first item. Have students compare their answers in pairs. After the form has been filled out, play the tape again and let students confirm their answers. (Point out that "city" and "state" are not mentioned on the tape but that students can get this from the form.)
(Answers: Name—Mike Frota; Address—24 Smith Street, San Francisco, California; Telephone—712-3847; Date of birth—November 11, 1975)

Task 4. (Page 11). Point out that, like listening, reading can be successful even if you do not understand every word.

Ask students to look through the post card and circle the words that describe people. Elicit responses from the entire class and write them on the board. (Answers: twenty, short, red, green, tall, dark, blue)

(Continued on page 11)

10 New People

Task Chain 1 Giving personal information

Conversation ....

Conversation ....

Conversation ....

Task 1
a Look at the people in the pictures. Where are they? In a train station? At an airport? How do you know?

b 🎧 Listen to conversations 1, 2, and 3. Write the number of each conversation under the picture that illustrates it.

c What happened to Mike's bag?

Task 2
a Check [√] the words or phrases you know. Compare your checklist with another student's list.

☐ Last name ☐ Telephone number
☐ First name ☐ Date of birth
☐ Address ☐ Occupation

b 🎧 Mike is talking to a police officer. Listen to the conversation. Look at the list above and circle the words you hear.

Task 3
🎧 Listen to the conversation again and then fill out the form below.

California State Police
San Francisco International Airport
Mon.–Fri. 10 a.m.–1 p.m. 2 p.m.–5 p.m.

Incident #: _____
Date: _____

Incident Report

Name: _____

Address: _____
         (Street)   (City)   (State)

Telephone: _____

Date of Birth: _____

Occupation: _____

Problem: black travel bag missing
_____

10 New People

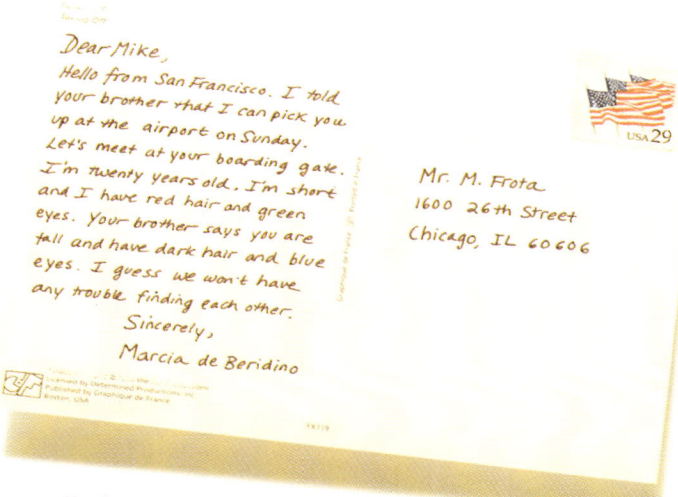

Task 4

Someone Mike does not know is meeting him at the airport. Read this postcard and circle the words that describe people.

Put the color, age, and size words from the postcard in the correct columns.

LEARNING STRATEGY
Classifying = putting similar things together in groups.

COLOR	AGE	SIZE

Task 5

"I'm twenty-one. I'm short and heavy. I have dark curly hair, blue eyes, and very big ears. My friends call me Shorty, but you can call me Dave."

Pair Work Now write some sentences about yourself. Exchange papers with your partner.

Task 6

Pair Work Marcia meets Mike and takes him to a party. Look at the photograph on page 9 and find Marcia and Mike.

Task 7

Group Work Discussion. Different cultures describe people in different ways. In North America, people use size, weight, eye and hair color, age. How do you describe people in your culture?

New People 11

📖 Student text page 10–11 (cont.)

Variation. In groups, get students to follow the model provided and describe the man that Mike is meeting. Elicit several responses from different students around the class.

Learning Strategy. Classifying = putting similar things together in groups. Remind students that learning and practicing different strategies is essential to learning, remembering, and using language. Good learners use strategies to make themselves understood, to understand others, to clarify, and to recognize and repair misunderstandings and communication breakdowns.

Explain the idea of classifying. If necessary, demonstrate by drawing different size squares, triangles, and circles on the board and having students put similar shapes together. Point out that classifying words makes them easier to learn. Encourage students to keep vocabulary notebooks, with words classified under key headings.

Students write the color, age, and size words from the post card in the correct boxes. If you think students might have difficulty, reproduce the boxes on the board or an overhead and do the task as a class activity. (Answers: color—dark, red, green, blue; age—twenty; size—short, tall.) You may want to have students add other words from the list on page 9 to the correct boxes.

Task 5. Using the model, students write descriptions of themselves. **Variation.** Have students omit their names from the descriptions. Circulate, helping out and checking work. Collect the papers and distribute them at random, so that each student has someone else's paper. Have them read the description and match it with the person. Check how accurately students read and matched the description with the right person. How many attempts did it take?

Task 6. Have students find Marcia and Mike in the photo on page 9. Did all pairs pick the same persons? What clues did they use?

Task 7. Introduce students to the idea that different cultures focus on, or pay special attention to different things about people and so describe people in different ways. Have students talk about how people are described in their culture.

New People 11

Student text page 12

Language Focus 1:
Statements and yes/no questions with *to be*

Explain that in this section, students will study and practice some of the grammar they have been using in the first task chain.

1. 🎧 In pairs, students listen to the tape and practice the conversation. Circulate and check pronunciation.

2. If necessary, demonstrate how to invert a sentence to make a question by writing the first sentence on the board, circling *am*, and drawing an arrow to the front of the sentence. Then have the students complete the eight items as you circulate and check their work.

I (am) Korean.

Elicit the rule from students and write it on the board. "To make yes/no questions with 'am,' 'is,' 'are,' move 'am,' 'is,' 'are' (alternatively, 'be') to the beginning of the question."

3. Read the instructions with the class and have students match the questions and answers. They then practice in pairs, asking and answering the questions. (Answers: c, e, d [or b], a)

4. In pairs, students simulate a telephone conversation in which they again describe themselves.

If students lack confidence, let them rehearse the conversation following the model in Activity 1.
Optional. With books closed, students repeat the conversation.

12 New People

Language Focus 1
Statements and yes/no questions with *to be*

1 🎧 **Pair Work** Listen. Then practice this conversation.

A: So I'll meet you at Gate 11 at 9:30. Now, what do you look like?
B: Well, I'm twenty-one. I'm of average height and weight. I have dark curly hair and brown eyes.
A: OK.
B: And I'm with my girlfriend. She's nineteen. She's tall, and she has blond hair and blue eyes. You can't miss us!

2 **Pair Work** Which words do you move to make questions? Draw arrows to show your answers.

a You (are) Tomoko.   e It is early.
b I am late.   f You are students.
c His girlfriend is nineteen. g Your name is Mike.
d Mike is from Chicago.   h They are from Korea.

Do you know the rule?
To turn statements with *to be* into yes/no questions, move *am, is, are* to ....

3 Match these questions and answers and then practice with another student.

Questions   *Answers*
a Are you Alex?   .... Yes, you are.
b Is Sandra your girlfriend? .... Yes, he is.
c Am I right?   .... Yes, they are.
d Is your girlfriend nineteen? .... Yes, she is.
e Are they students?   .... Yes, I am.

4 **Pair Work** Someone is meeting you at the airport. Describe yourself. Use the conversation in activity 1 as an example.

Task Chain 2: Making new friends

Task 1

🎧 Mike arrives at a party for new students. Listen to the conversation. How many people does he meet? Circle your answer.

1   2   3   4   5

Task 2

🎧 Listen again and complete the statements.

a Mike introduces himself. He says: "_Hello, I'm Mike_."
b John introduces Anna. He says: "_____."
c Mike greets Anna. He says: "_____."
d John introduces Maggie. He says: "_____."

Task 3

Here are some ways to introduce yourself and other people. Write the letters in the correct columns in the chart.

a I'm Pete Carlton.
b I'd like you to meet Paula.
c My name's Nina.
d This is Carmel.
e I want you to meet Ms. Shaw.

INTRODUCING YOURSELF	INTRODUCING SOMEONE ELSE

Task 4

You choose: Do **A** or **B**.

A Pair Work Discussion. How do you introduce yourself in your own language? How do you introduce someone else?

B Pair Work Discussion. How do you feel when you meet new people? Embarrassed? Shy? Frightened? Interested? Bored? Excited? Talk about how you feel.

A I'm very shy. I'm embarrassed when I meet new people.
B Oh, really? Not me! I'm interested in new people.

New People   13

📖 Student text page 13

Task Chain 2: Making new friends

Task 1. 🎧 This is a selective listening exercise. Play the conversation and ask students to identify the number of people that Mike meets at the party. Elicit responses from the class.
(Answer: 3)

Task 2. 🎧 Play the tape again and have students complete the statements. Play the tape once more if necessary. Have students compare their answers with those of others. Then elicit the answers from the class and write them on the board.
(Answers: a—"I'm Mike," b—"This is Anna," c—"Hello Anna. Good to meet you," d—"This is Maggie.")

Task 3. In pairs, students fill in the box. Circulate and check their responses.
(Answers: Yourself—a, c. Someone else—b, d, e)
Optional. Have students practice making the statements.

Task 4. In pairs, students complete the chosen task. Point out the language model for students doing **B**.

If you feel that your students will have difficulty choosing at this point in the course, explain both tasks and get the class as a whole to choose.

New People   13

Student text page 14

Task 5. (a) This task is meant to promote a free discussion and to encourage students to express their own ideas.

Discuss the chart with the class. Explain that singles parties and dances are especially for single (unmarried) people to meet one another.

Elicit reactions to the chart from the class. Ask about differences between men and women. Are any of the percentages surprising? Why?

(b) Working in small groups, students discuss and check their responses. Have the groups add some additional items to the list, then work together to compare their responses.

Elicit responses from around the class, and encourage students to talk about them.

Task 5

a **Group Work** Discussion. This chart shows where single people meet each other in the United States. What do you think the percentages are in your country?

How do single men and women meet each other?

	% of men	% of women
Through friends	30%	36%
At parties	22%	18%
At bars, discos	24%	18%
At singles parties/dances	14%	18%
At work	10%	9%
Through newspaper ads	1%	1%
Don't remember	1%	2%

Adapted from: Margaret K. Ambry, *The Almanac of Consumer Markets*, Probus Publishing Co. Chicago, Ill., 1989.

b **Group Work** Discussion. Where can you meet new people?

	Yes	No
At school?	☐	☐
At a party?	☐	☐
At the movies?	☐	☐
At a shopping center?	☐	☐
At a sports event?	☐	☐
At a concert?	☐	☐
At a friend's home?	☐	☐
....	☐	☐
....	☐	☐
....	☐	☐
....	☐	☐

Add to the list and ask some other students.

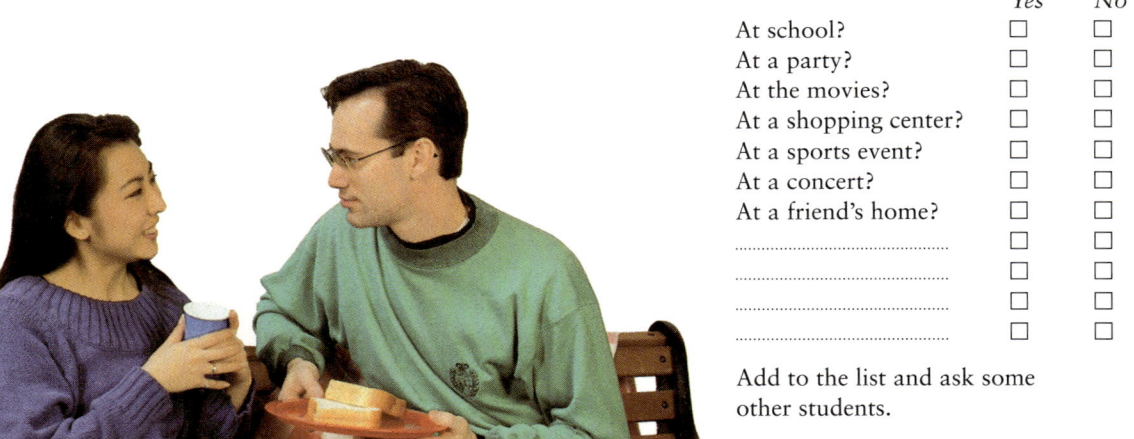

14 New People

Language Focus 2
Wh questions: what and where + to be

1 a 🎧 **Pair Work** Listen. Then practice the conversation.

   A: Hi! I'm Yongsue. What's your name?
   B: Vera.
   A: Where are you from?
   B: Chicago. What about you?
   A: I'm from Seoul, Korea. What do you do?
   B: I'm a student. What do you do?
   A: I'm a student, too.

  b **Pair Work** Now use information that is true for you.

2 Fill in the blanks.

Questions

a What's .... name?
b Where .... you from?
c Where .... he from?
d What .... name?
e Where .... she from?
f What .... his name?
g What .... their names?
h Where .... they from?

Answers

My .... Mike.
Mike .... from Chicago.
He .... from France.
Her .... Yumi.
.... from Japan.
His .... Michael.
.... names are Miguel and Mercedes.
They .... from Spain.

3 **Pair Work** Ask and answer these questions.

Questions

a What is Mike's last name?
b Where is Mike from?
c Where are Miguel and Mercedes from?
d Where is Yumi from?

Answers

His last name is Frota.
....
....
....

4 **Pair Work** Ask and answer these questions.

Questions

a What's .... ?
b Where .... from?
c What .... do?

Answers

My name ....
I'm ....
I ....

Now describe your partner to another pair.

Example: "This is Angela. She's from Mexico City, and she's a nurse."

New People **15**

📖 Student text page 15

Language Focus 2:
Wh questions: what and where + to be

1. (a) 🎧 In pairs, students listen to the tape with books closed, and then practice the conversation. Circulate and check pronunciation.

   (b) Students practice the conversation again, this time substituting information that is true for them. One pair member plays Yongsue, the other plays Vera. **Variation.** Students underline the words in the conversation that will change when they practice the conversation using information that is true for them.

2. Students fill in the blanks. You may want to reproduce the exercise on the board or an overhead. Solicit responses from around the class.
(Answers: a. Q—your, A—name is; b. Q—are, A—is; c. Q—is, A—is; d. Q—is her, A—name is; e. Q—is, A—She is; f. Q—is, A—name is; g. Q—are, A—Their; h. Q—are, A—are)

3. Put the following contractions on the board and review them:

I am = I'm	it is = it's
you are = you're	we are = we're
he is = he's	they are = they're
she is = she's	

Tell students to do the exercise using information from Exercise 2.
(Answers: b—He is from Chicago. OR He's from Chicago. c—They are from Spain. OR They're from Spain. d—She is from Japan. OR She's from Japan.)

4. In pairs, students practice the controlled conversation. If all are from the same country, they can answer "Where are you from?" with their town, suburb, or neighborhood. Then each student describes his or her partner to another pair, using the model at the bottom of the page. Have several students describe their partner to the class.

New People **15**

📖 Student text page 16

Self-Check

Communication Challenge

The Communication Challenge tasks provide opportunities for students to use, in a freer context, the language they have been learning. Challenge 1 is on page 111 of the Student Text, and suggestions for its use are on that page in this Teacher's Extended Edition.

1, 2, 3. If possible, have students complete the first three tasks without looking back at the unit. Some of these tasks can be done out of class and brought to the next session. For task 3, you may want to have students bring in photos of family members; in small groups they can introduce and give information about the people in the photos. Circulate to ensure that students use the forms taught in the unit.

4. Have students individually compile their lists of areas needing more practice, then compare their lists with others'. Elicit responses from the class. **Variation.** Have the whole class brainstorm ideas for getting more practice. List responses on the board for students to copy. Make a list for yourself and decide how and where you can include this review and/or extension work.

• Tell the class that summaries of the grammar points covered in each unit can be found at the back of their texts. The summary for Unit 1 is on page 129.

5. Remind students that the language strategy in this unit is classifying. Point out that the vocabulary list is already classified according to parts of speech, but that it could also be classified in other ways. Suggest some other categories, for example, words beginning with the same letter, long words, or words with the same number of syllables. Elicit other categories. You may want to have the class reorganize the words in the vocabulary list under two or three different headings.

16 New People

Self-Check

COMMUNICATION CHALLENGE

Look at Challenge 1 on page 111.

"I do workbook exercises to practice filling in personal information on forms."

"I practice describing myself in front of a mirror."

"I practice introductions with a partner after class."

1 Write down five new words you learned in this unit.

2 Write down three new sentences or questions you learned.

3 Review the language skills you practiced in this unit. Check [√] your answers.

CAN YOU:

Exchange personal information?	☐ yes	☐ a little	☐ not yet
Find or give an example:			
Describe yourself and others?	☐ yes	☐ a little	☐ not yet
Find or give an example:			
Introduce people?	☐ yes	☐ a little	☐ not yet
Find or give an example:			

4 What areas need more practice? How can you get more practice? Make a list.

5 Vocabulary check. Check [√] the words you know.

Adjectives			Adverbs	Conjunction	Nouns			
☐ big	☐ green	☐ right	☐ here	☐ or	☐ address	☐ eyes	☐ name	☐ people
☐ blond	☐ middle-	☐ tall	☐ too		☐ airport	☐ friends	☐ newspaper	☐ police
☐ blue	aged	☐ teenage	☐ very		☐ beard	☐ girlfriend	☐ occupation	☐ student
☐ dark	☐ new	☐ wrong	☐ with		☐ conversation	☐ hair	☐ partner	☐ telephone
☐ early	☐ old				☐ date	☐ information	☐ party	☐ weight
☐ elderly	☐ red							

Prepositions	Pronouns			Questions	Verbs		
☐ at	☐ he	☐ it	☐ they	☐ what	☐ am	☐ does	☐ work
☐ from	☐ her	☐ me	☐ us	☐ where	☐ answer	☐ introduce	☐ write
☐ in	☐ him	☐ my	☐ we		☐ are	☐ is	
☐ in front of	☐ his	☐ she	☐ you		☐ describe	☐ look	
☐ to	☐ I	☐ them	☐ your		☐ do	☐ practice	

16 New People

2 Meet the Family

Warm-Up

Unit Goals

In this unit you will:

Talk about your family
"I have a brother and two sisters."

Ask about other people's families
"How many sisters do you have?"

LEARNING STRATEGY

Predicting = saying what you think will happen.

1 Look at the title and the goals of this unit. They can help you predict what the unit is about. What do you think you will do in this unit?

This is what one student predicted:
"I'll listen to people talk about their families."
"I'll describe my family."

Pair Work Can you predict some of the things you will do in this unit? Now look quickly through the unit. Were you right?

Picture 1  Picture 2

Picture 3  Picture 4

Picture 5  Picture 6

2 Match these descriptions with the families in the pictures above.

Descriptions	Picture
a A family with one parent, one stepparent, and children	6
b A family with two parents and one adopted child	....
c A family with two parents and two children	....
d A family with two parents and three children	....
e A single-parent family	....
f A family with one grandparent, two parents, and children	....

3 a Which family photograph shows a "typical" North American family?

b What is a typical family in your country? Is the typical family changing?

Meet the Family **17**

---

2 Meet the Family

Student text page 17

Warm-Up

Unit Goals. In this section, students are introduced to language for talking about families. Read aloud, or have a volunteer read each of the goals and ask the students if they can do these things in English. Elicit responses from a representative group of students to get an idea of the range of ability in the class.

Learning Strategy. In this unit, we focus on predicting.

1. Explain the notion of predicting, using examples from everyday life. Then read aloud the first paragraph of instructions, ending with, "What do you think you will do in this unit?" Elicit student responses and write them on the board. Have students predict particular words they may meet in this unit and list them on the board. Divide the class into pairs. Have each pair predict some of the things they will be doing in the unit and then leaf quickly through the unit to see if they were correct.

2. Still in pairs, students then decide which picture matches each description and check their answers with another pair.
(Answers: a—6; b—5; c—3; d—4; e—2; f—1)

Give the class several minutes to think of other types of families and write them on the board as they are volunteered. **Optional.** Check responses and ask students how they made their choices, for example, father and mother are standing directly behind children. (Students will need to know the following regular and irregular plural noun forms in this unit: Regular: boys, girls, husbands, cousins, daughters, sons. Irregular: children, men, women, wives, families. Put these on the board and have students practice them. Focus on correct pronunciation, especially of the endings.)

(Continued on page 18)

Meet the Family **17**

Student text pages 17–18 (cont.)

3. (a) All the photographs can be called "typical American families" today since all are representative of families found in almost all middle-sized or larger American communities (and many smaller ones). Perhaps, as a *Newsweek* article states, "The American family does not exist. Rather, we are creating many American families."

(b) Answers will, of course, vary.

Task Chain 1: Meeting the family

Task 1. This is a classifying task. If necessary, demonstrate by doing the first item on the board. Circulate and check as students work. When they have completed the exercise, elicit answers from the class as students check their own responses.
(Answers: uncle—M; grandmother—F; son—M; niece—F; nephew—M; father—M; daughter—F; grandfather—M; sister—F; brother-in-law—M; aunt—F; brother—M; mother—F; stepfather—M)

Task 2. (a) 🎧 Play the tape as students check the words they hear. Remind students that with selective listening it is not necessary to understand every word. If necessary, play the tape a second time. Then have students, in pairs, compare their responses. Play the tape again for students to confirm their answers.
(Answers: grandfather, mom, sister, brother, niece, nephew)

(b) 🎧 Play the tape again and have students check the names they hear.
(Answers: Vera, Juan, José, Cristina, Sandra)

Task 3. 🎧 Have students listen once again and find and label the seven people in the picture.
(Answers: upper left [left to right]: José, Grandfather; upper right: Vera, Mom; lower left: Juan, Cristina; lower right: Sandra)

Task 4. In pairs, students complete the family tree. Elicit student responses and put the completed family tree on the board.
(Answers: brother—José; sister—Sandra; niece—Cristina; nephew—Juan)

18   Meet the Family

Task Chain 1   Meeting the family

Task 1
Are these family members male or female? Write *M* for male or *F* for female.

M uncle	..... father	..... aunt
F grandmother	..... daughter	..... brother
..... son	..... grandfather	..... mother
..... niece	..... sister	..... stepfather
..... nephew	..... brother-in-law	

Task 2
a 🎧 Vera is talking about the people in the photograph. Listen and check [√] the words you hear.

☐ grandfather   ☐ brother
☐ dad   ☐ daughter
☐ mom   ☐ niece
☐ sister   ☐ uncle
☐ son   ☐ nephew

b 🎧 Listen again and check [√] the names you hear.

☐ Maria   ☐ Cristina
☐ Vera   ☐ Bobbie
☐ Juan   ☐ Sandra
☐ José   ☐ Jean

Task 3
🎧 **Pair Work** Listen again and find these people: Vera, Vera's grandfather, Vera's mom, José, Juan, Cristina, Sandra. Label the people in the photo.

Task 4
Complete this family tree for Vera's family.

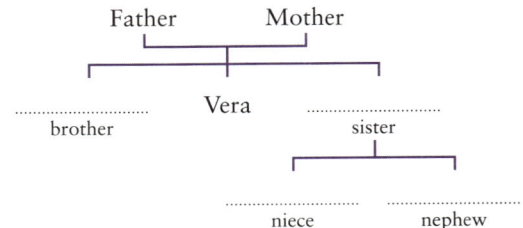

18   Meet the Family

Task 5
Now draw your own family tree.

A Do you have any sisters?
B Yes, I do. I have two sisters, Maggie and Janice.

Task 6
a **Pair Work** Ask questions about your partner's family. Now draw your partner's family tree.

b **Pair Work** Exchange roles and do the task again.

Task 7
Group Work Survey. Talk to four other students and complete the survey chart.

STUDENT'S NAME	BROTHER'S OR SISTER'S NAME	LIVE WITH PARENTS	WORK OR SCHOOL	JOB OR FIELD OF STUDY
Somchai	Suphat	no	work	doctor

a Do you have a brother or a sister?
b Does he or she live with your parents?
c Does he or she work or go to school?
d What is his or her job or field of study?

Pair Work Now work with a student from another group. Report on your survey.

Example: "Kenji has a sister. Her name is Tomoko. She lives in Kobe. She's a teller. She works in a bank."

Meet the Family 19

📖 **Student text page 19**

Task 5. Students work individually to complete a family tree diagram for their own family. Circulate and provide help as needed.

Task 6. (a) and (b) In pairs, students describe their family and draw each other's family tree. Tell students not to look at the family tree their partner drew in Task 5 at this time. When they have finished, let them compare the tree they drew with their partner's tree from Task 5. **Variation.** In small groups, have students describe and compare their family trees, with particular focus on different ideas of what constitutes a family. For example, who did they include in their family tree, and why? Did they include cousins, grandparents, spouses of relatives?

Task 7. Have students circulate and interview four other students to complete the survey. Make sure that every student gets interviewed by at least one other student. Then form pairs and have partners report to each other on their surveys. Finally, bring the whole class together and ask about the families of individual class members, using the question, "Can you tell me something about (Kenji's) family?" Have individual students respond, following the language model at the bottom of page 19.

Meet the Family 19

📖 Student text page 20

Language Focus 1:
Statements and yes/no questions with *do/does*

1. In this exercise, students fill in blanks to complete questions and answers. You may wish to write the first item on the board and do it with them as a class, asking, "What shall I write in the first blank?" and eliciting *Do* from the class. Continue with the other two blanks. Then divide the class into pairs to complete the exercise and practice the conversations with their partners. Circulate and check as the students work. When they have finished, call on individual students for responses and write them on the board.
(Answers: Line 1—Do, do, you; Line 2—Do, do, don't; Line 3—Does, she, doesn't; Line 4—Does, does, doesn't; Line 5—Do, we, don't; Line 6—Do, do, don't)

2. 🎧 In pairs, students listen to the tape and then practice the conversation. Circulate and check pronunciation. Students then use the conversation as a model to describe their own families to their partners.

3. Still in pairs, students now use information in the conversation about Helen to ask and answer questions. (Answers: a—No, she doesn't; b—Yes, she does; c—Yes, she does; d—No, she doesn't; e—Yes, she does; f—Yes, she does; g—Yes, they do)

4. Students walk around filling out the chart. Make sure that they understand that they are looking for both positive and negative responses to fill the chart. Monitor to check that students ask and answer in English, using the correct structures *(Do you…?; Yes, I do; No, I don't)*. In this kind of exercise students often simply repeat the item as printed instead of using the whole question form. **Optional.** Set a time limit of three minutes and see who fills in the most boxes.

20 Meet the Family

Language Focus 1
Statements and yes/no questions with *do/does*

1. **Pair Work** Fill in the blanks. Then practice the questions and answers.

Questions	Answers	
.... I have time to call?	Yes, you	No, ... don't.
.... you have a brother?	Yes, I	No, I ....
.... she have an aunt?	Yes, ... does.	No, she ....
.... he have an uncle?	Yes, he	No, he ....
.... you have a sister?	Yes, ... do.	No, we ....
.... they have children?	Yes, they	No, they ....

2. a 🎧 **Pair Work** Listen. Then practice this conversation.

   A: Do you have any brothers or sisters, Helen?
   B: Yes, I do. I have two brothers and three sisters. I also have six aunts and eight uncles and 25 cousins.
   A: Do you have nieces and nephews?
   B: Yes, I do—my sister's kids. They live with us.

   b **Pair Work** Now use information that is true for you.

3. **Pair Work** Ask and answer these questions.

   Example: "Does Helen have three sisters?" "Yes, she does."

   a Does Helen have five aunts?
   b Does she have a sister?
   c Does she have a brother?
   d Does she have six uncles?
   e Does she have any cousins?
   f Does she have nieces?
   g Do they live with her?

Do you know the rule?

Fill in the blanks with the correct pronouns from this list: *I, you, he, she, it, we, they*.

Use *do* with ....
Use *does* with ....

4. **Group Work** Class survey. Ask your classmates questions like this: "Do you go to the movies often?" Write one name in each box in the chart. See how many boxes you can fill.

FIND SOMEONE WHO . . .	YES	NO
likes hamburgers		
plays tennis		
speaks three languages		
likes classical music		
goes to the movies often		
wants to be an actor		
lives alone		
likes modern art		
drives a car		
works at night		

20 Meet the Family

Task Chain 2 Talking about your family

Task 1

These people are on a television game show. They are talking about themselves and their families.

a Can you predict some of words you will hear? Write them in the chart at left.

b 🎧 Listen. Check [√] the words you hear in the chart at left.

PREDICT	LISTEN
sisters	√

Task 2

🎧 Listen again and fill in this chart.

NAME	AGE	OCCUPATION	FAMILY
Eva	21	?	3 sisters, 4 brothers

Meet the Family 21

📖 Student text page 21

Task Chain 2: Talking about your family

Task 1. Ask students about TV game shows. What game shows do they know about? Which ones do they watch? Do they like game shows? Why or why not?

(a) In small groups, have students brainstorm some vocabulary they think they might hear in a TV game show when the contestants are talking about themselves and their families. Have them write these words in the chart under the heading "predict."

(b) 🎧 Students listen to the tape. When they hear one of the predicted words, they make a check mark next to it under heading "listen."

Task 2. 🎧 Working as individuals, students listen to the tape again and fill in the chart for each of the three contestants.
(Answers: Eva—21, no occupation given, 3 sisters, 4 brothers; Sylvia—19, student, only child; Pete—26, salesperson, 1 sister, 1 brother)

Student text page 22

Task 3. Before having students do this task, write the term *in-laws* on the board and make sure that students understand it. Do any of the students in the class have in-laws?

(a) Play the tape. Then call on students to state one rule of the game. Continue until all the rules have been presented.

(b) Divide the class into pairs. Play the tape again and have the pairs list the questions that the host asks. Circulate and check spelling, punctuation, and grammar.
(Answers: 1. Does your sister-in-law have children? 2. Where does your father-in-law work? 3. Where does your brother-in-law go to school? 4. Where does your mother-in-law work?) **Optional.** Have students practice asking the questions without referring to the written version.

(c) Again in their pairs, students listen to the tape and write the answers. Have one partner write James's answers and the other partner write Mary's. Circulate and check spelling, punctuation, and grammar. Have pairs compare their responses with two other pairs.
(Answers: James 1. No, he doesn't. 2. He doesn't work. He's retired. 3. He doesn't go to school. He works in a bank. 4. Can't remember. I think she changed jobs recently. Mary 1. Yes, he does. Three girls. 2. At a hospital. He's a doctor. 3. She goes to San Francisco State University. 4. In a publishing house.)

Task 4. Have the class brainstorm possible questions for the "interview." Make notes on the board as questions are suggested. Have the whole class practice asking the questions.

(a) Divide the class into pairs, and have them find out as much as they can about their partners' families.

(b) Have each pair work with another pair and ask and answer questions about the other partners' families.

(c) Have a class discussion. Who collected the most information? **Variation.** Have students take notes while interviewing classmates, then use these notes to write a short paragraph as homework. The paragraphs can be read and discussed at the next class session.

Meet the Family

Task 3

a In the next quiz show, the contestants are playing a game called *Know Your In-Laws*. Listen to the first part of the conversation and find out how the game is played.

b Listen again and write the questions in the chart.

c Listen once more and write the answers in the chart.

QUESTIONS	JAMES'S ANSWERS	MARY'S ANSWERS

A What does Tomoko's father do?
B He's a lawyer.
A Where is his office?
B I don't know.

Task 4

a **Pair Work** You have five minutes to find out as much as you can about your partner's family.

b **Group Work** Now work with another pair. Ask questions about the other partners' families.

c **Group Work** Discussion. Who collected the most information?

Meet the Family

Language Focus 2 *Wh questions with do/does*

1 🎧 **Pair Work** Listen. Then practice this conversation.

A: Who's that?
B: That's my brother.
A: Great-looking guy. What's his name?
B: Joe.
A: And what does he do?
B: He goes to school.
A: Oh, where does he go?
B: He goes to McGill University in Montreal.

2 **Pair Work** Fill in the blanks and practice the questions and answers.

	Questions	Answers
a	What .... I need?	You .... a work permit.
b	What do .... do?	I .... a teacher.
c	Where .... he work?	.... works in a bank.
d	Where .... you go to school?	We .... to Boston University.
e	What .... they do?	They .... students.

3 **Pair Work** Write questions for these answers. Then practice them.

	Questions	Answers
a	..........?	I live in Mexico.
b	..........?	She's a nurse.
c	..........?	They go to Hunter College.
d	..........?	We come from Tokyo.
e	..........?	They're students.

4 a Turn these statements into questions with *do/does*.

I need a work permit.
I need *what*
what .... I need
What do I .... need?

She lives in Tokyo.
she lives ....
.... she lives
.... live?

He studies engineering.
he studies ....
.... he studies
.... study?

You go to City University.
you go ....
.... you go
.... go?

b What is the pattern for these kinds of questions? Number the following words to put them in order.

.... **noun/pronoun**   .... **verb**   .... *wh* **word**   .... **do/does**

Meet the Family   23

📖 Student text page 23

Language Focus 2: *Wh questions with do/does*

Tell the class that in this section they will focus on some of the grammar used in Task Chain 1.

1. 🎧 Students listen to the tape and then practice the conversation. Circulate to check pronunciation.

2. Have students work in pairs to fill in the blanks. When all have finished, call on volunteers for their responses. Then have pairs practice the questions and answers.
(Answers: a—do, need; b—you, 'm/am; c—does, He; d—do, go; e—do, 're/are)

3. This is a new kind of exercise in this book. Instead of answering questions, the students read an answer and then write a question that fits the answer. If you feel it necessary, do the first item with the class; elicit that the correct question is "Where do you live?" When you are sure that all students understand what they are to do, have them complete the exercise.
(Answers: a—Where do you live? b—What does she do? c—Where do they go to school/college? d—Where do you come from? e—What do they do?)

4. (a) This is a discovery task. The purpose of the task is to transform statements into *wh* questions using the verb *do*. Write these examples on the board.

She works [in Seattle].
She works? [where].
[Where] she works?
Where does she work?

The information in brackets should be the answer to the *wh* question. When using she, he, or it the verb at the end of the sentence changes by losing the *s*.

(b) Have students number the words in the correct order. Elicit responses from the class.
(Answers: 3, 4, 1, 2)

Meet the Family   23

📖 Student text page 24

Self-Check

Communication Challenge

Challenge 2 is on page 112 of the student text, and suggestions for its use are on that page in this Teacher's Extended Edition.

- Emphasize to the students that the Self-Check sections are an extremely important element of the course. Not only do they help students keep track of what they have learned in each unit, they also encourage them to think about where they need more practice and to consider how to get this practice. This self-assessment is valuable not only to the student but also to you, the teacher.

1. Have students write the words. **Variation.** After they choose the five words, have students use each of them in a sentence.

2. Have students write their new sentences or questions. Then, in pairs, they practice saying what they have written without reading it.

3, 4. Have students do these tasks as homework and bring them to the next class session for discussion. **Variation.** For Task 4, have the class brainstorm areas in which they believe they need more practice—for example, Vocabulary, Grammar, Strategies. Elicit responses from the class.

- Where do your students need additional help? Make a list of areas that you feel the whole class needs to review,—grammar items, language functions, vocabulary, etc. Put your list on the board and talk about it with the class.

5. Have students check the list and select nouns that describe family relations. (This is nearly all the nouns.) Have them reorganize this selected list under gender headings: Male, Female, Either male or female.

- The grammar summary for this unit is on pages 129–130.

24 Meet the Family

Self-Check

COMMUNICATION CHALLENGE
Look at Challenge 2 on page 112.

"I listen to the cassette tape at home and repeat the conversations."

"Tomoko and I practice the conversations outside of class."

"I talk about my friends' families during coffee break."

1 Write down five new words you learned in this unit.

2 Write down three new sentences or questions you learned.

3 Review the language skills you practiced in this unit. Check [√] your answers.

CAN YOU:

Talk about your family?   ☐ yes   ☐ a little   ☐ not yet
Find or give an example: _____

Ask about other people's families?   ☐ yes   ☐ a little   ☐ not yet
Find or give an example: _____

4 What areas need more practice? How can you get more practice? Make a list.

5 Vocabulary check. Check [√] the words you know.

Adjective	Conjunction	Nouns				Verbs		Prepositions
☐ typical	☐ and	☐ aunt	☐ family	☐ male	☐ school	☐ ask	☐ have	☐ about
		☐ brother	☐ father	☐ mom	☐ sister	☐ come	☐ live	☐ for
		☐ child	☐ female	☐ mother	☐ son	☐ draw	☐ need	
		☐ children	☐ grandfather	☐ nephew	☐ television	☐ find	☐ predict	
		☐ dad	☐ grandmother	☐ niece	☐ uncle	☐ give	☐ study	
		☐ daughter	☐ home	☐ parent	☐ work	☐ go	☐ talk	
		☐ dictionary	☐ kids	☐ photograph		☐ has	☐ tell	

24 Meet the Family

3 Old Friends

Warm-Up

Unit Goals

In this unit you will:

Talk about friends
"Tomoko is kind."

Ask for information about other people
"Who is that?"
"Who do you work with?"

"Things I do with my friends? Well, I play tennis and go to movies with them. We study together, drink coffee together, and talk on the phone."

1 The photographs above show groups of friends. Which groups look interesting? Why?

2 🎧 Listen. Maria is talking about two of the pictures. Which ones is she talking about?

3 **Pair Work** Think of your best friends. What do you do together?

☐ play tennis   ☐ have coffee
☐ go to movies   ☐ talk on the phone
☐ go to parties

Add your own.

....
....
....

Old Friends   25

---

3 Old Friends

📖 Student text page 25

Warm-Up

Unit Goals. Read, or have a volunteer read the goals to the class; have other volunteers read the examples under each goal.

1. This task requires the students to focus on the photographs, which are also used in the first Task Chain. Tasks 1 and 2 in this Warm-Up build familiarity with the photographs in preparation for the Task Chain.

Ask students to look at the five groups of friends. Ask the class which groups look interesting and why. (You may need to encourage students by suggesting factors such as gender mix.) **Optional**. Ask students to compare the groups in the photos with their own friendship groups. Elicit similarities and differences.

2. 🎧 Selective listening. Have students listen to the tape in small groups and decide which pictures Maria is talking about. Elicit responses, and ask students why they chose the pictures they did.
(Answers: The first two pictures in the second row)

3. Working in pairs, students discuss what they do with friends. Each partner checks the appropriate items and adds others, following the model used for the printed items. You may want to ask individual students what they checked and added, and write their responses on the board. This could encourage students to realize that they do more things with their friends than they had thought of; they could add these new items to their lists.

Old Friends   25

📖 Student text page 26

Task Chain 1: Close friends

Task 1. (a) Divide the class into pairs. Have partners individually circle the words they would use to describe their best friends, then compare their ideas and discuss the qualities they believe are most important in a friend.

(b) Ask the pairs to think about other words to add to the list, and write them down.

(c) Have partners tell each other about the qualities of three of their friends. They can use the quotation in the upper left corner of the page ("Charlie is smart....") as a model. Circulate, checking fluency and pronunciation.

• Have the whole class brainstorm responses to Task 1, in particular the extra words that they added to the list. Brainstorming—rapidly sharing as many thoughts, ideas, and words as one can think of about a topic—is a good way for students to practice English. It is also a good learning strategy, because, by hearing other students' opinions or ideas, students can broaden their own views and learn about other ways of thinking.

Task 2. 🎧 Explain that students are to listen for people's names, and that only some of the names printed in the list are on the tape. Play the tape and have students check the names they hear. Then play the tape a second time and have them fill in the occupations of the people whose names they checked.

26 Old Friends

Task Chain 1   Close friends

"Charlie is smart and good-looking, Tomoko is serious and intelligent, and Somchai is funny and outgoing."

Task 1

a Pair Work Which words would you use to describe your best friend? Circle them. What qualities are most important in a friend?

happy	serious	smart	good-looking
romantic	funny	sexy	intelligent
outgoing	interesting	kind	

b Pair Work Can you add any other words to the list?

c Pair Work Think of three friends and make statements about them. Use words from the list above.

Task 2

🎧 Listen to the conversation. Tony is talking about his best friends. Check [√] the names you hear and write occupations next to them.

Occupations

☐ Dave ....
☐ Victor ....
☐ Tina ....
☐ Tony ....
☐ Maria ....
☐ Pete ....
☐ Pamela ....
☐ Maggie ....
☐ Steve ....

26 Old Friends

Task 3

Group Work Look at the photographs on page 25. Find a picture of Tony and his friends. Give a reason for your choice.

Task 4

Group Work Discussion. What does Tony do? Is this an unusual occupation for a man? What about in your country? Do men do this job? What jobs do men rarely do? What jobs do women rarely do?

Task 5

a **Pair Work** Read these messages and write the missing names in the blanks. Use the conversation in Task 2 and the messages to figure out the names.

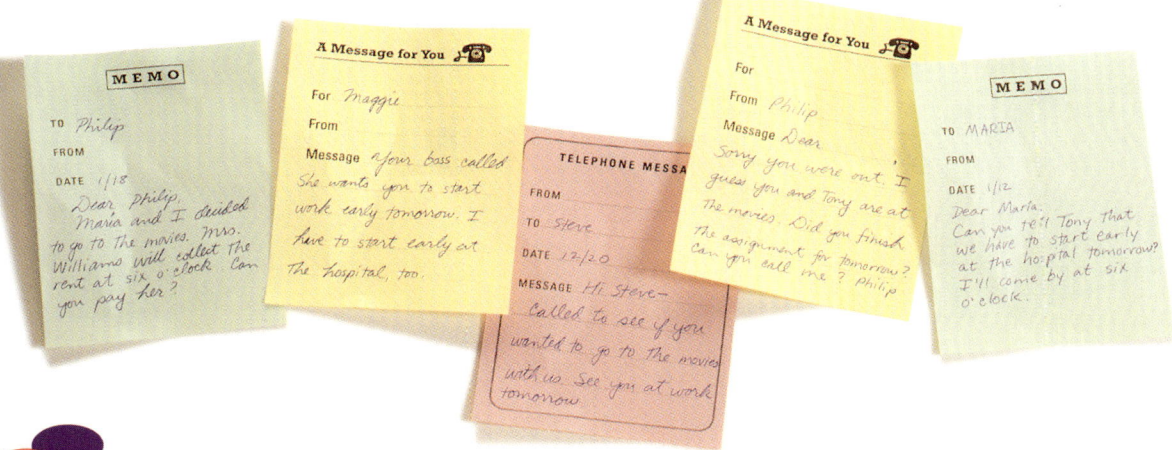

"One of my best friends is Vanessa, who is a photographer. We met in college. We go swimming and dancing together, and we talk about work, money, and our other friends."

Task 6

a Think of three good friends, and then complete the chart.

b **Pair Work** Now use the information to talk about your friends with a partner.

NAME	THINGS YOU DO TOGETHER	THINGS YOU TALK ABOUT	OCCUPATION	WHERE YOU MET
1				
2				
3				

Old Friends 27

Student text page 27

Task 3. Have students turn back to page 25 and find the picture of Tony and his friends. Ask them to give reasons for their choice.
(Answers: The first picture in the second row on page 25. This is the one that Maria chose as her "favorite picture" and the "very best friends" in it are the same people that Tony named.)

Task 4. Tony is a nurse. This task provides students with the opportunity for a free discussion in which they can express personal opinions about the roles of men and women in different societies. Traditionally, nursing has been an occupation for women in the United States, but the number of male nurses is increasing.

Task 5. In this task, students work in pairs to make inferences based on information from preceding tasks. Elicit responses from the pairs and put them on the board. Encourage students to give reasons for their choices.
(Answers, left to right: Pamela, Steve, Tony, Maria, Steve)

Task 6. (a) Students complete the chart individually. If possible, these should be different friends from those described in earlier tasks.
(b) In pairs, students talk about the three friends, using the information on the chart, and modeling their talk on the paragraph in quotation marks at bottom left on the page ("One of my best friends is…").

Old Friends 27

Student text page 28

Language Focus 1:
Present-tense questions with *do/does:* a review

1. 🎧 Play the tape, then have students practice the conversation in pairs. Circulate and check for fluency and pronunciation. **Variation.** Have students practice the conversation using information that is true for them. Make sure they remember the questions and responses and do not just read them.

2. In groups, students discuss the questions about dating customs after reading the article printed on this page. **Variation.** The discussions could take place at home or elsewhere outside the classroom. If all students are from the same country, they could talk about how customs differ from region to region or from one cultural group to another. In any case, open this up for a whole class discussion of students' responses.

3. Have students fill in the blanks individually before practicing asking and answering the questions in pairs. (Answers: a—Do, do, you; b—answers will vary; c—Does, she, doesn't; d—he, answers will vary; e—Do, do, you; f—they, do, they)

4. In pairs, have partners ask each other the questions and write their partners' answers. As they work, circulate and check both information and grammar. **Variation.** Working in pairs, small groups, or as a class, students can construct new questions, changing them from second person [you] to third person [he/she/they]. They can then ask others about a close friend or friends, or a classmate or group of classmates. For example, "Do they like pop music?" or "Does his mother speak English?"

Language Focus 1 Present-tense questions with *do/does:* a review

1 🎧 **Pair Work** Listen. Then practice the conversation.

A: Do you have a best friend?
B: Yes, Tomoko.
A: What does she do?
B: She's a student.
A: What do you do together?
B: Oh, we study together. Sometimes we go to the movies.

2 **Group Work** Discussion. Read the newspaper article at left and discuss the questions that follow.

In your country . . .
- do young people go on dates alone or in groups?
- when do people start dating?
- do men go out with each other in groups?
- do women go out with each other in groups?
- where do people usually go on dates?

> Most people form their closest relationships in high school, at college, or at work. In North America, many high school students have a boyfriend or a girlfriend. Many people start dating in their early teens, and they have a steady boyfriend or girlfriend by the time they are 16. The average North American has his or her first "puppy love" at age 13 and first serious love at age 17.
>
> In some countries, it is unusual for young people to have a steady boyfriend or girlfriend until they finish high school. In fact, in some countries, young people are not allowed even to talk to members of the opposite sex. In these cultures, it is common to see young men going out with other young men and young women going out with other young women.

3 **Pair Work** Fill in the blanks. Then practice the questions and answers.

	Questions	Answers	
a	.... I need a student card?	Yes, you	No, ... don't.
b	What does your sister do?	She	
c	.... she have a close friend?	Yes, ... does.	No, she ....
d	Where does .... work?	He	
e	.... we need a ticket?	Yes, you	No, ... don't.
f	Do .... have girlfriends?	Yes, they	No, ... don't.

4 **Pair Work** Ask and answer these questions.

	Questions	Answers
a	Do you like pop music?	
b	Where does your best friend live?	
c	Do you have a brother?	
d	Does your mother speak English?	
e	When do you get up in the morning?	
f	Do you like sports?	
g	What do you usually do after class?	
h	Do you have a girlfriend/boyfriend/ wife/husband?	
i	Does your best friend go to school?	

Old Friends

Task Chain 2 Social networks

Task 1

🎧 Pair Work Listen. Then practice the conversation.

A: Hi, Jenny. How is school?
B: Fine.
A: It must be lonely in a new city.
B: It is a little lonely. But I have some new friends.
A: That's nice.
B: And I see my classmates every day.

Task 2

🎧 Listen. Victor is doing a survey. What does he want to know?

Task 3

🎧 Listen again. Check [√] the names you hear.

- ☐ Tony
- ☐ Victor
- ☐ Maria
- ☐ Mary
- ☐ Steve
- ☐ Sophie
- ☐ Sonia
- ☐ Nina
- ☐ Agnes
- ☐ Annie
- ☐ Uncle Charles
- ☐ Karen
- ☐ Uncle Carlos
- ☐ Ms. Mills
- ☐ Ms. Miller
- ☐ Sam
- ☐ Mrs. Williams

Old Friends

📖 Student text page 29

Task Chain 2: Social networks

Before doing Task 1, explain the concept of the social network. You can illustrate this by talking about some of the social groups you belong to, for example, your family, school friends, sports teams, clubs, church or temple, fellow workers, your neighbors. Have the class brainstorm their own social groups. Then have small groups of students make a list of all the people they talk to every day. Choose one member of the group to do the writing. Have groups compare their lists. Then discuss them as a whole class.

Task 1. 🎧 In pairs, students listen to the recorded conversation and then practice it while you circulate to check fluency, intonation, and pronunciation.

Task 2. 🎧 Have students listen to the conversation between Victor and Tony and identify what Victor wants to know.
(Answer: Victor wants to know who Tony talks to every day.) [This is a continuation of the conversation in Task 2 of Task Chain 1, page 26.]

Task 3. 🎧 Play the tape again and have students check the names they hear.
(Answers: Tony, Victor, Maria, Steve, Sophie, Karen, Agnes, Uncle Carlos, Ms. Mills, Sam, Mrs. Williams)

Old Friends

Student text page 30

Task 4. In pairs, students listen to the tape once more and complete the social network diagram. Point out that "friends" are not mentioned in this tape, but students may find their names by looking at their answers to Task 2 of Task Chain 1 on page 26.

Task 5. Working individually, students complete their own social networks and then discuss them in small groups, using the conversation in the left margin as a model. **Variation.** Students can draw diagrams to show themselves in a number of different social groups, for example, a family-tree type diagram for the immediate family, the hierarchy at work, or one or more religious, social, or sports groups of which the student is a member. Have students "read" and discuss diagrams in pairs or small groups, with emphasis on where the student sees himself or herself in the group, and what the hierarchy is. Are some people in the group more important than others? (Sometimes the official hierarchy and the actual hierarchy are different; group members are usually very aware of this and how it affects them.)

Task 6. (a) Reproduce the box on the board or on an overhead. Read the questions with the class. Then have students work in groups to make their lists. Ask a representative from each group to report on who each member of the group talks to.

- Group work can be more focused if students are asked to concentrate on some specific questions, for example, What do you usually talk about in the coffee breaks or lunch breaks at work? What do you talk about while you're on the job? What topics do you never talk about with workmates or other casual acquaintances that you do talk about with friends?

(b) Have each group meet with another and compare their lists, noting similarities and differences. **Variation.** This can be done as a reading activity in which, before students discuss other groups' lists, they read them silently individually and make notes that will form the basis of a whole-class discussion.

30 Old Friends

Task 4

Pair Work Who does Tony talk to every day? Complete the social network below.

(Boss)   *Parents*

(Girlfriend)

TONY

(Coworkers)   (Friends)

(Landlady)   (Bus driver)

(Uncle)

A Who do you talk to every day, Julio?
B Well, I talk to my parents, the people at work, and my girlfriend. What about you?
A I talk to my landlady, the guy in the coffee shop, and my roommate.

Task 5

Group Work Who do you talk to every day? Make your own social network and share it with several classmates.

YOU

> **LEARNING STRATEGY**
> *Brainstorming* = thinking of as many new words and ideas as you can.

Task 6

a Group Work What do you talk about with your close friends? Your classmates or coworkers? Teachers? Make lists.

What You Talk About With . . .

CLOSE FRIENDS	CLASSMATES OR COWORKERS	TEACHERS OR BOSSES

Here is what one group said that close friends talk about: *money, movies, what to do on the weekend, changing jobs, the environment, relationships, other people, vacations, learning English, growing old, accidents.*

b Group Work Compare your lists with another group's lists and note similarities and differences.

30 Old Friends

Language Focus 2 Wh questions: who + do/does

1 🎧 Pair Work Listen. Then practice the conversation.

A: Excuse me. I'm doing a survey for *People* magazine. Can I ask you some questions?
B: Sure.
A: First of all, what do you do?
B: I work in a bank. I'm a teller.
A: Uh-huh. And who do you spend most of your time with?
B: My friends and family.
A: Who is your best friend?
B: My husband, I guess.
A: OK. And who do you talk to every day?
B: Well, now, let's see. My husband, my children, the people I work with, and the bank customers.

2 Now practice the conversation using information that is true for you.

3 Make questions for these cues.

Cues	Questions
a I like someone.	Who do you like ?
b Someone likes me.	Who likes you ?
c Molly works with someone.	?
d Peter lives with someone.	?
e Someone studies with Tomoko.	?
f They go out with someone.	?
g Someone studies with me.	?
h We play tennis with someone.	?

4 Pair Work How many statements and questions can you make from these words?

every day	do	who	talk to
work with	he	does	they
every week	she		you

5 Pair Work Look at the pictures at left. Who does Maria talk to each week? Take turns asking and answering the following questions. Choose your answers from this list:

parents   friends   neighbor   bus driver   storekeeper

Who does Maria talk to at home? At school? On the bus? At the deli? At the coffee shop? On the way to school?

Old Friends 31

📖 Student text page 31

Language Focus 2:
Wh questions: *Who + do/does*

1. 🎧 Play the tape. Students then practice the conversation in pairs.

2. 🎧 Still in pairs, students repeat the conversation, with speaker B answering using information that is true for them. **Optional.** You may wish to analyze the dialogue in more detail with the class before students do this task. For example, speaker A explains his or her objectives and then asks permission to carry out the survey. Speaker B gives permission, then speaker A asks the survey questions and speaker B answers them. **Variation.** With books closed, students practice the conversation again.

3. In Unit 2, students were given answers and asked to write questions to go with them. In this exercise, they are given statements, here called "cues," and asked to write questions that one might logically ask on hearing the statements or cues. Go over the first two items with the class to be sure all the students understand what they are supposed to do. Then have them complete the task.
(Answers: a—Who do you like? b—Who likes you? c—Who does Molly work with? d—Who does Peter live with? e—Who does Tomoko study with? f—Who do they go out with? g—Who studies with you? h—Who do you play tennis with?)

4. In pairs, students see how many questions they can make. Elicit responses and then put the following table on the board to show the question pattern.

| Who | does | he/she | work with | every week? |
| | do | you/they | talk to | every day? |

Optional. You can make this a competitive game by putting a time limit on the task.

5. Students complete the task in pairs. Point out that they need to interpret the pictures to find the answers. Ask for responses from the class.
(Answers: home—parents; school—teacher; bus—students; deli—storeclerk; coffee shop—friend; on the way to school—neighbor)

Old Friends 31

📖 Student text page 32

Self-Check

Communication Challenge

Challenge 3 is on pages 113 and 115 of the student text, and suggestions for its use are on page 113 in this Teacher's Extended Edition.

1, 2, 3. Have students collaborate in pairs on the first three tasks so they can discuss what they feel they have learned. If possible, have them complete these three tasks without looking back at the unit.

4. Have students complete this task individually, then compare their responses with another student. The quoted statements in the left margin suggest the kinds of ways some students get additional help and practice. Elicit responses from the class.

- Where do you feel the class as a whole needs additional help? Make a list for yourself. Decide how/where you can include this review and/or extension work.

- This unit has been concerned with the strategy of brainstorming. As a whole class, have students brainstorm ideas for getting more practice. List these on the board and have students write them down. **Variation.** In small groups, have students list areas in which they believe they have made progress.

5. Have students look at the list of *nouns* and think of headings under which they might classify them; they can then relist the words under these headings. Then have them think of three friends and three family members and write them on a piece of paper with enough space to write a description of each beside the name. Students then choose at least one word from the *adjective* list that accurately describes each person. If there are no words in the list that describe the person, students should provide an adjective of their own.

- The grammar summary for this unit is on page 130.

32 Old Friends

Self-Check

COMMUNICATION CHALLENGE

Pair Work Student A: Look at Challenge 3A on page 113. Student B: Look at Challenge 3B on page 115.

"I have a Canadian friend. She tells me when I make mistakes."

"This week, I'm going to ask five *who* questions every day."

1 Write down five new words you learned in this unit.

2 Write down three new sentences or questions you learned.

3 Review the language skills you practiced in this unit. Check [√] your answers.

CAN YOU:

Talk about friends?	☐ yes	☐ a little	☐ not yet

Find or give an example: ....

Ask for information about other people?	☐ yes	☐ a little	☐ not yet

Find or give an example: ....

4 What areas need more practice? How can you get more practice? Make a list.

5 Vocabulary check. Check [√] the words you know.

Adjectives		Conjunction	Nouns		Preposition	Question	Verbs	
☐ best	☐ kind	☐ but	☐ actor	☐ nurse	☐ with	☐ who	☐ brainstorm	☐ drink
☐ close	☐ lonely		☐ bank	☐ quality			☐ change	☐ grow
☐ funny	☐ outgoing		☐ bank teller	☐ secretary			☐ compare	☐ like
☐ good-looking	☐ romantic		☐ bus driver	☐ singer			☐ date	☐ play
	☐ serious		☐ coworker	☐ sports			☐ discuss	
☐ happy	☐ sexy		☐ culture	☐ teacher				
☐ intelligent	☐ smart		☐ hospital	☐ tomorrow				
☐ interesting	☐ unusual		☐ movies	☐ vacations				

32 Old Friends

4 Interesting People

Unit Goals

In this unit you will:

Talk about occupations
"My brother is an actor."

Talk about likes and dislikes
"I don't like classical music."

Warm-Up

Picture 1

Picture 2

Picture 3

1 Do you know these words to describe things? Circle the words you do not know and discuss them with your teacher.

strange	good-looking	beautiful	cute	good	old
funny	interesting	unusual	kind	silly	sad
young	handsome	energetic	ugly	lonely	evil
boring	intelligent	exciting	stupid	happy	

2 **Pair Work** Classify the words above into three groups: positive words, negative words, and neutral words.

POSITIVE	NEGATIVE	NEUTRAL
good	boring	unusual

3 Find two words to describe each of the pictures above.

Picture 1: .... Picture 2: .... Picture 3: ....

4 **Group Work** Pick three words to describe yourself and the other students in the group. Share these words with the rest of the class.

Interesting People **33**

---

4 Interesting People

📖 Student text page 33

Warm-Up

Unit Goals. Have volunteers read the two unit goals and the sample statements under each of them. Then have the class as a whole brainstorm as many occupations as they can think of from the previous unit. List these on the board, and add any others that students volunteer from their own knowledge and/or experience.

1. Give students several minutes to look through the list of adjectives and circle the words they do not know. Then have pairs of students compare their lists, explain to each other words that one partner knows and the other doesn't, and look up the remaining unknown words in the dictionary.

2. Remind students of the strategy of classifying. Point out that whether a word is considered positive or negative or neutral is partly subjective. (In the example the word "unusual" is placed under the heading "Neutral." Some people might consider it positive, however, while others might see it as negative.) Now have the students classify the words into the three groups and write them under the appropriate headings. (Suggested answers: *Positive:* good, beautiful, cute, handsome, kind, good-looking, intelligent, exciting, energetic, interesting, happy. *Negative:* boring, ugly, silly, stupid, sad, lonely, evil. *Neutral:* unusual, young, old, strange, funny)

3. In pairs, students find adjectives from the list and match them to the three pictures. Each partner then chooses one of the pictures and talks about it to the other partner. (The left picture is a detail from a painting by Paul Gauguin, the center picture is a poster by Henri de Toulouse-Lautrec, and the right picture is by Pablo Picasso.)

(Continued on page 34)

Interesting People **33**

📖 Student text pages 33–34 (cont.)

4. Students choose three words from the list in Task 1 to describe themselves. Have each one tell the class which words he or she chose. **Variation.** Have students try to find words to describe themselves that begin with the same letter as their names. (They will probably need to use other adjectives in addition to those on the list.)

Task Chain 1: I like it a lot

Task 1. Before looking at the list of words, students should turn back to page 33 and choose one of the three pictures. Each student should then write ten adjectives that the picture suggests to her or him. Have them find others who chose the same picture and in pairs or small groups, compare and discuss the words they chose for the picture. (**a**) Then have students turn to page 34 and, in pairs, look at the list of adjectives. Have them check those that they feel describe "their" picture and (**b**) add three others. How does each student's original list compare with the new list on page 34? (**c**) Have them exchange their lists with another pair and guess which picture that pair looked at.

Task 2. 🎧 Play the tape and have students listen and answer the three questions. They will need to use inference to answer questions b and c. (Answers: a—2; b—a museum or art gallery; accept other possibilities; c—paintings or photographs; accept other possibilities)

Task 3. 🎧 Play the tape again and have students check each of the expressions as they hear them. **Optional.** Have students in pairs practice saying the expressions from memory, not reading them.

Task 4. 🎧 Have students turn back to page 33. Play the tape once more and have them discuss with their partners which two pictures the speakers are talking about. Remind them of the strategy of selective listening: it is not necessary to understand every word to do the task.
(Answer: the right [Picasso] and left [Gauguin] pictures)

34 Interesting People

Task Chain 1 I like it a lot

Task 1

a **Pair Work** Brainstorm. Look at one of the pictures on page 33 for a few minutes, and check [√] all the words it reminds you of.

☐ beautiful   ☐ funny   ☐ exciting
☐ good   ☐ stupid   ☐ colorful
☐ ugly   ☐ boring   ☐ strange
☐ interesting   ☐ unusual   ☐ lonely
☐ sad

b Add three words of your own.

....

c **Group Work** Exchange lists with another pair, and guess which picture they looked at.

Task 2

🎧 Listen and answer the questions.

a How many people are talking? ....
b Where are they? ....
c What are they talking about? ....

Task 3

🎧 Listen again and check [√] these expressions when you hear them.

☐ I don't like it much.
☐ Yes, I like that one too.
☐ Which one do you like?
☐ I like that one.
☐ I like it a lot.
☐ I like it because of the colors and the shapes.

Task 4

🎧 **Pair Work** Listen again. Look at the pictures on page 33. Which two pictures are they talking about?

34 Interesting People

Task 5

a Pair Work Read these descriptions of the pictures on page 33 and guess which ones they are.

Pictures	Descriptions
………	This painting is interesting because of the colors and shapes. In fact, it doesn't even look much like a woman, but that doesn't matter.
………	This picture shows a beautiful young dancer at a famous night club.
………	This picture is very interesting because it's not clear what the women are looking at.

A The third picture is interesting.
B Well, it's unusual. But I think it's silly. It doesn't look like a girl at all.

b Pair Work Talk about the pictures on page 33. Follow the model, but use your own ideas.

Task 6

Group Work Survey. Find people who like the pictures on page 33 and people who dislike the pictures. Ask and answer questions.

Example: "Do you like picture 1?" "Yes, I do."
                                     "No, I don't."

Write the people's names in the chart below.

	LIKES	DISLIKES
Picture 1		
Picture 2		
Picture 3		

35

Student text page 35

Task 5. (a) Review the difference between scanning for key words and reading for detail. In this task encourage students, working in pairs, to read carefully for detail. Have students read and underline the words that link the description to the picture.

(b) This is an opportunity for free expression of ideas—but controlled, so that it also provides an opportunity to practice the model structure in the right margin of the page: *The first picture is …Well, it's … But I think it's … .* **Optional.** Assign this as a written task for homework.

Task 6. Have students find people in the class who like the pictures on page 33 (all from the end of the nineteenth or first part of the twentieth century) and those who dislike them. Have them ask and answer the questions and record the answers in the box. Students should circulate freely in the classroom and find at least four others to interview. Make sure this is true speaking practice and not simply an information gathering task.

Interesting People 35

📖 Student text page 36

Language Focus 1: Simple present with *like*

1. (a) 🎧 Play the tape and have students listen and write down all the words they hear that describe music and movies. Write the words on the board and have students pronounce them. Students then practice the conversation. Circulate and check pronunciation.

(b) Have students look at the two lists of words; check that they understand them. For example, do they know what country music is and what westerns are? Then have them repeat the conversation, with speaker B giving answers that are true for himself/herself and using words from the two lists. **Optional.** Have students practice the conversation again, this time with books closed.

2. Individually students match questions and answers by writing the letter of the correct question in front of the answer. Then in pairs, they practice the questions and answers.
(Answers: c, e, f, a, b, d)

3. Individually students fill in the blanks in the questions and answers. Circulate and check their work. Then in pairs, students practice the conversation taking turns to ask and answer the questions. **Optional.** Have students substitute the names of people they know for *he*, *she*, and *they* in the questions and answer them as they believe those people would answer.
(Answers: a—Do, do, don't; b—Does, does, doesn't; c—Does, does, doesn't; d—Do, do, don't)

4. Working in pairs, students take turns using the cues to ask questions and then giving answers that are true for them. **Optional.** If you think some students are likely to have difficulty with the on-the-spot transformation of clues into questions, suggest that they write the questions out first. You could also do the first item on the board, and elicit that the clue "what/movies/like" becomes the question "What movies do you like?"
(Answers: a—What movies do you like? b—Do you like horror movies? c—What is your favorite [kind of] music? d—Do you like jazz?)

36 Interesting People

Language Focus 1 Simple present with *like*

1 a 🎧 **Pair Work** Listen. Then practice the conversation.

A: Do you like modern art?
B: No, I don't like it very much. Do you like it?
A: Yes, I do. What about music?
B: I like rock music and jazz.
A: So do I. I like classical music, too.
B: What kind of movies do you like?
A: I like thrillers.

b Pair Work Now give your own answers using words from these lists.

MUSIC	MOVIES
classical	comedies
jazz	thrillers
rock	westerns
country	romances

2 Pair Work Match these questions and answers. Then practice them.

Questions *Answers*
a Do you like movies? .... No, she doesn't. She likes jazz.
b What kind of art do you like? .... I don't have one.
c Does she like classical music? .... No, they don't. They like classical ballet.
d Does he like country music? .... Yes, I do. I like westerns.
e Who is your favorite singer? .... I love modern art.
f Do they like modern dance? .... Yes, he does. He likes rock music, too.

Do you know the rule?
Fill in the blanks with the correct pronouns from this list: *I, you, he, she, it, we, they*.
Use *like* with ....
Use *likes* with ....

3 Pair Work Fill in the blanks and practice the questions and answers.

Questions *Answers*
a .... you like classical music? Yes, I .... No, I ....
b .... she like rock music? Yes, she .... No, she ....
c .... he like jazz? Yes, he .... No, he ....
d .... they like modern art? Yes, they .... No, they ....

4 Pair Work Use these cues to ask and answer questions.

Example: you / like / classical music
"Do you like classical music?" "Yes, I do." "No, I don't."

a what / movies / like
b you / like / horror movies
c what / favorite / music
d you / like / jazz

36 Interesting People

Task Chain 2 An unusual occupation

Task 1

a Do you know these occupations? Ask your teacher about the ones you don't know.

actor	lawyer	architect
musician	painter	doctor
receptionist	engineer	
writer	computer programmer	

b *Pair Work* Find an occupation that takes place . . .

in an office ....
in a TV studio ....
in a factory ....
at home ....
in a hospital ....

Task 2

Pair Work Check [√] the words that describe each occupation.

	INDOOR	OUTDOOR	HIGH-PAID	LOW-PAID	INTERESTING	BORING
actor						
architect						
computer programmer						
doctor						
engineer						
lawyer						
musician						
painter						
receptionist						
writer						

Task 3

🎧 Listen. Check [√] what kind of a program it is.

☐ a news broadcast   ☐ an interview   ☐ an advertisement

Task 4

🎧 Listen again. Check [√] the phrases you hear.

☐ a boring person   ☐ an interesting occupation
☐ an interesting person   ☐ a young man
☐ an unusual occupation   ☐ a strong man

LEARNING STRATEGY

Selective listening = listening for the most important words and information.

Interesting People 37

📖 Student text page 37

Task Chain 2: An unusual occupation

Task 1. (a) In small groups have students discuss the list of occupations and mark any that no one knows. Ask someone from each group to tell which occupations are unknown, and write them on the board. Where possible, ask other students to explain these occupations. Explain any that are unknown. **Optional.** Have the whole class brainstorm occupations that are not on the list; let students explain or discuss any that others do not know.

(b) Give students time to think individually of people they know who work in these locations; then in pairs, students complete the written list. Circulate and provide help if necessary—some students may know what a person does but not know the job title.

Task 2. This is a classification exercise. Have students, working in pairs, discuss each occupation and make a check mark (√) in the boxes that they believe fit that occupation. When all have finished, ask for answers from the class. Point out that in some occupations, such as actor or musician, a few famous individuals are well paid, but many less famous are not. (Remember that in many instances students' answers represent their own subjective opinions. The "answers" below are suggestions; students may have excellent reasons for choosing others.)
(Suggested answers: Actor—indoor, high/low, interesting; architect—indoor, high, interesting; computer programmer—indoor, high, boring; doctor—indoor, high, interesting; engineer—outdoor/indoor, high, interesting; lawyer—indoor, high, boring; musician—indoor, high/low, interesting; painter—indoor/outdoor, low, interesting; receptionist—indoor, low, boring; writer—indoor, low, interesting)

Task 3. 🎧 Selective listening. A key strategy. Play the tape and have students check the kind of program they heard.
(Answer: an interview)

Task 4. 🎧 Play the tape again and have students check the phrases they hear.
(Answers: an interesting person, an unusual occupation, a young man)

Interesting People 37

📖 Student text page 38

Task 5. 🎧 Play the tape again. Have students listen and check True or False for each statement. Then play the tape once more for students to check their answers. (Answers: a—F; b—T; c—F; d—T; e—T)

Task 6. Have students read the newspaper letter and underline phrases that mention contributions to society. Then have them transfer this information to the box, and compare in pairs. Check responses with the class and put them on the board.
(Answers: Madonna—entertains people; College professors—produce cures for cancer, add to knowledge, train people to work for society) **Optional.** Have the class discuss the relative contributions to society made by people in different occupations. The purpose of this discussion is to give students opportunities to practice giving their own opinions. The aim of the task is not to get students to agree or disagree with each other, but to honestly state their opinions and listen to—and respect—those of others. You may wish to set a time limit of only a few minutes or allow the discussion to continue up to a maximum of ten minutes if students are interested and actively involved.

38 Interesting People

Task 5

Are these statements true or false? Check [√] the correct answer.

		True	False
a	The interviewer is talking to Elvis Presley.	☐	☐
b	The person pretends to be Elvis Presley.	☐	☐
c	He earns $60,000 a year.	☐	☐
d	He plays the young Elvis.	☐	☐
e	Gary was a university professor.	☐	☐

Task 6

a Read this letter to a newspaper and complete the chart.

> Dear Sir,
> In Tuesday's newspaper, there was an article titled "Madonna, the $60 Million Woman." Everyone knows that she is a very rich woman. On the same page is an article about the salaries of college professors, who earn much less. Is it true that Madonna is much more important to society than a college professor? She entertains people, and they buy her CDs, play them a few times, and then forget them. What do professors do? They produce cures for cancer, they add to our knowledge, they train people to work for society. It seems that the more people earn, the less they help society.
>
> (Professor) J. Stephen Smith

How Do They Help Society?

MADONNA	COLLEGE PROFESSORS
	produce cures for diseases

b **GroupWork** Discuss these questions. Give reasons for your answers.

- Do you think pop stars earn too much?
- Is it true that the more money people earn, the less they help society?
- What occupations are the most valuable to society?
- What occupations are the least valuable to society?

38 Interesting People

Language Focus 2 Adjectives

1 🎧 **Pair Work** Listen. Then practice the conversation.

A: Sandy, would you like to go on a date with my brother?
B: What's he like? Is he interesting?
A: Oh, yeah. He's an artist.
B: Is he good-looking?
A: Yes—very.
B: And is he nice?
A: Of course.
B: He sounds too good to be true!

2 **Group Work** Combine the following sentences.

a Madonna is rich. Madonna is a young woman.
   Madonna is a rich young woman.

b Paul is talented. Paul is a young actor.

c The *Mona Lisa* is famous. The *Mona Lisa* is an old painting.

d Eri is hard-working. Eri is a young tour guide.

e Sonia is Italian. Sonia is an interpreter.

3 Now make up five statements of your own using some of the following words.

beautiful	good	ugly	cute	dull	handsome
funny	kind	young	silly	sad	good-looking
intelligent	happy	old	boring	evil	unusual
energetic	strange	lonely	exciting	stupid	interesting

4 a **Pair Work** What do these people do?

Descriptions   *Occupations*
I have a boring job. I work in an office, and I do
the same things every day. I write letters and I
answer the telephone.

I have an unusual and exciting job. I travel all
over the world. I work with a camera, but I'm
not an actor.

b **Pair Work** Now describe an occupation and ask your partner to guess what it is.

Student text page 39

Language Focus 2: Adjectives

1. 🎧 Have students listen to the tape and practice the conversation. **Optional.** Have students close their books and practice the conversation again.

2. Sentence combining. Have students work in small groups to combine the sentences. Put the first item on the board and show the students how the two sentences became one. **Variation.** Elicit the rule for word order using adjectives.
(Answers: a—Madonna is a rich young woman. b—Paul is a talented young actor. c—The *Mona Lisa* is a famous old painting. d—Eri is a hard-working young tour guide. e—Sonia is an Italian interpreter.)

3. One of the most challenging language practice tasks for students is to create their own language from models and examples they have been working with. That is what they must do here. In groups, give students several minutes to consider the task, in particular the form and content of the sentences they will produce. A "scribe" in each group should write the sentences the group comes up with. When the groups have finished have each scribe read his or her group's five sentences to the class.
(Answers will vary, of course, but check that "age" words usually come after other adjectives—however see item e, where an age word, if used, would precede "Italian.")

4. **(a)** In pairs, students read the descriptions and decide what the occupation is.
(Answers: receptionist [or secretary]; news photographer)
(b) Students use the models in part (a) to describe an occupation with which they are familiar.

Student text page 40

Self-Check

Communication Challenge

Challenge 4 is on pages 114 and 125 of the student text, and suggestions for its use are on page 114 in this Teacher's Extended Edition.

1, 2. Have students complete these tasks without looking back at the unit. You may want to have these done outside of class and then brought in for checking by you.

3. This task should also be completed without looking back at the unit. For the first item, you may want to have students make a list of occupations from the item—no more than ten. In small groups, students find two qualities one needs to do each job well. For example, "Teachers need to be intelligent and patient." For the likes and dislikes item, you might use these occupations as subjects for such sentences as "I would like to be a teacher because…." or "I wouldn't like to be a computer programmer because…."

4. Follow the procedure as in the earlier Self-Checks. Find ways to help students get more practice and note areas in which most of the students appear to need review and/or extension work.

5. Have students check the word list. Tell them to add any additional occupational names they know. Ask the class for words that any of the students left unchecked, and have these explained by students who know them or, if nobody does, by you. **Optional.** Write the following occupational titles on the board or an overhead: architect, computer programmer, dancer, doctor, engineer, lawyer, musician, painter, professor, receptionist, writer. Have students decide, in small groups, which occupations are *most difficult to enter, most highly regarded in the community, most highly paid,* and *most enjoyable.* Have them list these occupations under the headings they think appropriate. (The purpose of this task is not for the students to arrive at consensus, but to exchange ideas and explore ways of classifying new words that will help in remembering them.)

- Grammar summaries for this unit are on page 131.

40 Interesting People

Self-Check

COMMUNICATION CHALLENGE

Pair Work Student A: Look at Challenge 4A on page 114. Student B: Look at Challenge 4B on page 125.

"My friends and I talk outside of class about our likes and dislikes."

"I try to learn new words by writing them down."

1 Write down five new words you learned in this unit.

2 Write down three new sentences or questions you learned.

3 Review the language skills you practiced in this unit. Check [√] your answers.

CAN YOU:

Talk about occupations? ☐ yes ☐ a little ☐ not yet
Find or give an example: ....

Talk about likes and dislikes? ☐ yes ☐ a little ☐ not yet
Find or give an example: ....

4 What areas need more practice? How can you get more practice? Make a list.

5 Vocabulary check. Check [√] the words you know.

Adjectives			Adverb	Nouns			Quantifier	Verbs
☐ beautiful	☐ exciting	☐ silly	☐ a lot	☐ architect	☐ engineer	☐ painter	☐ much	☐ buy
☐ boring	☐ famous	☐ strange		☐ art	☐ impersonator	☐ professor		☐ impersonate
☐ colorful	☐ good	☐ stupid		☐ computer	☐ lawyer	☐ receptionist		☐ use
☐ cute	☐ handsome	☐ ugly		programmer	☐ music	☐ writer		
☐ dull	☐ rich	☐ young		☐ doctor	☐ musician			
☐ energetic	☐ sad							
☐ evil	☐ selective							

40 Interesting People

5 Review

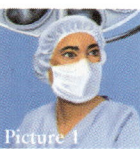
Picture 1

Picture 2

Picture 3

Picture 4

Picture 5

Picture 6

Picture 7

Task 1
How many occupations do you know? Label the pictures.

Task 2
Circle the word that doesn't belong in each line.

a name, address, friend, occupation, nationality
b uncle, father, son, nephew, daughter
c tall, happy, blond, female, handsome
d big, interesting, difficult, easy, boring
e movie, concert, singer, video, album

Task 3

a 🎧 Listen. How many different conversations do you hear?

1   2   3   4   5

b 🎧 Now listen again and fill in the chart.

	NAME	NATIONALITY	OCCUPATION
Conversation 1	Chuck		
Conversation 2	Tomoko		
Conversation 3	George		
Conversation 3	Anita		
Conversation 4	Cynthia		

c **Group Work** Student A: Keep your book open. Other students: Close your books. Student A: Say a nationality or an occupation. Other students: Make questions like the following ones.

What does .... do?
Where is .... from?

Example: Student A: France.
Student B: Where is Anita from?

Task 4

🎧 **Pair Work** Listen and fill in the missing information in the form at left.

ENROLLMENT FORM — Pacific Language School

Personal Information
Last name ....
First name *Carmen*
Citizenship *Argentinean*
Local address ....
Telephone *555-4083*
Occupation ....
Employer *Aerolineas Argentinas*
Highest level of education ....
Passport number *E6599139*

Language Needs
understand native speakers
talk to passengers!

Review   41

📖 Student text page 41

This is the first of three review units. It is designed to consolidate some of the key vocabulary grammar, and language functions introduced in Units one through four. In particular, this unit reviews personal identification and *wh* questions.

Task 1. Have students work in pairs or small groups to identify the occupations of the people in the photos and write the name of the occupation under each photo. Then have students practice asking and answering questions about the pictures, for example, "What does this person do? She's a doctor."

Task 2. Working individually, students find the word in the line that doesn't belong and draw a circle around it. This "Odd Man Out" item is basically a classification exercise, since four of the items belong under one heading and the fifth one belongs under another. Have students check their work in pairs; then elicit responses. Have students tell why they think the word does not belong. **Optional.** If there are clear differences of opinion, this would be a good time to discuss how meaning in language is interpreted and negotiated. Students should realize that interpretation is an important part of our understanding of language. (Answers: a—friend; b—daughter; c—happy; d—big; e—singer [or, perhaps, movie])

Task 3. 🎧 (a) Play the conversations and have students circle the number they hear.
(Answer: 3)
　(b) Now play the conversations again and have students fill in the box.
(Answers: 1—Canadian, teacher; 2—Japanese, student; 3—Argentinean, student; 4—French, student; 5—Taiwanese, doctor)
　(c) Have students follow the instructions. Let different students be "Student A."

Task 4. 🎧 Have students look at the enrollment form. If necessary, explain the heading, "Language

(Continued on page 42)

Review   41

Student text pages 41–42 (cont.)

Needs." Language needs can be described in terms of things you have to or want to do in English. These can be transactional tasks where you have to find out information or get things done. But needs may also be social such as meeting and chatting to other people, making friends, having fun…

Have students note what Carmen has filled in. In pairs, students listen to the conversation between Carmen and the Language School interviewer and fill in the missing information on the form.

Task 5. (a) Tell students that they are to ask and answer questions using the cues. They will work in pairs. One partner will ask a question about Carmen Costas, and the other partner will answer it. Partners will take turns asking and answering. Students may refer to the completed form in Task 4 for the answers if necessary. Have a volunteer phrase the first question: "What is her last name?" Ask another student to answer in a full sentence: "Her last name is Costas." Call attention to the fifth cue, "what/qualifications." Remind students that the interviewer at the language school asked Carmen, "Any qualifications?" Elicit that she answered, "I have a high school diploma." (Answers: Her last name is Costas; Her first name is Carmen; She's a flight attendant; She works for Aerolineas Argentinas; She has a high school diploma; She lives at 39 Silver Street, Apartment 40; She wants to understand native speakers, talk to passengers, fill in forms, understand TV, buy things in shops.)

(b) After all the questions have been asked and answered, have the partners interview each other, using the same cues, and fill in the form for their partners.

Task 6. Each partner writes the first names of the designated three people on a piece of paper. Partners then exchange papers and ask and answer "Who is…" questions. As they work, circulate and check pronunciation.

Task 7. Students think of or write questions for the answers, then, with a partner, take turns asking and answering them. (Suggested answers: What does she do? Do you like English? Do you like classical music? Where are you from? Where are they from? What is/What's his first name? Do you have a/any sister/sisters? What does Anya do?)

42 Review

Task 5

a Pair Work Ask and answer questions using these cues.

- what / last name
- what / first name
- what / do
- who / work for
- what / qualifications
- where / live
- why / want / study English

b Fill in the following form for your partner.

ENROLLMENT FORM .... (Name of your school)

Personal Information   *Language Needs*
Last name ....
First name ....
Citizenship ....
Local address ....
Telephone ....
Occupation ....
Employer ....
Highest level of education ....
Passport number ....

Task 6

a Pair Work On a piece of paper write the first names of three of the following people: your favorite actor, your father, the person who sits next to you in class, your best friend, your favorite singer, your mother.

b Pair Work Exchange papers and ask questions.

Example: "Who is Paul?" "The person who sits next to me in class."

Task 7

a Think of questions for these answers.

1. She's a student.
2. Oh, yes. I just love English.
3. No, I don't like classical music much—I prefer pop music, actually.
4. New York.
5. I guess they're from Japan.
6. Tony.
7. No, I don't have a sister—but I have three brothers.
8. Who, Anya? Oh, she's an artist. She's really well known.

b Ask and answer the questions.

42 Review

6 A Place to Stay

Warm-Up

Unit Goals

In this unit you will:

Ask for permission and make requests
"Can I stay with you?"

Talk about ability
"They can both swim."

Talk about quantity
"How many bedrooms are there?"
"How much is the two-bedroom apartment?"

Statement ....

Statement ....

Statement ....

Statement ....

1 Match these statements with the places above.

a I live in an apartment in Hawaii. We have fabulous views of the ocean.
b My parents live in a mobile home. They love it.
c Now, this place should be good for you. It has four bedrooms, two bathrooms, and a study.
d The Bedouin live in tents in the desert.

2 **GroupWork** Discussion. Which of these places would you like to live in? Give reasons.

3 **GroupWork** Discussion. Talk about the furniture in your bedroom at home. Compare your room with the bedrooms of other students.

"I have a bed, a dresser, a desk, and two chairs in my room."

A Place to Stay 43

Student text page 43

Warm-Up

Unit Goals. Read or ask individual students to read each of the three goals and the sample language aloud. Ask students to think about when they would need to ask permission to do something. Can they do this, and the other goals, in English?

1. Students can do the matching tasks individually and then compare their responses with other students in small groups. **Variation.** Have four students read the statements aloud; after each is read, the rest of the class guesses which picture matches it. Make sure the students who read the sentences provide a good model of pronunciation and, in particular, of correct stress and intonation.
(Answers: a—upper right; b—lower left; c—lower right; d—upper left)

2. Have students work in small groups to tell which of the pictured places they would like to live in and to give reasons for their choice. Break the discussion into two parts: first, the kind of house or dwelling they would like to live in, and second, the kind of room they would like to have as their own. **Optional.** As a class, discuss different kinds of housing. What sort of "house" is most common in big cities in the United States? What sort in small towns? In the countryside? If possible, include discussion of cultural differences; for example, are some types of housing more common or typical in some countries or regions than in others? What factors influence the kind of housing found in students' own countries and in the United States?

3. Before putting the class into small groups to describe their rooms, have them brainstorm vocabulary of furniture that you would find in a bedroom. Write words on the board. **Variation.** Rather than

(Continued on page 44)

A Place to Stay 43

📖 Student text pages 43–44 (cont.)

doing the brainstorm as an oral exercise have students come to the board and write a word. Encourage more than one student to come up at once, and students can approach the board more than once. Students may need to be encouraged to do this at first, especially if they feel unsure about spelling. You can encourage them by beginning the brainstorm yourself—write a single word on the board and move away. Approach the board again, write another and move away. Let students see that you are prepared to wait for them to think of and write up ideas of their own. Quietly correct any spelling mistakes on the board without discussing them. When the board is full have the class sit and silently read the words. Answer any queries about the meaning of any of the words.

- Call attention to the quoted statement in the lower left margin as a model for the discussion of students' bedroom furniture.

Task Chain 1: Alone in L.A.

Task 1. This is a selective reading task. Remind students that it is not necessary for them to understand every word. Before starting, make sure that students know what a fax is—a written document sent by telephone—and that "fax" is an abbreviation of "facsimile," which means an exact copy of something.

Have students work individually, writing their answers, then discussing them with others. (Suggested answers: a—Bill Jennings; b—Mary Sellers; c—Los Angeles; d—have a business meeting)

Task 2. 🎧 You may want to explain to students that when they take a phone message, they should write down only the essential information and use abbreviations. It would be useful to show the students a model of a telephone message to use as a guide. Play the tape, and have students write messages for each call. Pause after each message. You may need to play the tape several times to allow students time to listen and write. (Suggested answers: See top of page 45 of student text. Students' answers should approximate these.)

44 A Place to Stay

Task Chain 1 Alone in L.A.

Task 1
Read the fax, and answer the questions below.

```
FACSIMILE TRANSFER

To: Bill Jennings, Pacific Holdings, Hawaii
From: Mary Sellers
Date: Thursday, November 8

Dear Bill,
Our business meeting is confirmed for next Monday, November 12,
in Los Angeles. I have booked us rooms at the following hotel:

Beverly Inn
1829 Wilshire Boulevard
Beverly Hills, 90018
Tel: (310) 555-2020
Fax: (310) 555-0486

Looking forward to seeing you again. (And to some warm weather!)
Kind regards,


Mary


Eastern Holdings Ltd. – Park Plaza – Boston – Massachusetts
```

a Who is the fax addressed to? ....
b Who is it from? ....
c Where are they going to meet? ....
d Why? ....

Task 2
🎧 Listen to the four phone conversations. Take the messages.

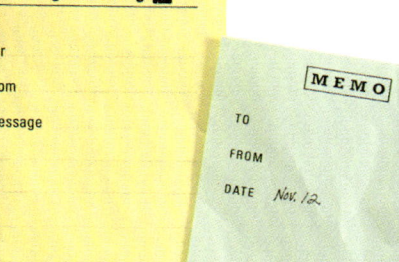
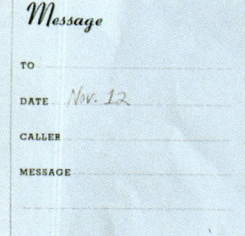

44 A Place to Stay

Task 3

🎧 Now listen to the telephone conversation between Bill and his secretary. Here are the messages for Bill. Which one does his secretary give him?

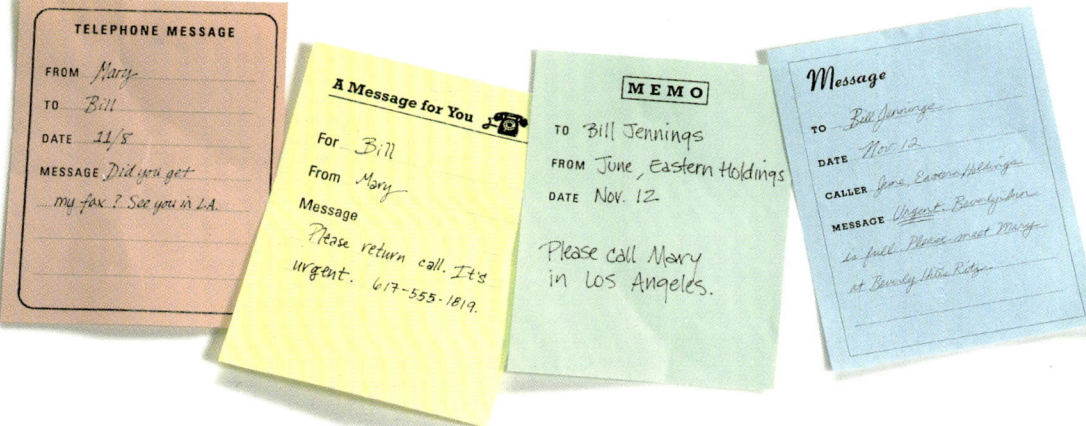

Task 4

a 🎧 **Pair Work** Listen. Bill is talking to a taxi driver in Los Angeles. What is the problem?

b **Group Work** What can Bill do? Make a list of possibilities.

Example: Perhaps he can stay in another hotel.

Task 5

Read the following letter from Mary. What was the problem?

Mr. W. Jennings
Pacific Holdings
1250 Punahou Street
Honolulu, Hawaii

Dear Bill,
I am very sorry about the mix-up in Los Angeles last week. I want you to know that it was not my fault. The hotel I booked rooms in changed its name, and the travel agency gave me the wrong name. Can we meet next week instead?

Sincerely,
Mary
Mary Sellers

A Place to Stay 45

📖 **Student text page 45**

Task 3. 🎧 Students listen to the tape.
(Answer: The secretary gives him the fourth message, about the change of hotel.)

Task 4. 🎧 (a) Play the tape. In groups students listen, and identify the problem.
(b) Have students make a list of things Bill might do. Ask them to tell their solutions to the class, if possible speaking without reading from their lists.

Task 5. Working individually, students read Mary's letter and underline the words that say what the problem was.
(Answer: The hotel I booked rooms at changed its name and the travel agency gave me the wrong name.)

A Place to Stay 45

Student text page 46

Language Focus 1: Modal: *can*

1. 🎧 Play the tape. In pairs, students listen, then practice the conversation, using their own names. Circulate and check pronunciation. **Optional.** Have students practice the conversation with books closed.

2. Point out that "can" can be used both to show ability and to make requests or give permission to do something. Use the first two items to show the difference. Then have students complete the exercise, writing 1 when "can" means ability and 2 when it means granting permission or making a request.
(Answers: 1, 2, 2, 2, 1, 2, 1, 2, 2)

3. Working in pairs, students write requests with "can" and then compare with another pair. Circulate and check responses, which may vary somewhat from the suggested answers below. **Optional.** Have individual students open their books and read aloud one of the statements at random. The rest of the class calls out an appropriate request.
(Suggested answers: a—Can I speak to Silvia, please? b—Can I borrow your car? c—Can you turn the music down, please? d—Silvia, can you teach me Portuguese? e—Can I have something to drink, please? f—Can I leave class early, please?)

4. Students work in pairs or groups to make up about 10 survey items using "can," following the model in the left margin. Then they interview classmates, asking questions in the form used in the example. As the students ask and answer the survey questions, circulate, monitor, and correct pronunciation. **Variation.** Students circulate and choose the people they want to survey.

46 A Place to Stay

Language Focus 1 Modal: *can*

1 🎧 **Pair Work** Listen. Then practice the conversation. Use your own name.

A: Can I speak to Terry, please?
B: Sure. Who's calling?
A: Sally.
B: OK. Wait a minute—I'll get her.
A: Thanks.
C: Terry here.
A: Hi! This is Sally.
C: Hi, Sally!
A: Can I come over and visit?
C: Sure.

2 Ability or requests? Write the number. 1 = ability; 2 = requests/permission.

..*1*.. Can you swim, Tony?
..*2*.. Yes, you can leave the room.
.... Can I speak to Maria?
.... No, you can't stay home today.
.... Maria can speak five languages.
.... Can I smoke in here?
.... They can play tennis really well.
.... You can't leave your bag in the hall.
.... We can come over after school.

3 **Pair Work** Make requests with *can*.

a You want to speak to Silvia.   *"Can I speak to Silvia, please?"*
b You want to borrow your friend's car.
c Your roommate is playing music very loudly.
d You want to learn Portuguese from Silvia.
e You are visiting a friend and want something to drink.
f You want to leave class early.

FIND SOMEONE WHO . . .	NAME
can speak Italian	Tony
can drive a car	

4 **Group Work** Class survey. Ask classmates questions with *can* and fill in the survey chart at left.

Example: "Can you speak Italian, Tony?" "Yes, I can."

46 A Place to Stay

Task Chain 2 Where would you like to live?

LEARNING STRATEGY
Personalizing = sharing your own opinions, feelings, and ideas about a subject.

Task 1
a Complete the following survey.

Where would you like to live?

1. Where do you think is the best place to live?
   a. in the center of the city
   b. in a suburb
   c. in a small town or village
   d. in the country
   e. _____ (other)

2. What sort of place would you like?
   a. a large house
   b. a small house
   c. an apartment
   d. a single room
   e. _____ (other)

3. Who would you like to live with?
   a. alone
   b. with a family
   c. with one friend
   d. with several friends
   e. _____ (other)

4. How much would you like to spend per month? _____

5. What would you like near your house?
   a. a park
   b. a shopping mall
   c. a library
   d. a health club

A Where do you think is the best place to live, Pat?
B I prefer the center of the city.

b **Group Work** Survey. Now ask two other students for their opinions.

Task 2
a 🎧 Listen for three people answering the questions in the survey. Write their answers.

	PERSON 1	PERSON 2	PERSON 3
Question 1			
Question 2			
Question 3			
Question 4			
Question 5			

b Who is the most like you? Who is the least like you?

c **Group Work** Compare your responses with the responses of three other students.

A Place to Stay

📖 Student text page 47

Task Chain 2: Where would you like to live?

Task 1. Introduce students to the strategy of personalizing, which means expressing your own opinions, feelings, and ideas in English. Then have them, working individually, complete the survey form. In groups of three, they share their ideas using the model in the left margin of the page. Call attention to the "other" possible answers for items 1, 2, and 3. Point out that if students aren't happy with any of the four choices (a, b, c, d) they can write in another answer. When students have completed the survey, carry out a "straw poll" around the class to find out what most students prefer.

Task 2. 🎧 (a) Play the tape. Students listen and write their answers in the box. You may need to play the tape more then once, pausing at key places.
(b) Have students interview others to find who is the most like him or her and the least.
(c) When they have completed the task, have them compare answers with those of three other students.

📖 Student text page 48

Task 3. Remind students that making choices is an important part of learning. Divide the class into pairs, and have each pair choose to do A or B. **Variation.** Negotiate with the whole class to do either or both tasks.

(A) Task A is a word association activity. Have partners brainstorm what other words they think of when they hear or read the word "HOME." Have them list these. Then, working individually, students check the statements in the book and add their own. Have them compare their responses with those of another pair.

• It is important to provide choices for learners, and this kind of activity allows for choice. Let students choose how they will compare ideas. Three possible ways to do this are:

1. reading their responses to each other
2. exchanging papers and reading other people's ideas
3. telling rather than reading

(B) 🎧 Have students listen to the tape and, in pairs, decide which room is being described. (Answer: Room 2)
Optional. Play the tape again and have students name the pieces of furniture that helped them to identify the room.

Task 4. (a) and (b). These discussions can be either of two kinds: They can be very open, giving students the chance to air their views freely and gain more confidence in speaking English; the focus is on content, what is said and not how it is said. Or they can be more controlled, with focus not only on what students think but also on how they express their thoughts, that is, with more attention paid to use of correct grammar and pronunciation. Both kinds of discussions are useful. They are best done in small groups rather than as a whole class; that way, more students have more opportunities to speak. Circulate and listen. If you have chosen the second kind of discussion, you may wish to correct both grammar and pronunciation—or make a note of things to be talked about later.

48 A Place to Stay

Room 1

Room 2

Room 3

Task 3

You choose: Do Ⓐ or Ⓑ.

Ⓐ Pair Work What does the word *home* mean to you? Check [√] the following statements and add some of your own.

A home is somewhere . . .

☐ I can be safe.
☐ I can keep my things.
☐ I can have parties.
☐ I can take care of my parents/children.
☐ I can make a lot of noise.
☐ I can invite my friends.
☐ ....
☐ ....
☐ ....

Now compare your statements with another pair's statements.

Ⓑ 🎧 Pair Work Listen. Teresa is calling about a room to rent. Which room?

Task 4

a Group Work Discussion. Look at the following information. Is any of the information surprising or unusual? Do you think the information would be similar or different in your country? How?

Where do North Americans live?

Houses	57%
Apartments	40%
Other	3%

Who do young North Americans live with?

- 4% of people aged 15 to 24 live alone.
- 25% of people aged 25 to 44 live alone.
- 77% of people aged 18 to 24 have never married.
- 66% of unmarried people aged 18 to 24 live with their parents.

b Group Work Discussion. Where do you live? In an apartment? In a house? When do young people usually leave their parents' homes in your country? Do they live alone or with friends? Do young people live together before they get married?

48 A Place to Stay

Language Focus 2 *How much? How many?*

1 🎧 **Pair Work** Listen. Then practice the following conversation.

A: I'm calling about the apartment you have for rent.
B: Yes?
A: How many rooms does it have?
B: Five.
A: OK. How many bedrooms does it have?
B: Two.
A: Oh, I want a three-bedroom apartment. How much is the rent?
B: $800 a month.
A: Oh, I'm sorry, that's too much.

2 Number these sentences to make a conversation.

.... Let's see—eight.
.... $700 a month.
.... Well, it has a yard. And there are shops nearby.
.... How much is the rent?
.... What do you want to know?
.... You're welcome.
.... What else does it have?
.... Well, how many rooms does it have?
.... Thank you.
.... Can you tell me about the house?

3 **Pair Work** Ask and answer questions about these places.

To let:
Studio Apartment
One bedroom
Share bathroom
Close to shops
$600 per month
555-9192

Four-bedroom apt./2 bathrooms
Men or women welcome
No smokers
Call Kelly
$300 per month
555-3042

4 **Group Work** Survey. Fill in the first row below. Then ask three other students about their homes and fill in the other rows.

NAME	APARTMENT OR HOUSE	NUMBER OF ROOMS	NUMBER OF BEDROOMS
1. you			
2.			
3.			
4.			

Do you know the rule?

Circle *can* or *can't* to complete each sentence correctly.

Use *how much* to ask questions about things you **can / can't** count.

Use *how many* to ask questions about things you **can / can't** count.

A Do you live in an apartment or a house?
B I live in a house.
A How many rooms does it have?
B Let's see, six.

A Place to Stay 49

📖 Student text page 49

Language Focus 2: *How much? How many?*

1. 🎧 Students listen to the tape and, in pairs, role-play the conversation, where possible from memory, memorizing two lines at a time. As they practice, circulate and check pronunciation. **Optional.** Students practice the conversation, with Speaker B substituting information that is true for where he/she lives. Students then change roles.

2. Students read the statements and say which one they think should start the conversation. Explain that it would be the last one, "Can you tell me about the house?" Then have students number the remaining sentences in the order in which they would occur in the conversation. When they have finished, discuss any differences.
(Answers: 4, 8, 6, 7, 2, 10, 5, 3, 9, 1)

3. This task gives students an opportunity to practice asking and answering "How much"/"How many" questions within a freer context. Remind them of the structures "*How much* is the rent?" and "*How many* rooms does it have?" Call attention to the rule in the left margin of the page.

Together with one student as respondent, model for the class one or two questions about the first advertisement, using "how much" and "how many." Then have pairs of students practice asking about both apartments. **Optional.** Have each pair of students choose one of the advertisements and practice the conversation from Task 1, using information from the advertisement.

4. Have students fill in the first row with information about their own homes. With the whole class, practice asking the survey questions, focusing on pronunciation, i.e., correct stress and questioning intonation. Then question three other students to complete the survey form.

A Place to Stay 49

Student text page 50

Self-Check

Communication Challenge

Challenge 6 is on pages 116 and 118 of the student text, and suggestions for its use are on page 116 in this Teacher's Extended Edition.

- The learning strategy in this unit is personalizing, sharing your own opinions, feelings, and ideas about a subject. In small groups, have students discuss their feeling about the Self-Check exercises. How useful are they as a way of reviewing what they have learned? How well are students using the Self-Check sections to maintain a learning diary or journal?

1, 2, 3. Have students complete the first three tasks without looking back at the unit. These can be done out of class and brought to the next session.

4. Have students compare their written responses with those of at least three others. Then call on individual students at random to tell you their responses; ask enough students to find out what areas seem to need more practice, and make plans for review and extension.

5. With the whole class discuss words that individual students did not know. Where possible, have other students explain them; provide explanations yourself if necessary.

- Grammar summaries for this unit are on page 131.

50 A Place to Stay

Self-Check

COMMUNICATION CHALLENGE

Group Work Group A: Look at Challenge 6A on page 116. Group B: Look at Challenge 6B on page 118.

"I practice speaking on a cassette tape. Then I listen to myself and find my own mistakes."

"I practice making requests with other students."

1 Write down five new words you learned in this unit.
....
2 Write down three new sentences or questions you learned.
....
....
....
3 Review the language skills you practiced in this unit. Check [√] your answers.

CAN YOU:

Ask for permission and make requests?	☐ yes	☐ a little	☐ not yet
Find or give an example:			
Talk about ability?	☐ yes	☐ a little	☐ not yet
Find or give an example:			
Talk about quantity?	☐ yes	☐ a little	☐ not yet
Find or give an example:			

4 What areas need more practice? How can you get more practice? Make a list.
....
....
....

5 Vocabulary check. Check [√] the words you know.

Adjectives	Nouns					Quantifiers	Verbs	
☐ alone	☐ ability	☐ bedroom	☐ health club	☐ mobile home	☐ table	☐ a lot of	☐ can	☐ personalize
☐ married	☐ apartment	☐ chair	☐ furniture	☐ wardrobe		☐ several	☐ mean	☐ rent
	☐ bathroom	☐ facsimile/fax	☐ garden	☐ permission			☐ meet	☐ stay
	☐ bed		☐ house	☐ study				

50 A Place to Stay

7 In My Neighborhood

Warm-Up

Unit Goals

In this unit you will:

Ask about and say where things are located
"Where's the supermarket?"
"It's on Fourth Avenue."
"It's next to the bank."
"It's near the subway."

Talk about what people are doing
"I'm watching a movie."

A I'd like a health club because I like to work out. What about you?
B I'd like a fast-food restaurant.
A Why?
B Because I love to eat, but I hate to cook.

1 Pair Work Look at the picture above and find places where you can . . .

- have lunch
- mail a letter
- catch a bus
- buy a newspaper
- buy traveler's checks
- buy some toothpaste
- buy some fruit
- borrow a book
- see a movie

2 Pair Work You are moving to a new neighborhood. Talk about all the things you want nearby.

3 Group Work Discussion. How many different neighborhoods have you lived in? Which did you like best? Why?

In My Neighborhood 51

---

7 In My Neighborhood

📖 Student text page 51

Warm-Up

Unit Goals. Read aloud or have volunteers read aloud the two goals. Discuss them. Ask students to think about whether they can ask for and give directions in English. Read aloud the direction words: "Where's the…"; "on the…"; "next to…"; "near…." Ask students to make sentences using these as a check on their understanding of them.

1. In pairs, students write on the picture itself where they could do each of the things in the list. Then have them make questions using the items as cues. With one student as respondent, do one as an example. Have the pairs ask and answer the questions; make sure both partners get a chance to ask and to answer. **Variation.** Have students ask the question using "I" rather than "you," i.e., "Where can I have lunch?" **Variation.** Have students switch pairs after three questions.

2. Have pairs brainstorm all the things they would like to have nearby, such as a fast-food restaurant, a park with a baseball diamond, a record store, a health club, a swimming pool, a skating rink. **Variation.** You can structure the task by asking students to list their ideas under certain headings, for example, transportation, stores, restaurants, sports facilities, parks or gardens. **Optional.** Have students ask their partners why they would like the items nearby. The conversation in the lower left corner of the page can be used as a model.

3. Individually, students list the different neighborhoods they have lived in, then star those they have liked best. Then in small groups, they talk about these neighborhoods and why they liked them. Encourage them to be specific in describing the neighborhoods and what they liked about them.

In My Neighborhood 51

📖 Student text page 52

Task Chain 1: Where's the Subway?

Task 1. This is another "Odd Word Out" exercise. Accept different answers if the students can justify them. (Suggested answers: a—on the roof; b—city; c—taxi; d—go to; e—park)

Task 2. (a) This is a different kind of word association exercise. Working in small groups, have students add to the "word map" on the page.

(b) Do this group discussion as a class. Be sure students know what the word "ideal" means. Then ask what they understand by the word "facilities." Elicit or suggest such things as services, shops, restaurants, playgrounds, parks, swimming pools, skating rinks, and any others the students can think of. Talk about which of these they would like to have in the "ideal" neighborhood, and why.

Task 3. 🎧 (a) Introduce the task by explaining that different people have different needs and wants—and people's needs and wants change during their lives. Then have students listen to the tape and fill in what Silvia would like and would not like in her neighborhood. They can use more paper if necessary.

(b) Have them compare their lists with others. (Answers: Would like: close to center or good transportation, bank, post office, shops, church, park for jogging. Would not like: noise, freeway nearby, bars, nightclubs)

(c) 🎧 Have students listen to the tape and, working individually, fill in the advantages and disadvantages of each location. They can use more paper if necessary. (Answers: Barker St. advantages: near city center, can walk to the city, has shops, banks, is fairly quiet; disadvantages: no parks. Beaker Hill advantages: close to city center, has shops, etc., park nearby; disadvantages, bars. Kellyville advantages: quiet, parks, shopping malls; disadvantages: pretty far out of town, poor transportation)

(d) In pairs, students discuss the advantages and disadvantages, from Silvia's point of view, of each of the three neighborhoods. Which one do they think is the best for her? Have the pairs report their decisions to the class.

52 In My Neighborhood

Task Chain 1 Where's the subway?

Task 1
Circle the word or phrase that doesn't belong.

a on the left, on the hill, on the corner, on the roof
b street, city, avenue, boulevard
c subway, bus stop, airport, taxi
d next to, across from, go to, on top of
e park, museum, church, theater

Task 2

a **Group Work** What does the term *neighborhood* mean to you? Build a word map.

b **Group Work** Discussion. Think of the "ideal" neighborhood. What would it look like? What facilities would it have?

shops — safe — NEIGHBORHOOD — friends and neighbors — somewhere to come home to

Task 3

a 🎧 Listen. Silvia is talking about the sort of neighborhood she would like to live in. Make a list of the things she would like and the things she would not like.

b **Group Work** Share your lists with other students.

WOULD LIKE	WOULD NOT LIKE

c 🎧 Listen to Silvia and Charlie talking about different neighborhoods. Note the advantages and disadvantages.

	ADVANTAGES	DISADVANTAGES
Barker Street		
Beaker Hill		
Kellyville		

d **Pair Work** Now decide which is the best neighborhood for Silvia.

52 In My Neighborhood

Task 4

a Pair Work Silvia finally decides to rent an apartment in the Beaker Hill neighborhood. Here is a map of the neighborhood.

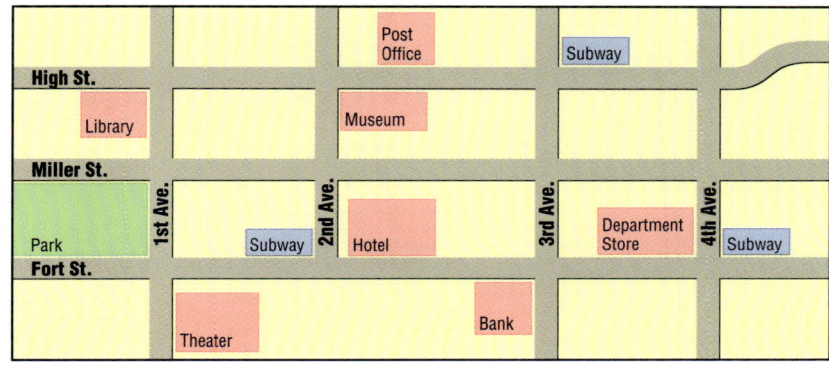

Student A: Ask questions about whether certain places are in the neighborhood, and ask where they are. Use the following words.

| museum | post office | hotel | library | park |
| video store | theater | bank | gym | |

Student B: Look at the map and answer the questions.

A Is there a museum?
B Yes, there is.
A Where is it?
B It's on the corner of Second Avenue and High Street.

b Pair Work Now change roles and do the task again.

Task 5

Group Work Create your own ideal neighborhood. Make suggestions, and have one student fill in the map.

Example: "There's a pizza parlor on Second Avenue."
"There's a subway on every corner."

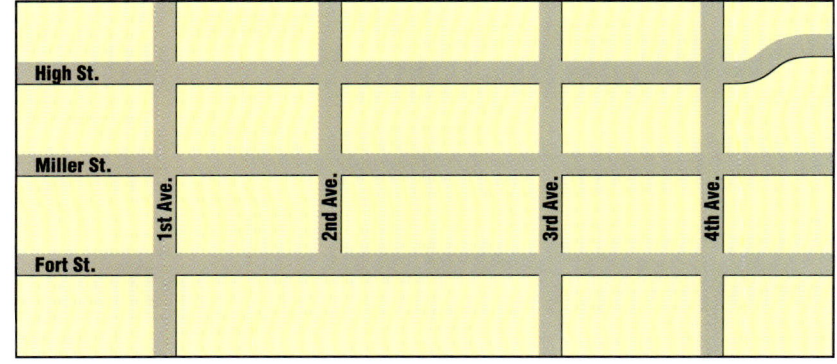

In My Neighborhood   53

Student text page 53

Task 4. (a) and (b) In this task, students, working in pairs, ask and answer questions about where particular places in a neighborhood are. Make sure students use complete questions and answers, following the model in the left margin. Students need to ask both questions, "Is there a …?" and (if the answer is yes) "Where is it?" Note that the answer is *no* for video store and gym. Students should switch roles after each item so that both partners have the opportunity to answer as well as to ask the questions.
(Answers: museum—It's on the corner of Second Avenue and High Street; post office—It's on High street, near the corner of Second Avenue; theater—It's on First Avenue, near the corner of Fort Street; hotel—It's on Fort Street, near the corner of Second Avenue; bank—It's on the corner of Fort Street and Third Avenue; library—It's on the corner of High Street and First Avenue; park—It's on First Avenue, on the corner of Miller Street and Fort Street) **Optional.** Students can also ask about the department store and the subway entrances (three of them).

Task 5. Have students, working in small groups, create their own neighborhood. What facilities would they include, and where would they locate them? Have each group appoint one person to draw in the facilities after the whole group has agreed on them. Point out that if a student says, "There's a pizza parlor on Second Avenue," the person doing the drawing can answer, "Where is it on Second Avenue?" and be told, for example, "It's at the corner of Second Avenue and Fort Street." **Variation.** In small groups, have students discuss how their wants or needs have changed. Can they think of times in their lives when they liked to do different things, go to different places, from those they like to do or go to now? How would their ideal neighborhood THEN differ from their ideal neighborhood NOW? **Optional.** Discuss what the ideal neighborhood for them would have been when they were 5 years old, or 10, or 15. Do these differ from one another? Why?

In My Neighborhood   53

📖 Student text page 54

Language Focus 1: Prepositions: *on, next to, near*

1. 🎧 Play the first conversation ("nearest subway entrance") and have students practice it in pairs, then switch roles so that each partner has the opportunity to be Speaker A and to be Speaker B. Then do the same with the second conversation ("the bank, please"). Monitor for pronunciation.

2. Have students individually make up statements and questions, writing them as they think of them. (Some students may realize that statements can be converted easily to questions: the skill learned on page 23 works with other kinds of questions as well as those with *do* and *does,* so "The bank is on Smith Street" can be converted to "Is the bank on Smith Street?") Point out that "the" is not used before street names. Accept any grammatically correct statements and questions that use only words from the list.

3. This exercise can be done in pairs or with the whole class. Make it clear that not all the statements have mistakes in them. Elicit responses from around the class, calling on different students for each statement. (Answers: a—false [see the example in the text]; b—false, the hotel is on the corner of Fort Street and Second Avenue; c—false, there are subways on Second, Third, and Fourth Avenues but none on First Avenue; d—false, the library is on First Avenue, not near a subway; e—true, the department store is on the corner of Fourth Avenue and Fort Street; f—false, the park is on Miller Street and Fort Street)

4. In pairs, students look at the map on page 53 again and answer the questions. Circulate and monitor performance. **Optional.** Students do this as a writing task, perhaps as homework.
(Answers: a—It's on Second, Third, and Fourth Avenues OR It's on Fort Street and High Street; b—They're on Fort Street; c—It's next to the Post Office; d—It's on First Avenue; e—It's near Miller Street [It's ON High Street and First Avenue, but NEAR Miller Street]) Students can talk about where similar facilities are in their home neighborhoods.

54 In My Neighborhood

Language Focus 1 Prepositions: *on, next to, near*

1 🎧 **Pair Work** Listen. Then practice these conversations.

A: Excuse me.
B: Yes?
A: Where's the nearest subway entrance?
B: It's on High Street.
A: And is there a post office anywhere near here?
B: Yes, there's a post office next to the museum.

A: Where's the bank, please?
B: It's on Third Avenue.
A: Thank you.
B: You're welcome.

2 How many statements and questions can you make up from the following words?

is	post office	Smith Street	where are	it	on
and	the	bank	next to		they

3 **Pair Work** Look at the map on page 53 and find the mistakes in the following statements.

a The post office is next to the theater.
b The hotel is on the corner of Fort Street and Fourth Avenue.
c There is a subway on First Avenue.
d The library is near a subway.
e There is a department store on Fourth Avenue.
f The park is on High Street.

Now take turns making correct statements.

Example: "The post office isn't next to the theater. It's next to the museum."

4 **Pair Work** Look at the map again and answer these questions.

Questions	Answers
a Where is the subway?	It's on ....
b Where are the hotel and the department store?	They're on ....
c Where's the museum?	It's next to ....
d Where's the theater?	It's on ....
e Where's the library?	It's near ....

Now talk about where these things are in your own town or neighborhood.

"In my neighborhood, the subway is on 21st Street."

In My Neighborhood

Task Chain 2 Garbage in Hunterville

A What can you do in your neighborhood?
B We can go skating at the Ice Palace.
A What can you buy in your neighborhood?
B Well, you can get good coffee at the Belaroma Café.
A What can you see in your neighborhood?
B There are good movies at the Roseville Cinema.

Task 1

a Think about things you can do, buy, and see in your neighborhood and where. Fill in the chart.

DO	BUY	SEE	WHERE?
ice skating			Ice Palace
	good coffee		Belaroma Café
		movies	Roseville Cinema

b *Group Work* Ask each other questions about your neighborhoods.

Task 2

a Jerry, Mike, and Helen are talking about the good and bad things in their neighborhood. Listen and fill in the chart.

	GOOD	BAD
Jerry		
Mike		
Helen		

b *Pair Work* Compare your notes with another student's notes.

Task 3

a *Group Work* Talk about the things Jerry, Mike, and Helen don't like about their neighborhoods. Suggest possible solutions and list them.

b *Group Work* Compare your list of solutions with another group's list.

A There's no parking in Helen's neighborhood.
B Maybe they can get better public transportation. Then they won't need cars.

Task 4

Look at the neighborhood picture on page 51. Who lives in this neighborhood—Jerry, Mike, or Helen?

In My Neighborhood 55

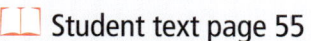 Student text page 55

Task Chain 2: Garbage in Hunterville

Task 1. **(a)** Give the students a few minutes to consider the three questions, "What can you do in your neighborhood?" "What can you buy in your neighborhood?" and "What can you see in your neighborhood?" Then, working as individuals, have them fill in the chart, using the example answers as models.

(b) This is a speaking practice task. In pairs, students ask and answer questions about their neighborhoods. They should use the sample conversation in the upper left margin as a model. If possible, they should answer from memory, without reading from the chart.

Task 2. **(a)** and **(b)** Play the tape and have students fill in the chart.
(Answers: Jerry: Good—safe; Bad—boring. Mike: Good—stores and restaurants, exciting and fun; Bad—a lot of crime. Helen: Good—interesting architecture, good shopping; Bad—crowded, nowhere to park.)
Have students compare their notes with another's.
Optional. Students brainstorm the good and bad things about their neighborhoods and make a list.
Variation. Have students discuss not only the good and bad things about their neighborhoods but also the reasons they feel that way. Would these be the same choices made by your parents? Your brothers and sisters, people much older, young children, parents of big families?

Task 3. **(a)** and **(b)** In groups, students talk about possible solutions to the things that Jerry, Mike, and Helen don't like. Have them also discuss possible solutions to problems in their own neighborhoods. Call attention to the sample conversation in the lower left margin. Have them compare their solutions with those of others.

Task 4. Do this as a class exercise. Call on individual students to tell whose neighborhood this looks like and ask them to give their reasons. Is there a consensus? (Suggested answer: Helen: She's near the center of the city, there's good shopping, but probably little parking space.)

In My Neighborhood 55

Student text page 56

Task 5. Remind students of the importance of developing effective learning strategies. The key strategy in this unit is scanning, reading through a text rapidly to find specific information.

(a) Have students look quickly at the articles to determine if each talks about a problem or a solution; they are to write "P" next to each article about a problem and "S" next to each one about a solution. (Answers from top to bottom: P, S, P, S, P, S, S, P)

(b) Working in pairs, students fill in the chart. They will need to scan the articles to find the solution(s) that go with each problem. (Answers: Hunterville as shown in text. Grantham: P— high crime rate; S—more police patrols, neighborhood watch. Newtown: P—no public transportation; S—subway system planned. Strathfield: P—no sports facilities; S—new pool, gym, sports fields)

(c) Have pairs use information in the chart to ask and answer questions. **Variation.** Remind students that articles from a newspaper are easy to recognize because of the general format, layout, and print. Using the overhead projector, show them a variety of other kinds of written or printed material; show each long enough so that one can see what it is, but not long enough to read it; have the students identify what kinds of text it is. Suggested items are a utility bill, magazine article, business letter, personal letters, postcard, page from a travel brochure. Discuss the cues they used.

Task 6. (a) Do this task in small groups from the same neighborhood or town if possible; otherwise have students work individually. Give them time to think of specific examples from real life to illustrate the good and bad things about their town or neighborhood.

(b) Have groups or individuals compare their lists.

(c) This can be done as a whole class discussion, with each group describing a problem, what is being done to solve it, and what the group thinks should be done. This task should give students a chance for freer discussion focusing on sharing ideas rather than on language accuracy.

56 In My Neighborhood

LEARNING STRATEGY

Scanning = searching a text for specific information.

Task 5

a Scan these newspaper articles. Which are problems and which are solutions? Write *P* for problems and *S* for solutions.

b Pair Work Read the articles again and complete the chart.

PLACE	PROBLEM	SOLUTION
Hunterville	bad garbage collection system	new garbage collection and recycling system

Hunterville: The garbage collection system is so bad that city hall is finally doing something about it. Garbage gets collected late, or not at all. Last month 89 people called to complain about the problem.

In response to complaints from residents, city hall is improving facilities in the neighborhood. This year, they are building a pool and a gymnasium. Next year they will build some new sports fields.

Police records show that Grantham has the highest crime rate in the whole city. Major crimes include robbery and assault. Car thefts are so common that many people do not bother to lock their cars.

In response to complaints from residents, city hall is setting up a new garbage collection and recycling system. The new garbage contractors are putting recycling bins throughout the suburbs so that residents can recycle paper, bottles, and cans.

Residents of Newtown are upset because they don't have public transportation. People living in the suburb say that it takes two hours to get to the city by car.

We contacted the traffic authority and found that they are developing a new subway system for the suburb. This will cut traveling time to the city by over an hour.

Authorities are taking steps to deal with the problems. They are increasing the number of police patrols, and they are establishing a neighborhood watch, a citizen's action organization to watch out for and report crimes.

Strathfield: At a town meeting last night, residents complained that they don't have any sports facilities. Their children have to travel several miles to the nearest fitness center. They demanded that the town do something.

c Pair Work Use the information in the chart to take turns telling about a problem. Your partner will tell about the solution.

Task 6

a Group Work Choose a neighborhood in your city or town and describe it. Make a list of the good and bad things.

NEIGHBORHOOD	GOOD	BAD

b Group Work Compare your list with another group's list.

c Group Work Discussion. Is your city or town doing anything to solve the problems? What is it doing? What do you think it should do?

56 In My Neighborhood

Language Focus 2 — Present progressive for actions in progress

1 🎧 **Pair Work** Listen. Then practice this conversation.

A: Hi, Helen. What are you doing?
B: We're having a neighborhood cleanup.
A: Really? Sounds interesting. What does it involve?
B: Well, we're picking up all the trash, and the kids are painting a mural on that wall, and we're planting some trees along the sidewalk.
A: That's great. Can I help?
B: Sure. You can help Tina. She's emptying that trash can over there.

2 Underline all the progressive verb forms in the following letter.

> Dear Mary,
> I'm having a good time here in New York now that I have somewhere to live. As you can see from the photo, I'm living in a nice apartment. I had a party last night, and most of my friends came. It was great.
> I'm going out with a nice guy from school, and I'm studying hard, so everything is going well.
> Love,
> Teresa

Do you know the rule?

Look at the verbs. Then write the rule for changing the base form into the progressive form.

Base Form	Progressive Form
go	going
have	having
be	being
live	living
come	coming
work	working

....
....
....

3 **Group Work** Look at the picture of Helen and Michael above. How many present progressive statements can you make?

Examples: "Michael is talking to Helen."
"Helen is wearing a T-shirt."

4 **Group Work** Write down what you are wearing at the moment. Give the paper to your teacher. Your teacher will give you a classmate's paper. Read the sentences to the class and guess who wrote them.

Example: "I'm wearing a red jacket and a pair of jeans."

5 **Pair Work** Make statements about your perfect day. Your partner says a time, and you say what you are doing.

Example: "It's 1 p.m." "I'm having lunch with friends."

In My Neighborhood 57

📖 Student text page 57

Language Focus 2:
Present progressive for actions in progress

1. 🎧 Have students, in pairs, listen to the tape, then role-play the conversation. Have them memorize two lines at a time so that they can do the whole conversation without reading.

2. The aim of this task is to encourage students to discover a rule through a process of induction. In groups, students study the examples, and try to determine the rule for spelling progressive verb forms. Ask for suggestions from the class and put a rule formulation on the board. Possible formulation: "Add -*ing*. When the verb ends in 'e,' drop the 'e' and add -*ing*." Now have students read through the letter to Mary and underline all the progressive verbs in it. (Answers: having, living, going, studying, going)

3. Have students, working in groups, study the picture of Helen and Michael. Ask them to make as many present progressive statements as they can about the picture.

4. This can be done in groups or individually. In either case, call on individual students to read to the class the sentences they received and ask, "Who do you think wrote this?" When someone gives the correct answer, have the writer of the sentence stand up so the class can see that the sentence was correct: the writer is indeed "wearing a red jacket and a pair of jeans," for example. **Variation.** Have students write a statement about what someone else in the class is wearing. Monitor what they have written before they move into groups, both to ensure accuracy and to be certain that what they have written will not be offensive or embarrassing to others.

5. Model this task by describing your own (fictional) "perfect" day. Say, "It's (five) o'clock and I'm…" Add one or two other examples. Then have pairs take turns giving a time and responding with what they are doing at that time.

In My Neighborhood 57

Student text page 58

Self-Check

Communication Challenge

Communication Challenge 7 is on pages 121 and 123 of the Student text, and suggestions for its use are on page 121 of this Teacher's Extended Edition.

- The key strategy in this unit is scanning (reading for particular information). Duplicate or have students copy this list from the board or an overhead. Tell them, "We read different kinds of written or printed material in different ways. Which of the materials in this list would you read carefully for all the details? Which would you scan quickly for particular information?" Have them take the list home and think about which way they would read each kind of document. Then, in class, put them in small groups and have them discuss their responses and give reasons for them:

junk mail	the TV program
a newspaper article	a utility bill
a magazine article	a check
a letter from a bank	a street map
a letter from a friend	a guide book
a telephone message	a postcard

1, 2, 3. These items can be done outside the classroom and brought in at the next session.

4. Ask students to discuss in groups what problems they have with reading, and what they could do to improve it. The sentences in the lower left margin may be used as models for the discussion.

5. If any of the words are unknown, have a student who knows them help those who don't. Provide help yourself if necessary.

- Grammar summaries for this unit are on page 132.

58 In My Neighborhood

Self-Check

COMMUNICATION CHALLENGE

Pair Work Student A: Look at Challenge 7A on page 121. Student B: Look at Challenge 7B on page 123.

"I can't remember prepositions. So I draw pictures and stick them on my mirror."

"I'm collecting maps of American cities. I use these to practice directions and locations."

1 Write down five new words you learned in this unit.
....
....

2 Write down three new sentences or questions you learned.
....
....
....

3 Review the language skills you practiced in this unit. Check [√] your answers.

CAN YOU:

Ask about and say where   ☐ yes   ☐ a little   ☐ not yet
things are located?
Find or give an example: ....

Talk about what people are doing?   ☐ yes   ☐ a little   ☐ not yet
Find or give an example: ....

4 What areas need more practice? How can you get more practice? Make a list.
....
....
....

5 Vocabulary check. Check [√] the words you know.

Nouns					Prepositions	Verbs		
☐ bus stop	☐ gym	☐ map	☐ neighborhood	☐ subway	☐ near	☐ borrow	☐ mail	☐ sell
☐ church	☐ hotel	☐ museum	☐ park	☐ theater	☐ next to	☐ catch	☐ scan	
☐ department store	☐ library	☐ neighbor	☐ post office		☐ on	☐ hate	☐ see	

58 In My Neighborhood

8 New York, New York

Warm-Up

Unit Goals

In this unit you will:

Ask about and describe locations of places

"Is there a bookstore around here?"

"There's a bookstore near the subway."

Make, accept, and reject suggestions

"Why don't you go on the boat trip around Manhattan?"

"No, it's too cold today."

"Yes, that's a good idea."

LEARNING STRATEGY

Memorizing conversational patterns and expressions = learning phrases to start conversations and keep them going.

1 **Pair Work** Match these statements with the places pictured above. What does *it* refer to in each statement?

Pictures	Statements
....	We heard it at Radio City Music Hall.
....	We saw it from the Empire State Building.
....	We did it in Central Park.
....	We saw it in Times Square.
....	We caught it to the Statue of Liberty.

2 a **Pair Work** How many of these English expressions do you know? Check [√] your answers.

	Yes	Not sure	No
Sorry?	☐	☐	☐
Hi!	☐	☐	☐
See you later.	☐	☐	☐
Excuse me?	☐	☐	☐
See you.	☐	☐	☐
How are you doing?	☐	☐	☐

b **Pair Work** Which expressions do you use in these situations? Add some situations and have your partner give the correct expressions.

- you are greeting someone
- you are saying goodbye
- you do not understand

New York, New York **59**

Student text page 60

Task Chain 1: Making plans

Task 1. (a) Have students work collaboratively, circling the words they know and explaining any words they know that others in the group do not know.
(b) If any words are unknown to the whole group, have students look these up in their dictionaries. Circulate and make a note of words causing the most trouble. Put these on the board and go through them with the class.

Task 2. (a) Have students classify the words. Point out that there are no right and wrong answers for many of the words: for example it is a subjective matter whether "quiet" is considered positive or negative. Remind students that categorizing words is a good way of learning them. Reorganize the class into small groups and have the groups discuss which words they put into each category and why. **Variation.** Students invent other categories under which they might classify the words—for example the shape or form of the words; positive and negative words.

Task 3. Students brainstorm other words to describe places and add them to the list. **Variation.** Put several examples on the board and discuss them. Some possibilities: hot, cold, bustling, attractive, sprawling, unusual, strange.

Task 4. Give students several minutes to write down words to describe their own city or neighborhood. In pairs they discuss the words they have written, using the model dialogue in the left margin.

Task 5. 🎧 Students listen to the tape and check the words they hear. Let them listen again to check their answers.
(Answers: interesting, noisy, busy, nice, expensive, crowded)

Task 6. (a) 🎧 Have students listen again and summarize the suggestions and objections. You can play the tape several times.
(Answers: go to exhibition at museum / tired of looking at art; go shopping / stores crowded and expensive; walk through Central Park / busy at lunch time)
(b) (Answer: They decide to stay where they are.)

60 New York, New York

Task Chain 1 Making plans

Task 1
a Group Work These words describe places. Which words do you know? Circle them.

interesting	small	dirty	exciting
noisy	quiet	beautiful	horrible
crowded	ugly	busy	big
awful	wonderful	expensive	

b Group Work Use your dictionary to find unknown words.

Task 2
a Pair Work Classify the words in Task 1 into three groups: positive words, negative words, and neutral words.

POSITIVE	NEGATIVE	NEUTRAL
wonderful	awful	interesting

Task 3
Pair Work Can you think of other words to add to the lists?

Task 4
Pair Work Which words would you use to describe your city or neighborhood?

Task 5
🎧 Listen. Pauline and Ron are making plans for the day. Check [√] the words you hear.

☐ interesting   ☐ wonderful   ☐ noisy   ☐ beautiful
☐ busy   ☐ nice   ☐ expensive   ☐ exciting
☐ quiet   ☐ crowded   ☐ horrible

A My neighborhood is noisy and dirty.
B It sounds horrible.
A Yes, but it's also exciting. I like it.

SUGGESTIONS	OBJECTIONS

Task 6
a 🎧 Pair Work Listen again and note the suggestions and objections in the chart at left.

b What do they finally decide to do?

60 New York, New York

Task 7

Pair Work Study the following sample guidebook entries. Where can you go to . . .

- entertain your ten-year-old niece?
- eat a late-night meal?
- buy a new compact disc player?
- buy gifts to take home to your parents?

Children's Museum of Manhattan
212 W. 83rd St.
555-5904
The Children's Museum of Manhattan was the idea of Bette Korman, a kindergarten teacher who believed that children needed "laboratories" to explore the world during nonschool hours. The museum is extremely popular, and its newest location now provides even more space for hands-on exhibits.

Lyric High Fidelity
1221 Lexington Ave. (between 82nd and 83rd St.)
555-5710 and 555-1900
Mon.–Wed., Fri., Sat.: 10–6; Thurs.: 10–8
Lyric is the place for experienced sound fanatics. As Lyric's Michael Kays says, "We're not for beginners, but people who recognize fine equipment and great values can make their dreams come true at Lyric."

Carnegie Delicatessen and Restaurant
854 Seventh Ave. (at 55th St.)
555-2245
There's no other city on earth with delis like New York's, and the Carnegie is one of the best. Its location in the middle of the hotel district makes it the perfect place for midnight snacks. Everything on the menu is made at the deli, and Carnegie offers free delivery between 7 a.m. and 3 a.m. within a five-block area. Remember, come hungry! The sandwiches are huge!

Wanamaker's
1194 Lexington Ave. (between 81st and 82nd St.)
555-2492
Wanamaker's is the place for special household goods. It has unusual household gifts for friends and family—and you'll probably find something for yourself, too!

"I'd take my boyfriend to the Phoenix Restaurant. It's very cheap."

"For an evening of entertainment, we can go to the free concert in the park."

Task 8

Pair Work Talk about places in your own town. Where can you go for . . .

- a meal with your girlfriend/boyfriend/best friend?
- an evening of free entertainment?
- a new car?
- an interesting afternoon with your nine-year-old nephew?

New York, New York **61**

📖 **Student text page 61**

Task 7. This is a scanning task. Remind students that scanning means reading for key information, not trying to understand every word. In pairs students study the four guidebook entries and answer the questions.
(Answers: entertain 10-year old niece—Children's Museum of Manhattan; eat late night meal—Carnegie Delicatessen and Restaurant; buy a compact disc player—Lyric High Fidelity; buy gifts for parents—Wanamaker's) Note: These are fictional places, but are typical of those found in New York City.

Task 8. This task can be done in pairs or in small groups. Give students a few minutes to think about places in their own town, city, or neighborhood. Then, following the model in the lower left margin, have them practice both asking and answering. Circulate and monitor their performance. Choose three or four pairs to role-play their questions and answers for the class. Check and correct pronunciation and grammar if necessary.

New York, New York | **61**

Student text page 62

Language Focus 1:
Making suggestions with *Why don't you...?*

1. 🎧 Have students listen to the tape and role-play the conversation. Then have them exchange roles and role-play it again. Circulate and monitor pronunciation, intonation, and stress. **Optional.** With books closed, have the pairs practice the conversation again.

2. Have the pairs work together to put the conversation in order. Point out that there are two possible conversations that can be made from these sentences. When they have finished, have them practice the conversation, then exchange roles and practice it again. (Answers: Option a: 3, 6, 5, 1, 4, 8, 7, 2; Option b: 5, 6, 3, 1, 2, 8, 7, 4)

3. Have pairs of students match the suggestions and answers. They can draw lines or they can write the letter of each suggestion next to the appropriate answer. When they have finished, check answers around the class. Then have the pairs practice the questions and answers; each partner should have the opportunity to suggest and to answer (or object).
(Answers: a—I don't like looking at paintings; b—It's quicker to walk; c—She doesn't like to go out at night; d—I'm not hungry; e—It's too expensive)

4. Call on four students to ask the questions; have the rest of the class volunteer answers. Try to get every student to participate, and elicit as many suggestions as possible. **Optional.** This can be made into a competitive game by awarding points for the most interesting, unusual, or ridiculous suggestions.

62 New York, New York

Language Focus 1 — Making suggestions with *Why don't you...?*

1 🎧 **Pair Work** Listen. Then practice this conversation with another student.

A: What are you planning to do today?
B: What do you suggest?
A: Why don't you go on the boat trip around Manhattan?
B: No, it's too cold today.
A: Well, why don't you go to a museum or gallery?
B: That's a good idea.

2 **Pair Work** Number these sentences to make a conversation. Then practice the conversation.

.... No, it's too cold.
.... I know what we can do.
.... No, it's too expensive.
.... What can we do this evening?
.... Why don't we go to the new show at Lincoln Center?
.... We can stay home.
.... What?
.... Why don't we go to the free concert in Central Park?

3 **Pair Work** Draw lines to match the suggestions and answers. Then practice them.

Suggestions	Answers
a Why don't you visit the gallery?	I'm not hungry.
b Why doesn't he take the subway?	It's too expensive.
c Why doesn't Tomoko go to the theater?	I don't like looking at paintings.
d Why don't we go out to eat?	It's quicker to walk.
e Why don't they stay at the Hilton Hotel?	She doesn't like to go out at night.

4 Make suggestions to someone who asks these questions.

Questions	Suggestions
a Are there any good places to take children?	Why don't you ....?
b All I want to do is eat out somewhere.	Why don't you ....?
c I need to buy a CD player.	Why don't you ....?
d I'd like to get something for my sister.	Why don't you ....?

62 New York, New York

Task Chain 2 Talking about location

Task 1
Read the paragraph about New York and underline the places and the locations.

Visiting New York

One of the best neighborhoods to stay in for visitors to New York is the Upper East Side. Here, the streets are lined with beautiful town houses, magnificent mansions, and apartment buildings. There are two <u>famous museums</u> (the Guggenheim and the Metropolitan) <u>on Fifth Avenue</u>. There is a famous store (Bloomingdale's) on Lexington Avenue, and there are many mansions on Carnegie Hill. Stop for a cup of coffee or a drink at one of the many cafés and bars on Central Park South. For people who like photography, there is the International Center of Photography on Fifth Avenue. Like most of New York's neighborhoods, the Upper East Side is best seen on foot.

[Source: Adapted from Gerry Frank, *Where to Find it, Buy it, Eat in New York*, Gerry's Frankly Speaking, Salem, Oreg., 1989.]

Task 2
Transfer the information in the text to the chart below.

PLACES	LOCATIONS
famous museums	on Fifth Avenue

Task 3

a 🎧 Listen to Ron talking about his trip to New York. What four things happened to him? Where did they happen?

Incident	Where
....	....
....	....
....	....
....	....

b **Pair Work** Compare your answers with another student's answers.

📖 Student text page 63

Task Chain 2: Talking about location

• Before doing Task 1 and 2, have the class brainstorm all the places in New York City that they know.

Tasks 1 and 2. Have students scan the paragraph and underline the particular places mentioned and their locations and transfer these to the chart. Have students check their responses with one or more other students. Then call on individual students to give their answers.
(Answers: famous museums / Fifth Avenue; famous store / Lexington Avenue; mansions / Carnegie Hill; cafes and bars / Central Park South; International Center of Photography / Fifth Avenue)

Task 3. (a) 🎧 Have students listen to the tape and write down what happened to Ron and where it happened.
(Answers: mixup in hotel reservations, had to find accommodations / various places; Went to Museum of Modern Art, but it was shut / Museum of Modern Art; lost wallet / Macy's Department Store; problem with return flight, stuck 8 hours / airport)
(b) Have students compare answers with a partner.

New York, New York

Student text page 64

Task 4. Have students write on the postcard on the page. Suggest they describe places they went to in New York and what they did there. They do not need to describe catastrophes such as happened to Ron (Task 3), although they can if they wish to. **Variation.** Present students with a model of a postcard you have sent/someone else has sent from an airport while they were on vacation. Discuss with the class some of the features of a postcard—where the address is written, short sentences, some words left out to save space. Using this model have students write a postcard of their own. Give them time to think about where they are writing the postcard from and what they will say on it.
   Alternative. As a whole class activity brainstorm some places that people go to on vacation. List them on the board and students choose from the list.

Task 5. (a) Give students at least five minutes to think about the New York places they would like to visit and write them down. **Variation.** Have them do the exercise in pairs.
   (b) Put the class in small groups and have group members talk about the places they would like to visit and why they would like to visit them. Go around the room and check both content and pronunciation. **Optional.** Have several students make their statement to the rest of the class.

Task 6. Have students choose either **A** or **B**. This task provides students with an opportunity to talk about places they know a great deal about, either with a pair partner or in a group discussion. Option A is more structured and emphasizes one-to-one conversation. Option B encourages freer discussion and a greater variety of opinions, but limits the number of places a student can talk about in the group. In either case, students can use the quoted sentences on the lower left margin as models for their conversations or discussion.

64 New York, New York

Task 4
Imagine you are Ron. You are at the airport waiting for your flight. Write a postcard to a friend describing your holiday.

Task 5
a Make a list of all the places you would like to visit in New York. Write down why you would like to visit these places.

Places	Reasons
....	....
....	....
....	....

b Group Work Discussion. Talk about the places you would like to visit and say why.

Task 6
You choose: Do **A** or **B**.

A Pair Work List all of the places in your city you would like to show to a visitor. Share your list with another person.

B Group Work Discussion. Talk about three famous or interesting places in your city.

"I come from Bangkok. In Bangkok, there are many interesting Buddhist temples. There's a famous hotel, the Oriental, by the river, and there are lots of jewelry shops on Silom Road."

64 New York, New York

Language Focus 2
There is/there are and *one, any, some*

1 🎧 **Pair Work** Listen. Then practice this conversation.

A: Is there a bookstore around here?
B: No, there isn't. But there's one near the subway. Why?
A: I want to get a guidebook.
B: Oh, there are some guidebooks on the shelf—help yourself.
A: Thanks a lot.

2 **Pair Work** Fill in the blanks and then practice the questions and answers with another student.

A: .... there a subway near here?
B: Yes, ... is. There's one near the hotel.

A: .... there a restaurant around here?
B: No, there ...., but there's .... in the hotel.

A: .... there any bookstores nearby?
B: Yes, there .... There .... some on Lexington Avenue.

A: .... there .... bars near here?
B: No, there .... But there are .... opposite Central Park.

3 **Pair Work** Look at the guidebook entries on page 61. Make up questions for these answers and then practice them.

Questions	Answers
....?	Yes, there is. There's one on Seventh Avenue and 55th Street.
....?	No, there isn't. But there's one at 212 West 83rd Street.
....?	Yes. There's one on Lexington between 82nd and 83rd Streets.
....?	Yes. There's one on Lexington between 81st and 82nd Streets.

4 **Pair Work** Write five interesting questions to ask classmates about places in their neighborhood.

5 **Group Work** Survey. Ask other students the questions and write their answers. Share the information with the class.

New York, New York **65**

📖 Student text page 65

Language Focus 2:
There is/there are and *one, any, some*

1. 🎧 Have students listen to the tape and then practice the conversation.

2. Students fill in the blanks working individually; then they practice the questions and answers with a pair partner. Have them exchange roles so that each student practices both asking and answering. When they have finished, check the answers with the class. (Answers: A—Is, B—there; A—Is, B—isn't, one; A—Are, B—are, are; A—Are, any, B—aren't, some)

3. Have students turn back to page 61 and look at the Guidebook entries. Using these, they make questions to match the answers given. They can either write their answers in the blanks or give them orally to their partner. **Variation.** Do this as a whole class exercise, writing the questions on the board as students agree on them; try to ensure that all students participate actively. (Suggested answers: Is there a deli [restaurant] near here? Is there a museum for children near here? Is there a stereo equipment store near here? Is there a gift store near here?)

4. As preparation for this task, have students brainstorm the kinds of questions they might ask, both content and structure, i.e., what they could ask about and how they could phrase their questions. Then have them make up five questions to ask their partners, similar to those in Task 2 above. Circulate and check their questions and answers.

5. Have each student ask four or five other students and write their answers. Be sure that all students get the chance to answer as well as to ask questions and that the information gathering is done orally, not in writing.

New York, New York **65**

Student text page 66

Self-Check

Communication Challenge

Challenge 8 is on page 117, and suggestions for its use are on that page in this Teacher's Extended Edition.

1, 2, 3. Have students complete the first three tasks without looking back in the unit if possible; they may look back if necessary. These tasks may be completed outside of class.

- Remind students that the key strategy in this unit was using conversational patterns and expressions to start conversations and keep them going. Explain that different topics of conversation are appropriate for different situations—and also that what is considered appropriate may vary from one culture to another. In casual American conversations, the following topics are among the common ones: the weather, sports, TV programs or movies, books or magazine articles, what you did over the weekend (or on vacation), work, family, current events. In small groups have students discuss which of these topics they feel comfortable talking about in English. Are there words or expressions they need to use that they do not know in English? Would they talk about these topics in their own language?

4. Have a discussion with the whole class about the best ways of practicing conversation.

5. Have students check the words they know and work in groups to clarify any of which they are not sure. Then, as a whole class, have them provide opposites for the adjectives on the list. Write them on the board as they are given. Note that many words have multiple opposites; accept any that seem to apply. (Suggested answers: awful—very good, great; busy—relaxed, idle, quiet; crowded—uncrowded; dirty—clean; expensive—cheap; horrible—wonderful, lovely; nice—nasty; noisy—quiet; quiet—noisy, loud; small—large; wonderful—terrible, horrible, awful)

- Grammar summaries for this unit are on page 132.

66 New York, New York

Self-Check

COMMUNICATION CHALLENGE
Look at Challenge 8 on page 117.

"I have trouble learning grammar. So I choose one grammar point to study every week."

"Sometimes I practice my English at work."

1 Write down five new words you learned in this unit.

2 Write down three new sentences or questions you learned.

3 Review the language skills you practiced in this unit. Check [√] your answers.

CAN YOU:

Ask about and describe locations of places?   ☐ yes   ☐ a little   ☐ not yet
Find or give an example:

Make, accept, and reject suggestions?   ☐ yes   ☐ a little   ☐ not yet
Find or give an example:

4 What areas need more practice? How can you get more practice? Make a list.

5 Vocabulary check. Check [√] the words you know.

Adjectives			Nouns			Quantifiers	Question	Verbs
☐ awful	☐ expensive	☐ quiet	☐ bar	☐ compact	☐ guidebook	☐ any	☐ why	☐ entertain
☐ busy	☐ horrible	☐ small	☐ bookstore	disc	☐ location	☐ one		☐ suggest
☐ crowded	☐ nice	☐ wonderful	☐ café	☐ entertainment	☐ postcard	☐ some		☐ take
☐ dirty	☐ noisy			☐ gift	☐ suggestion			☐ understand
								☐ visit

66 New York, New York

9 Going Places

Warm-Up

Unit Goals

In this unit you will:

Talk about the weather/climate

"What's the weather like where you come from?"

"It's usually hot in summer."

Ask for and give opinions and advice

"What are the most interesting sights in Barcelona?"

"You should go to Kyoto when you visit Japan."

Caracas ....

London ....

Cairo ....

San Francisco ....

Seoul ....

Barcelona ....

1 **Group Work** Where are the cities in the pictures above? Write the country names above the pictures.

2 **Pair Work** Which places would you like to visit? List them in order. Can you give reasons for your choices?

3 a 🎧 **Pair Work** Listen to Tony and Fabio talking about the temperature, and complete the following:

To convert .... to .... you subtract .... , ... by 5, and .... by 9. To convert .... to .... , you multiply by .... , ... by 5, and add ....

b Complete the table at right.

CELSIUS	FAHRENHEIT
	28
38	

Going Places 67

---

9 Going Places

📖 Student text page 67

Warm-up

Unit Goals. Have students read the goals and sample language aloud. Or read them yourself.

• Before doing the three tasks on this page, have students brainstorm vocabulary relating to the weather. List the words on the board as they are given. Be sure the following are included: cloudy, cold, cool, day, dry, evening, fall, high, hot, low, morning, night, spring, summer, sunny, warm, wet, winter. If students have not suggested any of these, add them yourself.

1. Have students work in small groups to decide what country each city is in. Allow them to use dictionaries or an almanac, but do not suggest that they do so. (Answers: Caracas—Venezuela; London—England [or United Kingdom or Britain]; Cairo—Egypt; San Francisco—United States; Seoul—South Korea; Barcelona—Spain) Have them discuss how they arrived at their answers.

2. First have the students individually list the places they would like to visit; then in pairs, have them discuss their choices and their reasons.

3. (a) 🎧 Before doing the listening task, discuss the two different systems for measuring air temperature—Fahrenheit and Celsius (also called Centigrade). Then have them listen to the tape in pairs and fill in the blanks. You may need to play the tape more than once and/or pause it to give students the opportunity to write.
(Answers: Fahrenheit, Celsius, 32, multiply, divide; Celsius, Fahrenheit, 9, divide, 32.)

(b) In pairs students do the calculations and complete the table. Combine pairs to compare answers. (Answers, 28° F = -2.2°C; 38° C = 100.4°F)

Going Places 67

Student text page 68

Task Chain 1: What's the weather like?

Task 1. (a) Have students work individually or in pairs to match the words in the two columns. Check responses with the whole class. **Optional.** This can be made into a competitive game by imposing a time limit and the student or pair matching the most pairs of words in the allotted time is the winner. (Answers: hot/cold, high/low, day/night, wet/dry, summer/winter, sunny/cloudy, morning/evening, warm/cool, fall/spring)

(b) Have students underline any of the above words they find in the weather forecasts. (Answers: Note that "high" and "low" appear twice in each of the forecasts and are not included in this answer list. Montreal: cool, cloudy, morning; Los Angeles: sunny, warm, morning, cloudy; Vancouver: cool, cold; Miami: sunny, night; Nashville: warm, sunny, evening, sunny, night; San Diego: morning, sunny, sunny, dry; San Francisco: sunny, cloudy; New York: sunny, cloudy, night, cool, wet)

Task 2. The strategy underlying this task is cooperating. Call attention to the definition in the left margin. Students often feel that they can learn only from the teacher; they do not understand how they can learn from each other. Emphasize how valuable working together is to learning.

In groups of three have students use the information from Task 1 to complete the box. **Variation.** Some of the groups can record the information for today, some for tomorrow, and some record the key words. The groups then reformulate and share their information. Elicit responses and write them on the board, or have one or more students do this.

Task 3. (a) Have students guess when the forecasts were made and give reasons for their choice. (Answers: Spring, May 14. The temperatures are too warm for February and November, too cool for August.)

68 Going Places

Task Chain 1 What's the weather like?

Task 1

a Draw lines to match the words in column A with their opposites in column B.

Column A	Column B
hot	cool
high	cloudy
day	evening
wet	spring
summer	dry
sunny	low
morning	winter
warm	cold
fall	night

b Look at the words in columns A and B. How many of these words can you find in the weather forecasts shown here? Underline them.

Montreal Blue skies; very nice but cool weather continues; high 48, low 35. Tomorrow: Cloudy; morning showers; high 49, low 40.

Los Angeles Sunny; warm readings; high 75, low 58. Tomorrow: Sunny morning; cloudy afternoon; high 72, low 58.

Vancouver Damp and cool with periodic rain; a cold lake breeze; high 49, low 35. Tomorrow: Rain, then showers and sun later; high 56, low 46.

Miami Fine day with sun and mild ocean breezes; high 81, low 69. Tomorrow: Partly sunny; mild night; high, 84, low 70.

Nashville Warm; not as sunny; evening thunderstorm; high 81, low 58. Tomorrow: Partly sunny; showers at night; high 82, low 60.

San Diego After some morning clouds, milder; sunny afternoon; high 71, low 61. Tomorrow: Partly sunny; remaining dry; high 70, low 60.

San Francisco Sunny start, partly cloudy afternoon; high 74, low 56. Tomorrow: Some afternoon rain developing; high 68, low 56.

New York Another beauty—bright and sunny; cloudy night; high 54, low 39. Tomorrow: Cool morning, wet afternoon; high 49, low 43.

[Source: Adapted from *USA Today*.]

LEARNING STRATEGY

Cooperating = sharing ideas with other students and learning together.

Task 2

Group Work Cooperate with two other students. Use the information from Task 1 above to complete the following chart.

CITY	TODAY HIGH	TODAY LOW	TOMORROW HIGH	TOMORROW LOW	WEATHER
Montreal	48	35	49	40	cool, cloudy, showers
Vancouver					
San Diego					
San Francisco					

Task 3

a Look again at the forecasts in Task 1. Do you think it is spring, summer, fall, or winter? Can you guess what date the forecasts were made? Circle your answer.

February 26   May 14   August 8   November 2

68 Going Places

A I like nice weather, so I'd like to be in San Francisco today and San Diego tomorrow.

B Well, I like it warm, so I'd like to be in Miami or Nashville.

b **PairWork** Which place would you like to be in today? Which place would you like to be in tomorrow?

Task 4

Write a weather forecast for your town or city.

Task 5

a 🎧 Listen to these weather reports. Which weather words do you hear? Write them in the chart below.

b 🎧 Listen again. Which cities from the forecasts in Task 1 is the announcer talking about? Write them in the chart.

REPORT	WEATHER	CITY
1		
2		
3		

Task 6

Read the following postcard and look at the pictures at the beginning of the unit. Which place is Roger visiting?

Task 7

PairWork Choose a city and write your own postcard as if you're visiting that city. Exchange postcards with a classmate. Can you guess the name of your partner's city?

Going Places **69**

📖 **Student text page 69**

(b) In pairs, have students discuss which places they would like to be in "today" and "tomorrow" on the basis of the forecasts. The quoted language in the left margin can be used as a model. **Variation.** After they have discussed the forecasts, have students discuss which months relate to which seasons in the northern and southern hemispheres.
(Suggested answers: Northern: Spring = March, April, May; Summer = June, July, August; Fall = September, October, November; Winter = December, January, February. Southern: Spring = September, October, November; Summer = December, January, February; Fall = March, April, May; Winter = June, July, August)

Task 4. Individually, students choose a particular date in a particular season and write a forecast for the place where they live (or used to live). Have them follow the format of the forecasts in Task 1 or the abbreviated formats of Task 2. **Optional.** This task may be done outside of the classroom.

Task 5. (a) 🎧 Have students listen to the tape and write the weather words in the chart. You will probably need to play the tape several times. Check responses and put them on the board.
(Answers: see answers for Task 1 (b) for Nashville, Miami, and San Francisco)

(b) 🎧 Play the tape again and have students compare the forecasts with the printed forecasts in Task 1. (Answers: Nashville, Miami, San Francisco)

Task 6. Have students read the postcard silently. (Answer: Cairo)

Task 7. Have students individually choose a city and write a postcard home from that city. Then have them exchange postcards with a partner, who must guess where they are. Students draw a space the size of a normal postcard on their paper and write their postcard in that space, including the name and address of the person they are sending it to. **Variation.** Have students choose a city from the newspaper forecasts in Task 1 (b).

Going Places **69**

📖 Student text page 70

Language Focus 1: Adverbs of frequency

1. (a) 🎧 Have students listen to the tape and then role-play it with a partner. Circulate and monitor pronunciation.

(b) Have students practice the conversation again, with speaker B using information that is true for them. Then have students exchange roles and do the conversation once more.

2. Introduce or review adverbs of frequency. This can be a brainstorm exercise. List the following on the board and see if students can think of any others: most, least, frequently, always, usually, often, sometimes, hardly ever, never. Then, in pairs, have students underline the adverbs of frequency and number the sentences in order from most frequent to the least frequent. (Answers: never, often, hardly ever, always, sometimes, usually; 6, 3, 5, 1, 4, 2)

3. Have pairs of students discuss where the adverb should go in each sentence. Check responses around the class.
(Answers: a. Is it usually…? b. It is rarely…. c. Does it often…? d. It is always…. e. It never….) **Variation.** Discuss adverb placement and see whether students can recognize a pattern or figure out a rule.

4. (a) Have students write sentences that are true for them, using the cues and the appropriate adverb. For example, "I often write letters." Have them take turns telling their partners what they wrote. Encourage them to tell, not read their sentences. This will be easier if both students do one and tell their partners before going on to the next one.

In pairs have students practice the sentences from memory, referring to their books as little as possible.

Focus on pronunciation as well as practicing short term memory.

(b) Have each student tell another pair about his/her partner, following the form of the example. Remind the class of the grammatical change necessary when talking about someone else (going from first person to third person): add the third person "s" to the verb.

70 Going Places

Language Focus 1 Adverbs of frequency

1 a 🎧 **Pair Work** Listen. Then practice the conversation with another student.

A: What's the weather like where you come from?
B: Well, it's always hot in summer—usually over 40° Celsius.
A: Wow, that's hot. What about winter?
B: It's usually warm in winter. And it hardly ever rains in summer or winter.

b Pair Work Now use information that is true for you.

2 Pair Work Underline the adverbs of frequency in these statements, and then number them from most frequent (1) to least frequent (6).

.... We never go away on long weekends.
.... It often rains when we plan a holiday at the beach.
.... I hardly ever go to parties.
...1... Susie always goes to the beach on the weekend.
.... They sometimes take vacations in winter.
.... He usually goes to the movies on Saturday night.

3 Pair Work Draw a line to show where each adverb should go in each sentence.

a Is it warm in the evening?   usually
b It is cold in Rio de Janeiro.   rarely
c Does it snow in New York?   often
d It is wet in London.   always
e It snows in Sydney.   never

Do you know the rule?
Complete the statement.
"We usually place adverbs of frequency ...."

4 a Pair Work Take turns talking about how often you do the following things. Use these words in your answers.

never   rarely   sometimes   often

- write letters
- arrive at work/school late
- cook dinner for friends
- sleep with the window open
- stay home on Saturday night
- go away for the weekend
- sing in the shower
- play a musical instrument

b Group Work Tell another pair about your partner.

Example: "Tomoko never writes letters."

70 Going Places

Task Chain 2 What should we do on our vacation?

Task 1

Pair Work Where should these people go on vacation? Take turns giving advice.

a Tony loves skiing.   He should _go to Switzerland_.
b Nancy likes Asian art.   She should _____.
c Peter studies French.   He should _____.
d Sonia is interested in Buddhism. She should _____.
e Carmen likes Italian food.   She should _____.
f Tomoko studies modern art.   She should _____.

Task 2

Group Work Make a list of each person's interests and then decide where he or she should go for vacation.

NAME	INTERESTS	WHERE THEY SHOULD GO
Claudia	the environment, hiking	Nepal or Australia

Task 3

a You are going to listen to a doctor talking about the things you should and shouldn't do when you travel in foreign countries. Before you listen, can you predict some of his advice?

b 🎧 Listen to the doctor's advice and fill in the chart.

THINGS YOU SHOULD DO	THINGS YOU SHOULDN'T DO
take medicine	

c **Pair Work** Do you agree with the doctor's advice? Add your own advice to the list.

d **Group Work** Share your ideas with another pair.

A You know a lot about Japan, don't you?
B I guess so. Why?
A I need some advice. My cousin is visiting Japan next month. She's interested in art and architecture. Where should she go?
B Well, she should definitely visit Kyoto. She should also go to Tokyo.

A We agreed that you should take medicine with you. We disagreed that you shouldn't eat uncooked food.
B We think you should have an emergency health care number you can call.

📖 Student text page 71

Task Chain 2:
What should we do on our vacation?

Task 1. Individually, students fill in the blanks in their books. Ask several students for their responses and put them on the board. Then have pairs take turns giving advice, following the model. (Possible/Probable answers: a. go to Switzerland [or Colorado, Vermont]; b. go to Tokyo [Kyoto, Beijing, Agra]; c. go to Paris; d. go to Thailand; e. visit Rome [Naples, Milan]; f. visit New York [Paris])

Task 2. Individually group members write three of their interests or hobbies. They pass the papers around the group so that each person has someone else's paper. Each student writes on the paper where that person should go for his/her vacation. Return the papers to the original writers and in the group discuss reactions to the vacation suggestions. Do the students like the places suggested? Are they interested in going there? Have they been there?

Task 3. (a) Do this as a group exercise. Have students try to predict some of the advice the doctor might give. If doing this in groups appears too difficult, do it as a teacher-led task, writing student responses on the board as they are given. **Variation.** Have students brainstorm in small groups what the doctor may advise, then bring the groups back for a whole-class feedback of ideas.

(b) 🎧 Play the tape and have students fill in the chart. They can use more paper if necessary. (Answers: Should: take medicine, find out about common local diseases, take out medical insurance, carry card with name and medical history. Shouldn't: drink well or tap water, eat uncooked food)

(c) In pairs, students should add their own advice. As models they can use the sentences in the lower left margin.

(d) Have them share their ideas with another pair. You could also discuss the doctor's advice, and students' additions to it, as a whole class.

📖 **Student text page 72**

Task 4. (a) Have each group of students, select a city to visit and choose the essentials they would take with them. Limit the choice to five items. Circulate and monitor pronunciation as they decide which items to take. Have each group report their choices to the class.

(b) Have the groups brainstorm and add other items. Again, you may wish to have the groups report to the class.

Task 5. (a) Have students list their cities/places and reasons individually; they can use more paper if necessary. Then have them discuss their choices in small groups, using the quoted sentences in the lower left margin as a model. **Variation.** Have group members read each other's work.

(b) Working from memory, have each student share his/her ideas with three other students. Circulate, monitor, and if necessary, correct language, both grammar and pronunciation.

72 Going Places

Task 4

a Group Work Choose a city to visit. Then choose five things from the following list to take with you. Give reasons for your choice.

guidebook	bus schedule	money	shopping bag
sunglasses	passport	hat	umbrella
camera	watch	phrase book	map
driver's license	credit card	raincoat	sweater

Example: "I think we should take sunglasses because the weather is going to be nice."

b Group Work Can you add more items to the list?

Task 5

a List the three most interesting cities or places in your country and why people should visit them.

City/Place	Why is it interesting?
....	....
....	....
....	....

b Group Work Share your ideas with three other students.

"You should visit Chiang Mai, in Thailand. It's a beautiful city, and you can visit the hill tribe villages."

72 Going Places

Language Focus 2: Modal: *should*

1 🎧 **Pair Work** Listen. Then practice this conversation with another student.

A: Where should we go for our vacation?
B: Why don't we go to Mexico?
A: No, we went there last year.
B: You're right. I guess we should go somewhere new.
A: And somewhere interesting.
B: Why don't we go somewhere really different, like Thailand?
A: That's a good idea.

2 a **Pair Work** Number these questions and sentences in the correct order to make a conversation. Then practice it.

.... How about the Bahamas?
.... Then why don't you go to Australia?
.... What do you like to do?
.... No. It's too far.
.... Where should I go for my vacation?
.... Well, I like swimming and underwater diving.
.... No, everything is too expensive there.

b **Pair Work** Now have a similar conversation with information that is true for you.

3 **Pair Work** Choose one of the places from the weather forecasts in Task Chain 1. Give some advice for a visitor going to this place. Your partner then can try to guess the name of the city.

4 Write five things someone visiting your city should or shouldn't do. Use these things to talk about your city.

Example: "Well, you shouldn't visit in summer because it's too hot. You should come in spring, because the weather is great then."

A Today you should wear a sweater and a jacket. Tomorrow you should take an umbrella or a raincoat.

B I think that you're talking about Montreal.

📖 Student text page 73

Language Focus 2: Modal: *should*

1. 🎧 Play the tape; then have students role-play the conversation. Circulate and monitor pronunciation.

2. (**a**) Have pairs of students number the sentences in order to make a conversation. Elicit responses and put them on the board. Then have pairs practice the conversation, exchange roles, and practice it again. (Answers: 4, 6, 2, 7, 1, 3, 5; depending on where students are, another possibility is 6, 4, 2, 5, 1, 3, 7)

(**b**) Give the pairs time to think about two other places to talk about; then have them practice a similar conversation using information that is true for them. As they work, circulate and check accuracy. Encourage them to use the target structure with "should."

3. Have each partner individually choose one of the cities from the weather forecasts on page 68 and think of five pieces of advice for a visitor going to this place. The partners then tell each other the advice and try to guess the other's city. They can use the model sentences in the lower left margin of the page.

4. Have students write five pieces of advice for someone planning to visit their city. (This can be the city they chose in Task 3 or the city in which they live or used to live.) When they have finished, choose individuals to talk to the whole class about their city. Encourage them to talk from memory, not to read their sentences. **Optional.** You may wish to elicit corrections of grammar and pronunciation from the rest of the class.

Student text page 74

Self-Check

Communication Challenge

Challenge 9 is on page 119 and suggestions for its use are on that page in this Teacher's Extended Edition.

1 and **2.** These can be done outside of class and brought in at the next session. Try to have students do these, and Task 3, without looking back at the unit, although this is permissible if necessary.

3. Talking about the weather/climate: Review these words for describing weather and have students add any others of their own: temperature, sunny, showers, mild, cloudy, cool, rain, hot, windy, warm, cold, snowy, cloudy, dry, hot, wet, always, never, often, rarely, usually, sometimes. Then in threes, have students talk about (i) the weather today, (ii) the weather yesterday, and (iii) their hopes for the weather tomorrow. Circulate and make sure students use some of the words from the list.

Again in small groups and using combinations of words from the list, have students give opinions about the weather in the city or region where they live (or used to live) in the summer and in the winter.

4. Work with students to ensure that they can get more practice in the areas in which they feel they need it.

5. Using combinations of adjectives and adverbs from the vocabulary list have students write a few sentences about the weather in the city or region where they live a) in summer, b) in winter—e.g., *In spring it's warm and sunny.*

• Grammar summaries for this unit are on pages 132 and 133.

Going Places

Self-Check

COMMUNICATION CHALLENGE

Look at Challenge 9A on page 119.

"I buy an English-language newspaper and read about the weather around the world."

"My brother-in-law is Canadian. I practice with him."

1 Write down five new words you learned in this unit.

2 Write down three new sentences or questions you learned.

3 Review the language skills you practiced in this unit. Check [√] your answers.

CAN YOU:

Talk about the weather/climate?   ☐ yes   ☐ a little   ☐ not yet
Find or give an example:

Ask for and give opinions and advice?   ☐ yes   ☐ a little   ☐ not yet
Find or give an example:

4 What areas need more practice? How can you get more practice? Make a list.

5 Vocabulary check. Check [√] the words you know.

Adjectives
☐ cloudy   ☐ hot
☐ cold   ☐ mild
☐ cool   ☐ sunny
☐ dry   ☐ warm
☐ high   ☐ wet

Adverbs
☐ always   ☐ sometimes
☐ never   ☐ there
☐ often   ☐ usually
☐ rarely

Nouns
☐ advice   ☐ evening   ☐ passport   ☐ temperature
☐ camera   ☐ fall   ☐ raincoat   ☐ umbrella
☐ city   ☐ license   ☐ spring   ☐ watch
☐ country   ☐ money   ☐ summer   ☐ weather
☐ credit card   ☐ month   ☐ sunglasses   ☐ winter
☐ day   ☐ night   ☐ sweater

Verbs
☐ continue
☐ give
☐ know
☐ should

Going Places

10 Review

Photograph A

Photograph B

Task 1

a Pair Work Student A: Look at photograph A. Student B: Look at photograph B. How many differences can you find? Make statements like these:

Tony .... is standing up.
.... is sitting down.
.... is next to ....
.... is near the ....
.... is drinking a soda.
.... is eating a sandwich.
.... is eating an apple.
.... is wearing a .... sweater.

b Pair Work Make a list of all the differences you found.

c Group Work Now compare your list with another pair's list. Who found the most differences?

Task 2

Classify the following words.

interesting	usually	rarely	crowded	on
often	exciting	quiet	near	always
expensive	next to	sometimes	beautiful	never

Words You Can Use To . . .

SAY HOW OFTEN THINGS HAPPEN	DESCRIBE PLACES OR THINGS	SAY WHERE THINGS ARE LOCATED
usually	interesting	on

Review 75

Student text page 76

Task 3. (a) This is a controlled small group discussion with a focus on accuracy in grammar and pronunciation as well as on content. Students use the model as a guide to what they say. Give students time to think about a city they wish to talk about and what they want to say about it. Listen to the various groups and monitor accuracy. **Optional.** Select several students to talk to the class about their favorite city.

(b) Have students individually write postcards from—and about—their favorite city. They can use Tina's postcard on the page as a model. Encourage students to mention the climate or weather, as Tina did on her card.

Task 4. (a) and (b) 🎧 Have pairs of students listen to the conversation, then practice it, exchange roles, and practice again. **Variation.** Prepare a brief list of pairs of activities (to replace watching TV/going to a movie). Have students choose a pair from this list and practice the conversation using the new activities. Repeat with at least two more paired activities. **Optional.** Have students practice the conversation with books closed.

Task 5. Have individual students match the two parts of each conversation and choose the correct form of the verb in the second part. Elicit responses and put them on the board. Then have students practice the conversations with a partner, exchange roles and practice again.
(Answers: Q. Can I speak to Sally? A. I'm sorry—she's not home. She is shopping. Q. What does Paul do? A. He is a student. Q. Where does Sandy go to school? A. She goes to UCLA. Q. What is John doing? A. He is trying to study.)

76 Review

Task 3

a Talk about your favorite city.

Example: "Well, I just love San Francisco. The climate is good, although it's a little cool in winter. It's very pretty, and there's lots to do."

b Now study the model at left, and write a postcard about your favorite city.

Task 4

a 🎧 **Pair Work** Listen. Then practice this conversation with another student.

A: Hi, Maria, what are you doing?
B: Nothing much—just watching TV.
A: I'm not doing anything special either. Why don't we go to a movie?
B: No, not tonight. I'm tired.
A: Oh, that's what you always say.
B: Yes, I'm always tired when you call.

b **Pair Work** Change roles and practice the conversation again.

Task 5

Pair Work Draw lines to match the two parts of the conversations, and then circle the correct verb form in the second part of each conversation. Practice the questions and answers with another student.

1. Can I speak to Sally?
2. What does Paul do?
3. Where does Sandy go to school?
4. What is John doing?

5. He **tries / is trying** to study.
6. She **goes / is going** to UCLA.
7. I'm sorry—she's not home. She **shops / is shopping**.
8. He **is / is being** a student.

76 Review

11 Time Out

Warm-Up

Photograph 1

Photograph 2

Photograph 3

Photograph 4

Photograph 5

Photograph 6

Photograph 7

Unit Goals

In this unit you will:

Discuss hobbies and leisure activities
"What do you do in your spare time?"
"I play the guitar."

Ask and tell about past events
"What did you do over the weekend?"
"I went to the movies."

Describe a sequence of events
"I had a great time over the weekend. First I played tennis, then I went out to dinner, and then I went to the movies."

A I like sleeping late and having fun over the weekend.

B Unfortunately, I have to clean the house over the weekend.

1 Pair Work Look at the photos above. How many of these activities can you name?

2 a Group Work What do you usually do on the weekend? Brainstorm and write down all the words and phrases you can think of.

b Group Work Now talk about your weekend activities.

Time Out 77

---

11 Time Out

📖 Student text page 77

Warm-Up

Unit Goals. Have volunteers read aloud the three goals for this unit; choose other students to read the sample language and have the class repeat them. Or read the goals and sample language yourself.

1. Before doing this exercise, have students brainstorm words that describe hobbies and leisure activities. List these on the board. In pairs students discuss the pictures and choose from the list those words that describe the activities in the photos. If any of the activities from the photos are not on the brainstorm list add them. Check that students know each of these activities shown in the pictures.
(Answers: 1. Making model airplanes; 2. playing tennis; 3. playing guitar; 4. whale watching; 5. cleaning the house; 6. dancing at a disco; 7. gardening) **Variation.** Have students classify the activities into those done indoors and those done outdoors.

2. (a) This can be done in small groups or as a whole class activity. In small groups, have students brainstorm words associated with "weekend" and write them in the diagram form shown in the book. If done as a whole class option, write WEEKEND on the board and give students several minutes to brainstorm words associated with it. Write the responses on the board as they are given. **Optional.** Have students classify the responses into "fun" activities and "boring" ones.

(b) Have students use the conversation in the lower left margin as a model to talk with others in the group about what they do on the weekend. They should do this with books closed. **Variation.** In groups, students have a free discussion on (i) which leisure activities are most popular and least popular in their countries and (ii) which they feel are most and least popular in the United States. They will find answers to (ii) later in this unit. Set a time limit—maximum five minutes—for the discussion.

Time Out 77

Student text page 78

Task Chain 1: How was your weekend?

Task 1. Give students several minutes to look through the list of hobbies. Explain, or have a volunteer explain any they do not understand. Have them check the "do" or "would like to do" box for activities they either do already or think they would enjoy. They should make no check marks for activities in which they have no interest. Have them compare and discuss their responses with others. Check responses with the whole class and list some of the most popular ones on the board.

Task 2. In pairs students choose three or four hobbies and discuss what sort of person might like them. Remind students that this is an opinion task—there are no right or wrong answers. Check responses with the class. If there are answers that are very stereotypical, for example that old people play chess or children fly model airplanes, try to elicit real life examples to challenge these.

Task 3. (a) Have students work in pairs to name the hobbies and list the key words. Check responses with the class, then discuss the fact that knowing some of the key vocabulary of a subject can help you make intelligent guesses about the meaning of written and spoken language. This is an important language learning strategy. (Answers: gardening - grew, roses; play golf - set of clubs; cook Chinese food - rice, soy sauce; play guitar - broke, string; watch movies - best actor; gardening - cut dead flowers; watch birds - binoculars)

(b) Have pairs continue with the same kind of statements, using other hobbies listed.

Task 4. 🎧 Play the tape and have students look at Task 1 and circle the hobbies on the list that they hear Sophie, Teresa, and Ken mention. (Answers: cook Chinese food; gardening; play chess; go whale watching; watch movies; fly model airplanes)

78   Time Out

Task Chain 1 How was your weekend?

Task 1
Look at this list of hobbies. Which hobbies do you do? Which would you like to do? Check [√] your answers.

	Do	Would like to do
cook Chinese food	☐	☐
gardening	☐	☐
play chess	☐	☐
go whale watching	☐	☐
play the guitar	☐	☐
race cars	☐	☐
play golf	☐	☐
watch movies	☐	☐
watch birds	☐	☐
fly model airplanes	☐	☐

A Well, I think it's usually young men who race cars.

B I agree that it's often young people who race cars, but I think it's not just men—women race cars, too.

Task 2
Pair Work Pick three or four hobbies. What sort of person likes these hobbies? (Specify ages, men or women, children or adults, etc.)

Task 3
a Pair Work Look at these statements. What hobbies do they refer to? Which words helped you guess?

	Hobbies	Keywords
I grew some beautiful roses last year.	gardening	grew, roses
I tried out my new set of clubs.		
We need more rice and soy sauce.		
I broke another string last night.		
Where did I put my running shoes?		
Jack Nicholson was the best actor in it.		
Make sure you cut off the dead flowers.		
Could I borrow your binoculars?		

b Pair Work Take turns making statements like the ones above and guessing which hobbies your partner is thinking about.

Task 4
🎧 Listen to Sophie, Teresa, and Ken talking about their weekends. Which hobbies from Task 1 do you hear? Circle them.

78   Time Out

Task 5

Listen again, and look at these pages from a daily planner. Who wrote each entry?

Name ....

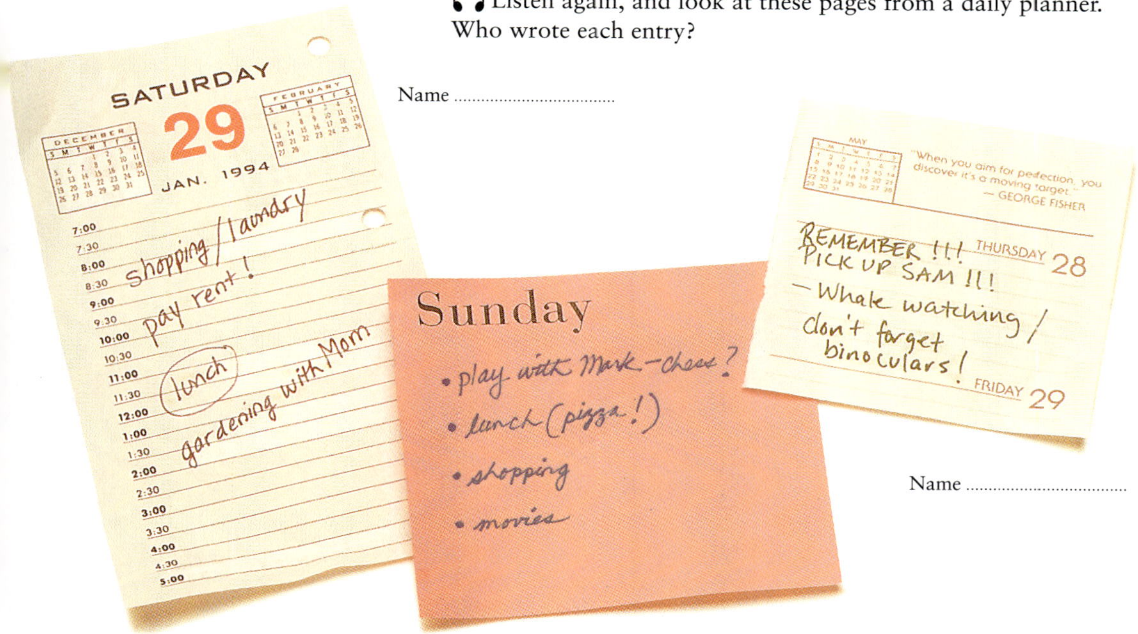

SATURDAY
29
JAN. 1994
7:00
7:30
8:00
8:30
9:00
9:30
10:00
10:30
11:00
11:30
12:00
1:00
1:30
2:00
2:30
3:00
3:30
4:00
4:30
5:00
shopping / laundry
pay rent!
lunch
gardening with Mom
Sunday
• play with Mark—chess?
• lunch (pizza!)
• shopping
• movies
"When you aim for perfection, you discover it's a moving target."
— GEORGE FISHER
THURSDAY 28
REMEMBER!!!
PICK UP SAM!!!
—Whale watching /
don't forget binoculars!
FRIDAY 29

Name ....

Name ....

Task 6

a GroupWork Discussion. Here are the three most popular and three least popular weekend activities in the United States. Guess which three are the most popular and which three are the least popular.

- going fishing
- visiting friends or relatives
- seeing a play
- running errands
- exercising, jogging, walking, or biking
- going to a sporting event

b GroupWork Discussion. What do you think are the most and least popular weekend activities in your country?

Student text page 79

Task 5. Play the tape again, and have students write the names of the people who wrote each note. (Answers: Left—Teresa; Middle—Ken; Right—Sophie)

Task 6. (**a**) Have groups of students discuss the six activities. Tell them that they will find answers later (in the Communication Challenge at the end of the unit). **Variation.** Have students expand the discussion topic to include reasons why certain activities might be popular or unpopular in the United States, i.e.,what factors in the society and/or the natural surroundings in the United States might make this so.

(**b**) Have students discuss what sort of weekend activities are popular or unpopular in their own countries, and why.

📖 Student text page 80

Language Focus 1:

Simple past: statements and *yes/no* questions

1. 🎧 Have students listen to the conversation and discuss as a whole class which words would change if students were to take the roles of the speakers for themselves. Have them practice the conversation in pairs. Then have them change partners with one or more other pairs and practice the conversation again. Circulate and monitor language forms and pronunciation.

2. This task can be done individually in writing or in pairs orally. Do one example on the board. Then have students complete the remaining items.
(Answers: b. Did you go out last night? c. Did he do anything special on/over the weekend? d. Did they see their friend on the weekend? e. Did they meet you at the movies last night? f. Did we get an invitation to the party?)

• The key learning strategy in this unit is discovering. Point out that this strategy means recognizing patterns in language. Looking for patterns can help in figuring out grammar rules, and understanding how language works.

3. Have pairs of students study the conversation and try to discover the rule for forming the simple past tense. Elicit responses from the class.
(Answer: add -ed to form the past tense.) Explain that those verbs that follow this rule are called *regular* verbs.

4. The aim of this exercise is to have students focus on regular and irregular past tense forms of verbs. This is best done as a whole class task. Point out that all the words are past tense verbs; then call on students for responses, and ask them to give reasons for their choice.
(Answers: a—saw; b—went; c—studied; d—wanted)

5. Have students ask others about their weekend activities. Monitor for grammar and pronunciation.

80 Time Out

Language Focus 1 Simple past: statements and yes/no questions

1 🎧 **Pair Work** Listen. Then practice the conversation with another student using information that is true for you.

A: What did you do over the weekend, Pete?
B: Well, on Saturday, I played golf, and then I went shopping. After that, I worked in the yard. On Sunday, I ran a marathon. What about you?
A: Well, on Saturday, I read a book. After that I took a nap. On Sunday, I watched videos and listened to music.

2 Make simple-past questions from these cues.

Cues	Questions
a you / see / the doctor / yesterday	Did you see the doctor yesterday?
b you / go out / last night	
c he / do / anything special / weekend	
d they / see / their / friend / on / weekend	
e they / meet you / movies / last night	
f we / get / invitation to / party	

LEARNING STRATEGY
Discovering = finding patterns in language.

3 **Pair Work** Study the conversation and discover the spelling rule for the simple past tense of these verbs.

stay   watch   talk   play   work   visit   listen   want

A: I stayed home last night.
B: Oh, yeah? What did you do?
A: I watched the basketball game on TV. What about you?
B: I stayed in and listened to music.

4 Circle the word that doesn't belong in each line.

a called, saw, looked, rented
b went, cooked, started, talked
c studied, walked, climbed, happened
d was, wanted, did, had

A Did you go to the movies this weekend, Eric?
B No, I didn't. I went to a concert, though.

5 **Group Work** Ask some other students about their weekend activities.

80   Time Out

Task Chain 2 A wild time!

Task 1

Group Work You are going to hear a story containing these phrases. What do you think it is about?

wild time . . . . won $5,000 . . . . crazy rock station . . . . identify the songs . . . . win $5,000 . . . . took Jerry and Kay out to dinner . . . . went to the theater . . . . went to that new disco . . . . danced all night . . . . took a limo home . . . . crashed into bed . . . . next morning . . . . no money . . . .

Task 2

🎧 Listen to the conversation and circle the words that are different from the ones you hear.

a I had a really wonderful time yesterday.
b You won five thousand?
c Well, there's this crazy pop station, and every hour they invite people to call in.
d I took Terry and Kay out to lunch to celebrate.
e Then we went to the movies.
f Then I took a taxi home.
g I fell into bed.
h Did you contact the police?
i I went back to sleep.
j We might have spent it all the night before.

Task 3

🎧 Listen again and number these pictures in the order each event happened.

Picture ....

Picture ....

Picture ....

Picture ....

Picture ....

📖 Student text page 81

Task Chain 2: A wild time!

Task 1. Read the instructions aloud with the students. Encourage the groups not only to discuss what the story might be about but also to give their reasons for thinking so.

Task 2. 🎧 Play the tape and have students circle the words that are different from those they hear. Then play the tape again, pausing at key points for them to confirm or correct their responses.
(Answers: a. really, wonderful; b. thousand; c. pop, hour; d. Terry, lunch; e. movies; f. taxi; g. fell; h. contact; i. sleep; j. might)

Task 3. 🎧 Play the tape again. Individually or in pairs, students sequence the pictures. Play the tape once or twice more as students are rearranging the pictures. (Answers, top to bottom, left to right: 4, 1, 6, 7, 2, 5, 3)

Time Out 81

📖 Student text page 82

Task 4. (a) Have the groups brainstorm the various possibilities and make a list of them. **Optional.** This can be done as a whole class task, with the list being written on the board and discussed.

(b) In their groups or as a whole class, have students tell what they would do and recount any similar things that may have happened to them, for example, winning money or other prizes in a lottery or losing their wallet or pocketbook and later finding it (or not finding it). Encourage them to use such connecting words as "first" and "and then."

Task 5. Have students retell the story. When they get to the end, encourage them to use the structure "Maybe...." to describe the various ways in which the money might have disappeared. **Optional.** Ask students whether they think that it is a true or realistic story. Have them say what they would do in this situation.

Task 6. (a) Have students number the statements. (Answers: 5, 7, 3, 6, 4, 8, 2, 1) Call attention to the following words that act as cues to the sequence: this morning, last week, the first thing, next, however, in a week.

(b) Encourage the students to think of unusual or amusing titles for the story. This will give them an opportunity to experiment and play with the language.

82 Time Out

Task 4

a Group Work Work with three or four other students. What happened to the money? Make a list of possibilities. Which group has the most interesting or unusual list?

b Group Work Discussion. What would you do in this situation? Has anything like this ever happened to you?

Task 5

Pair Work Retell the story in your own words.

Task 6

a Number these sentences to make a story.

.... However, the limo company owners said that no one had reported any missing money.
.... They told him that if no one claimed the money in a week he could keep it.
.... He counted it and found that the bundle came to $2,500.
.... Next, he went to the police, but they said the same thing.
.... Of course, the first thing he did was to go to the limo company to return the money.
.... No one claimed the money, so Jimmy was able to keep it.
.... Last week he found a large bundle of money under the seat of a limo he was riding in.
.... Jimmy Garcia is a little richer this morning.

b Pair Work Write a title for the story. ....

Language Focus 2 Simple past: connecting words and *wh* questions

1 🎧 **Pair Work** Listen. Then practice the conversation.

A: What did you do on your vacation, Sandra?
B: Oh, I had a great time. I did lots of different things.
A: Where did you go?
B: Well, first I went hiking in Nepal, and then I went scuba diving in Australia. Finally, I went skiing in Switzerland.
A: Wow, it sounds like you had a great time.

2 a **Pair Work** Fill in the blanks with four of these connecting words.

then   after that   next   first   finally

A: Oh, great, it's working again. How did you fix it?
B: Well, ... I checked to see if there was a cassette inside.
.... I reread the instructions.
.... I called my repair shop.
.........., I discovered that it wasn't plugged in!

b What kind of machine are these instructions for?

3 **Pair Work** Fill in the blanks and then practice the questions and answers.

A: What .... you do Saturday night?
B: .... I had dinner, and .... I watched a video.

A: Where .... she go on Friday?
B: .... she went to school, and .... she visited friends.

A: What did he .... last night?
B: .... he .... dinner, ... he .... with a friend, and .... they saw a movie. .... he .... home and .... to bed.

4 a **Pair Work** Each of you will tell a story containing four events. Take notes on your partner's story here:

First, ...
Then, ...
Next, ...
Finally, ...

b **Pair Work** Ask *wh* questions about your partner's story.

Example: "Where did it happen? When did it happen?"

Time Out **83**

📖 Student text page 83

Language Focus 2:
Simple past: connecting words and *wh* questions

1. 🎧 Play the tape and have students practice the conversation, exchange roles, and practice it again. **Variation.** Have them substitute place names and hobbies for those in the book. You may want to give them time to write out the new conversation before they practice it. **Optional.** Have students practice line for line until they can do the whole conversation from memory.

2. (**a**) Put the five connecting words on the board or an overhead. Discuss what purpose such words serve in a sentence. Explain that they show the order in which things happened. Point out that "then" and "next" can sometimes be interchanged. Then have pairs work together to decide which connecting word to put where in the conversation.
(Answers: first, Then, After that, Finally)
   (**b**) A cassette player.

3. In pairs, have students fill the blanks and practice the conversations, playing both A and B roles.
(Suggested answers: did, First, then; did, First, then; do, First, had/ate, next, met, then. After that, went, went)

4. Telling people about things that happened or things we saw or read about is an important element in everyday conversation. People talk about funny, serious, and mysterious things and things that are confusing and disturbing. This task gives the students a chance to practice this important feature of casual conversation.
   (**a**) Give students time to think of a story or event, to tell. Emphasize that they are not to write and memorize their story, but simply to *tell* it. Then have one partner tell his/her story to the other.
   (**b**) Explain that when one is telling a story or relating an event, it is natural for the other person to ask questions, even to interrupt the story to ask something about it. Encourage the listeners to ask questions such as those in the example. Then have students change roles.

Time Out **83**

Student text page 84

Self-Check

Communication Challenge

Challenge 11 is on pages 120, 122, and 124 of the student text. Suggestions for its use are on page 120 in this Teacher's Extended Edition.

1, 2, 3. Have students complete the first three tasks without looking back at the unit and then, in pairs, compare their word lists and sentences and discuss the language practiced in the unit.

- The key learning strategy in this unit is discovery. In the context of language learning, this means recognizing patterns. Looking for patterns can help in figuring out grammar rules and understanding how grammar works. A language pattern featured in the unit is the use of "ed" at the end of a base verb to form the simple past tense. You may want to put the following verbs on the board or an overhead and ask the class to tell you in which verbs the past tense is formed by adding "ed" and in which the past tense is irregular. (Do not underline any—the underlining here is the verbs whose past tense is irregular, for use as an answer key.)

sleep	break	talk	clean	put	work
cook	collect	listen	grow	buy	eat
go	visit	read	play	see	write
race	study	take	watch	want	walk
fly	stay	give			

4. Identify areas needing more practice and work with students to find ways of getting this practice, review, or extension. Direct attention to the quoted sentences in the left margin.

5. Have students check the words. Explain or have another student explain any that students are unsure of, and/or have students look them up in their dictionaries.

- Grammar summaries for this unit are on page 133.

84 Time Out

Self-Check

COMMUNICATION CHALLENGE

Group Work Student A: Look at Challenge 11A on page 120. Student B: Look at Challenge 11B on page 122. Student C: Look at Challenge 11C on page 124.

"I try to write something in English every day."

"I memorize lists of past-tense verb forms."

1 Write down five new words you learned in this unit.

2 Write down three new sentences or questions you learned.

3 Review the language skills you practiced in this unit. Check [√] your answers.

CAN YOU:

Discuss hobbies and leisure activities?	☐ yes	☐ a little	☐ not yet
Find or give an example:			
Ask and tell about past events?	☐ yes	☐ a little	☐ not yet
Find or give an example:			
Describe a sequence of events?	☐ yes	☐ a little	☐ not yet
Find or give an example:			

4 What areas need more practice? How can you get more practice? Make a list.

5 Vocabulary check. Check [√] the words you know.

Connecting Phrases and Words
- ☐ after that
- ☐ first
- ☐ then
- ☐ finally
- ☐ next

Nouns
- ☐ chess
- ☐ guitar
- ☐ taxi
- ☐ coffee shop
- ☐ hobby
- ☐ weekend
- ☐ discovering
- ☐ instructions
- ☐ whale
- ☐ flowers
- ☐ leisure
- ☐ game
- ☐ roses

Verbs
- ☐ clean
- ☐ hang gliding
- ☐ skiing
- ☐ cooked
- ☐ sleep
- ☐ did
- ☐ ran
- ☐ was
- ☐ discover
- ☐ saw
- ☐ watch
- ☐ fly
- ☐ scuba diving
- ☐ went
- ☐ were

84 Time Out

12 That's Entertainment

Warm-Up

Picture 1

Picture 2

Picture 3

Picture 4

Picture 5

Picture 6

Unit Goals

In this unit you will:

Talk about entertainment plans

"What are you doing tonight?"

"I'm going to the movies. What about you?"

Express opinions about entertainment

"That's a very boring movie."

1 a Group Work Think about the word *entertainment*. Brainstorm with three or four other students and write down all the words and phrases you can think of.

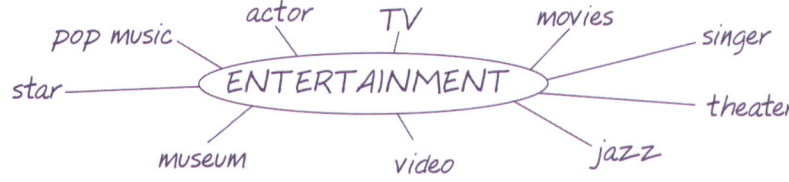

b Group Work Which words go together? Can you classify them?

2 a Look at the pictures above. Do you know where the photographs were taken? Write the picture numbers in the blanks beside the correct descriptions.

.... a late-night jazz club .... a street market
.... a zoo .... the movies
.... a theater .... a museum for kids

b Group Work Which places would you like to go to? Compare your choices with other students' choices.

A I'd like to go to the kid's museum.
B You're not a kid.
A I know, but it looks like fun.

That's Entertainment 85

---

12 That's Entertainment

📖 Student text page 85

Warm-Up

Unit Goals. Have volunteers read aloud the two goals, and call on other students to read the sample language under each goal. Or read them yourself.

1. (a) Write ENTERTAINMENT on the board. Have students, with books closed, call out any words and phrases they associate with the word "entertainment." Write them on the board as they are given; you may wish to use the "concept web" format in the text.

(b) Have students classify the words under category headings. **Optional.** Give groups of students several minutes to brainstorm words associated with "entertainment." Encourage them to include as wide a range of entertainment as they can. One person in each group should list the responses. At the end of the time limit, call on each group to give its responses. Put them on the board, omitting duplications. Then have the class suggest ways to classify the words. Elicit category headings and have students choose the words to go under each one. **Variation.** Write the following words on the board and ask students in small groups to determine whether they think they belong under the "entertainment" heading or not: wrestling; eating with friends; writing letters; receiving letters; comics; street musicians; museums; golf; art galleries; opera; shopping; sightseeing; flying.

2. (a) Have students match the pictures with the location names.
(Answers, reading down the columns: 1, 2, 3, 4, 5, 6)

(b) In groups, students discuss which places they would like to visit. **Variation:** Have them discuss which places the following people would probably like to visit: a five-year-old child; their grandparents; their parents; a teenage boy or girl. They should be ready to give reasons for their choices.

That's Entertainment 85

📖 Student text page 86

Task Chain 1:

What are you doing tonight?

Task 1. (a) Before having students do this task, review the different kinds of entertainment in the ads and the list in Task 1. Does everyone understand what these are? Explain, or have other students explain any that are unfamiliar. Then have students decide how they would rate each item on the list and write the appropriate number. Be sure students understand that this is an opinion question: there are no right or wrong answers. Some people would love to go to an opera or to a rock concert; others would hate to.

(b) Have students compare their responses with those of others. In talking about their choices, encourage them to use the four numbered structures. Tally the "scores" to find what kinds of entertainment the group as a whole enjoys.

Task 2. This task provides students with an opportunity to voice their opinions and gives you an opportunity to discuss cultural views and/or stereotypical attitudes.

(a) Direct attention to the six pictures at the bottom of pages 86 and 87. Have a student read the instructions aloud. In pairs, have students match each person with the person that he or she is going to go out with. Encourage students to give reasons for their choices. (In part [b] of the task they find out who is, in fact, going out with whom tonight.)

86 That's Entertainment

Task Chain 1 What are you doing tonight?

Task 1

a Look at these advertisements and rate them according to this scale.

1 = I would love to go.   2 = I would like to go.
3 = I wouldn't like to go.   4 = I would hate to go.

.... country music festival   .... classical music
.... opera   .... hot gospel group
.... ballroom dancing   .... modern dance group
.... late-night jazz club   .... rock concert
.... ballet   .... musical

b Group Work Compare your ratings with the ratings of three other students.

Task 2

a Pair Work Each of these people is going out with one other person tonight. Try to match each person with the person he or she is going out with.

Eva   David   Kiti

86 That's Entertainment

b 🎧 Listen to the answering machine messages and write the correct responses in the blanks.

John is going out with ....
Kiti is going out with ....
Eva is going out with ....

Task 3

a *Pair Work* look at the advertisements in Task 1. Where do you think each pair is going tonight?

b 🎧 Listen to the telephone conversations and write the correct responses in the blanks.

Harvey and John are going to ....
David and Kiti are going to ....
Lorraine and Eva are going to ....

c *Group Work* Find out where your classmates are going tonight.

Task 4

a *Pair Work* These people are coming to town to visit you. Where will you take them?

- your uncle
- your 12-year-old niece
- your older brother
- a very close friend

b Compare your choices with another pair's choices.

Task 5

You have been to one of the events in Task 1. Write a letter to a friend describing it.

John

Lorraine

Harvey

Student text page 88

Language Focus 1:
Present progressive for planned future

1. 🎧 Call attention to the learning strategy box in the left margin. Point out that students have been using this strategy throughout the previous units but have perhaps not recognized it as an important learning strategy. Ask if any of them play musical instruments. If they do, they know how important practicing is. Tell them that it is just as important in learning a language as in learning to play the piano, violin, trumpet, or any other instrument. Play the tape and have students practice it with a partner, exchange roles, and practice it again. Then have them role-play the conversation substituting other movie titles. **Variation.** Have students practice a more open-ended conversation, substituting some other activity for "going to the movies" and choosing their own closing for the conversation. Monitor to make sure that the conversations are grammatically correct.

2. This can be done orally or in writing. Remind students of the focus of the page: use of the present progressive tense for something that is going to happen in the future. They should use this structure in all their questions. Monitor the pairs as they work. Then run a feedback session with the whole class; ask for at least one example from each pair and at least one example using each of the given words.

3. In this task students must complete the sentences correctly and practice pronouncing them. Have them try to remember each pair of sentences without having to refer to the book.
(Answers [accept I'm for I am]: What, am going, read/I'm reading; Who, am seeing, going; What, seeing; Where, are going)

4. This can be done either as speaking practice, with each student asking and answering the questions, or as a writing task with students writing their answers and then reading the answers of others in the class. Check for use of present progressive for planned future.

88 That's Entertainment

Language Focus 1 Present progressive for planned future

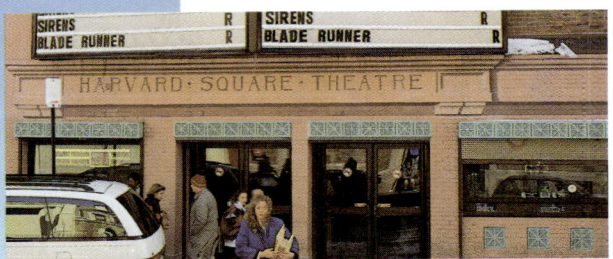

1 🎧 **Pair Work** Listen. Then practice this conversation with another student.

A: Hi, Artie. What are you doing tonight?
B: I'm going to the movies.
A: What are you seeing?
B: *Blade Runner.*
A: But that came out years ago. Haven't you seen it yet?
B: Yes, I've seen it five times before. I love it.

2 **Pair Work** How many questions can you make from the following words?

where	are	you	what	Tom
going	seeing	tomorrow	tonight	who

LEARNING STRATEGY
Practicing = listening or reading and repeating. Practicing improves your fluency and makes you a better speaker.

3 **Pair Work** Complete these conversations and practice them.

A: .... are you doing on Saturday?
B: Nothing much. I .... home and .... a book.

A: .... are you seeing tonight?
B: I .... Artie and Julie. We're .... to a movie.

A: .... movie are you seeing?
B: We're .... an old Humphrey Bogart movie.

A: .... are you taking your next vacation?
B: We .... to Hawaii at Christmas.

4 **Group Work** Ask and answer these questions. Then think of some questions of your own.

a What are you doing next New Year's Eve?
b What are you doing next Sunday?
c Where are you going on your next vacation?
d What is the next movie you are going to see?
e Who are you seeing tomorrow?
f What are you buying next time you go shopping?

88 That's Entertainment

Task Chain 2 Out and about

Review 1

This is a rather boring movie from Megafilms about two bank robbers who get away with money and murder—and some fairly bad acting. Eventually they are caught in a small western town, which looks like every small western town in every small western movie ever made. A complete waste of time!

Review 2

A middle-aged art critic becomes friendly with a young woman who is in a difficult relationship with a famous artist. Eventually she realizes that the critic is more sensitive and creative than the selfish boyfriend. The film is about the woman's inner struggle to break free from the power of her boyfriend and her fear of falling in love with the art critic. Highly recommended.

Review 3

This film was made for children, although parents may enjoy it as well. Four young children get locked in a Disney-type theme park overnight. When the sun goes down, all the creatures in the park come to life. Corny? Perhaps. But the young actors' remarkable performances make the movie well worth seeing.

Review 4

Shakespeare might like this film—or at least be flattered—because the plot has been stolen from several of his plays. A jazz musician strangles his wife to the music of the Phil Gould Big Band. Of course, the murderer gets caught in the end, but not before boring the audience to death. This movie should be shown only on airplanes. See it if you must.

Task 1

a *Pair Work* Think of an example of each of these types of movies.

Thriller: _____
Horror: _____
Comedy: _____
Romance: _____
Drama: _____
Adventure: _____
Western: _____

b *Group Work* Compare your answers with those of another pair.

Task 2

a Write brief answers to these questions.

Questions	Answers
Do you often go to the movies?	
What is your favorite type of movie?	
What are your five favorite movies?	

b How do you usually decide which movie to see? Check [√] your responses.

☐ I ask my friends.
☐ I read movie reviews.
☐ I look at movie advertisements.
☐ I watch previews.

c *Group Work* Discuss your responses with three other students.

Task 3

a Match the movie titles below with the reviews at left. Write the number of each review in the blank before the correct title.

…… *Creatures From the Past*
…… *The Power of Love*
…… *With These Hands*
…… *Wild Horses*

That's Entertainment **89**

📖 Student text page 89

Task Chain 2: Out and about

Task 1. (a) Before they open their books, have pairs of students brainstorm as many movie titles as they can. Then have them classify these under the headings in the book. **Optional.** Before students start to classify their titles, go through the category names to be sure students understand what type of movie would go under each heading.

(b) Have them compare their answers with another pair's. Discuss any differences in classification of particular films. Ask for answers from the different groups. What are the most popular types of movies for these students?

Task 2. (a) Have students write "brief" answers. (These can be as short as one word.) As they write, circulate quietly to monitor spelling or grammatical errors. Then have students move around the class reading each other's work. **Variation.** Collect all the papers and redistribute them so that each student gets someone else's paper. They read it silently, then move around the room to find who wrote it.

(b) Have students check their responses. Some may make only one check, some may check all the sources.

(c) Have them discuss their responses with three others. This is a free discussion focusing on exchanging ideas, comparing views, and getting to know each other better.

Task 3. (a) Brainstorm with the class what kinds of movie each of these might be, referring back to the list at the top of the page. Then give students several minutes to read the reviews individually, without asking any questions, understanding as much as they can. When they have finished reading, answer any questions about vocabulary or meaning. Then have them match the titles with the reviews.
(Answers: Creatures from the Past, Review 3; The Power of Love, Review 2; With These Hands, Review 4; Wild Horses, Review 1)

That's Entertainment **89**

Student text page 90

(b) Have students look back at the list of film types in Task 1 and the titles and reviews of the movies in part (a) of this task. What type of film is each? Is its review positive or negative? Have pairs discuss these questions and fill in the chart.
(Suggested answers: Creatures from the Past—thriller, positive. The Power of Love—romance or drama, positive. With These Hands—thriller or drama, negative; Wild Horses—Western, negative)

Task 4 (a) 🎧 Have students listen to the tape and check the phrases they hear.
(Answers: too long, pretty boring, very interesting, really good)

(b) 🎧 Play the conversations again, one at a time. After each conversation, have students fill in the chart. When all four lines have been filled, have students compare and discuss their choices. You may want to play the four conversations again for students to confirm or correct their initial choices.
(Answers: 1. Creatures from the Past, agree. 2. With These Hands, disagree. 3. Wild Horses, agree. 4. Power of Love, agree)

Task 5. As a whole class, look again at the reviews in Task 3 on page 89 and discuss some of the features of this kind of review. For example, such a review is short. It tells some of the important parts of the story but not all the story (and especially not the ending). It also gives the reviewer's opinion about whether this is a movie the reader should see or not, and why.

Then have each student choose a movie she or he has seen and enjoyed and, with the reviews on page 89 as a guide, write a rough draft review. Circulate as they write and correct errors in grammar or spelling or in content if it is not clear. Have students write a final draft incorporating the corrections. Have them read each other's reviews. Encourage them to ask questions about anything they do not understand or if they want more information. **Variation.** Have students share their drafts with a partner or a small group for feedback and correction before writing the final review. **Variation.** Model the task by writing your own review. Or have the class write a collaborative review of a movie all have seen. Write the review on the board or an overhead as sentences are given and agreed on.

90 That's Entertainment

---

b **Pair Work** Look at the list of film types in Task 1. Decide what type of film each of these is. Are the reviews positive or negative (good or bad)? Complete the chart.

TITLE	TYPE OF MOVIE	REVIEW

Task 4

a 🎧 Listen to these people talking about the movies. Check [√] the phrases you hear.

☐ very exciting
☐ too long
☐ pretty boring
☐ very interesting
☐ really good
☐ not too interesting

b 🎧 Now listen again and look at the reviews in Task 3. Which movie is each person talking about? Do the people agree or disagree with the reviews?

CONVERSATION	FILM TITLE	AGREE / DISAGREE
1		
2		
3		
4		

Task 5

Write a review of your favorite movie.

Language Focus 2   Intensifiers: *too, fairly, pretty, very*

1. 🎧 **Pair Work** Listen. Then practice this conversation with another student.

   A: Where do you want to go?
   B: Well, it's too cold to stay outdoors.
   A: Why don't we go to the movies? There's one at the Showcase Cinema that sounds pretty interesting.
   B: What is it?
   A: *Wild Horses*.
   B: Oh, with Kurt Russell. He's a very good actor. OK, let's go.

2. How many words can you delete from these questions and sentences?

   a There is a very good movie at the Odeon.   *There is a movie at the Odeon.*
   b Is there a very good movie on right now?
   c I saw a really boring show on TV last night.
   d Michelle Pfeiffer is a really good actress.
   e That movie is too old.
   f Those are pretty funny programs.

3. **Pair Work** Discuss famous entertainers, TV shows, movies, and songs. How many statements and questions can you make from these cues?

   a *I think talk shows are just* too boring.
   b .... a very exciting ....
   c .... pretty old ....
   d .... a fairly interesting ....

4. **Group Work** Take turns thinking of a movie, TV show, actor, or singer. State the category. The other students will ask you questions with *yes* or *no* answers to try to guess what you are thinking of. Answer each question only if it contains one of these words: *too, fairly, pretty, very*.

A I'm thinking of a movie.
B Is it very exciting?
A Yes, it is.
C Is it fairly new?
A No, it isn't.
D Is it *Home Alone*?
A No, it isn't.
B Was it shown on TV fairly recently?
A Yes, it was.
C Is it *Rear Window*?
A Yes, it is.

That's Entertainment   91

Student text page 92

Self-Check

Communication Challenge

Challenge 12 is on pages 114 and 127 of the student text. Suggestions for its use are on page 114 in this Teacher's Extended Edition.

- As a whole class exercise, review how individual students are using the Self-Check sections to develop a learning diary or journal.

1, 2, 3. Have students do the first three tasks without looking back at the unit. These may be completed outside of class and brought in at the next session.

4. Have students write four sentences describing their English. Ask them to use the word *too* in the first sentence, *fairly* in the second sentence, *pretty* in the third, and *very* in the fourth sentence. Encourage students to write about both their progress and the areas in which they feel they need more practice. Have students compare and discuss their sentences in pairs or small groups.

- Where do your students need additional help? Make a list for yourself. Decide how and where you can include this review and/or extension work.

5. Write the following words from the list on the board: long, fairly, free, pretty, club, critic, review, star. Remind students that words often have more than one meaning. Then put the class into pairs or groups to find at least two meanings for each word. Give them a time limit, perhaps five minutes, and then call for responses and discuss them, eliciting phrases or sentences using each meaning. Following the discussion, suggest that students look up the words in their English dictionaries and find even more meanings.

- Grammar summaries for this unit are on page 133.

92 That's Entertainment

Self-Check

COMMUNICATION CHALLENGE

Pair Work Student A: Look at Challenge 12A on page 114. Student B: Look at Challenge 12B on page 127.

"I read the entertainment pages of English-language newspapers."

"I watch English-language videos and sing songs in English."

1 Write down five new words you learned in this unit.

2 Write down three new sentences or questions you learned.

3 Review the language skills you practiced in this unit. Check [√] your answers.

CAN YOU:

Talk about entertainment plans?	☐ yes	☐ a little	☐ not yet

Find or give an example: _____

Express opinions about entertainment?	☐ yes	☐ a little	☐ not yet

Find or give an example: _____

4 What areas need more practice? How can you get more practice? Make a list.

5 Vocabulary check. Check [√] the words you know.

Adjectives	Adverbs	Nouns				Verbs	
☐ classical	☐ long	☐ fairly	☐ adventure	☐ jazz	☐ preview	☐ star	☐ classify	☐ enjoy
☐ creative	☐ selfish	☐ free	☐ club	☐ modern	☐ review	☐ thriller	☐ decide	☐ go out
☐ gospel	☐ sensitive	☐ pretty	☐ comedy	dance	☐ romance	☐ zoo		
			☐ critic	☐ opera				

92 That's Entertainment

13 Healthy Living

Warm-Up

Unit Goals

In this unit you will:

Talk about past experiences

"Have you ever been hang gliding?"

"Yes, I have."

"No, I haven't."

Talk about how often things happen

"How often do you exercise?"

"About three times a week."

A Have you stayed up past one o'clock in the morning?

B Yes, I have.

C No, I haven't.

1 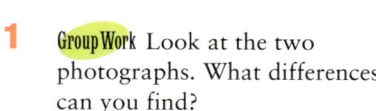 Look at the two photographs. What differences can you find?

2 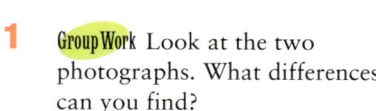 Compare these differences with those found by another group.

Example: "In the first photo, some people are drinking beer and wine. In the second, they're drinking juice."

3 Check [√] those things in the picture that you think are healthy. Put an [X] next to the things that are unhealthy.

4 Think about your habits over the last month. Check [√] your responses.

Have you . . .	Yes	No	Don't remember
• stayed up past one o'clock in the morning?	☐	☐	☐
• played any sports?	☐	☐	☐
• done some other kinds of physical activity?	☐	☐	☐
• eaten junk food?	☐	☐	☐
• drunk alcohol?	☐	☐	☐
• smoked?	☐	☐	☐

5 **Pair Work** Take turns asking and answering the questions in the previous activity.

Healthy Living 93

---

13 Healthy Living

📖 Student text page 93

Warm-Up

Unit Goals. Have volunteers read the goals aloud, and call on other students to read the language examples. Or read them yourself to the class.

1. Have students look at the two photographs and, in groups, discuss the differences between them. You may need to guide this activity: point out that students are to look for differences in what people are doing, not in what they look like, how many there are, etc. (Answers: Top photo: Photo of people at a party engaging in unhealthy activities, i.e., smoking cigarettes, drinking alcohol, eating junk food. Bottom photo: same people engaging in healthy activities, i.e., drinking mineral water and juice and eating fruits and vegetables.)

2. Have students compare their responses with those of another group. Encourage students to follow the model in the book. Check responses around the class.

3. Students check, on the pictures, the things they think are healthy and put an X on the things they think are unhealthy. Note: not all cultures have the same ideas about what is considered healthy and unhealthy. **Optional.** As a whole class activity, using the photographs as a starting point, have students brainstorm other healthy/unhealthy habits or behavior. This could also be done as a written activity with pairs or small groups compiling lists of healthy/unhealthy activities.

4. Give students several minutes to think about what they usually do, and then check the appropriate column for each of the activities listed. **Variation.** List responses on the board to create a class "health profile."

5. Have pairs ask and answer the questions from memory, taking turns as asker and answerer. They can use the quoted dialogue in the lower left margin as a model.

Healthy Living 93

Student text page 94

Task Chain 1: Talking about sports

Task 1. (a) Have students do this task individually, then compare their responses with those of two or three others. (Answers: icons in order are soccer, running, golf, volleyball, baseball, ice hockey, tennis, swimming, skiing)

(b) Give students time to think about how many different sports they play or have played. Have each student make a list and then ask and answer questions with a partner, using language similar to the dialogue in the upper left margin.

Task 2. Have partners work together to complete the chart. Tell students that their answers should reflect how and where the sport is usually played. Accept alternative answers if students can justify them. Note that some sports have yes answers for both indoors and outdoors, winter and summer. (Suggested "yes" answers: team sport—soccer, baseball, volleyball; outdoors—golf, soccer, running, baseball, skiing, volleyball; indoors—running, volleyball, baseball [in domed stadium]; winter—soccer, running, skiing; summer—golf, soccer, running, baseball, volleyball; court—volleyball)

Task 3. Students ask and answer yes/no questions similar to those in the model in the left margin at the bottom of the page. To prepare, have each student make a list of three to five sports with information about where each is played, what equipment is used, etc. Then have them work in pairs asking and answering questions, or have all group members quiz one until the sport is determined, then another, and so on. Encourage students to use the sentences, "Yes, it is" and "No, it isn't" rather than the simple "Yes" and "No."

Task 4. 🎧 Play the tape and have students listen and fill in the form. Then play the tape again, several times if necessary, for students to check and/or correct their responses. Check answers with the whole class. (Answers: 1. tennis—racquet, court, singles, doubles; 2. automobile racing—race track, speeding ticket; 3. soccer—ball, World Cup, goal)

94 Healthy Living

Task Chain 1 Talking about sports

Task 1

a Draw lines to match the symbols with the sports.

golf   baseball   swimming   ice hockey   tennis   skiing   soccer   volleyball   running

A Have you ever played golf?
B Yes, I have.

b Pair Work Ask your partner which sports he or she has played.

Task 2

Pair Work How well do you know these sports? Fill in the chart.

DESCRIPTION	GOLF	SOCCER	RUNNING	BASEBALL	SKIING	VOLLEYBALL
Uses a ball	yes	yes	no	yes	no	yes
Is a team sport						
Is played outdoors						
Is played indoors						
Is played in winter						
Is played in summer						
Is played on a court						

A This sport uses a ball. It's a team sport, and it's played outdoors.
B Is it played on a court?
A No, it isn't.
C Is it soccer?
A No, it isn't.
B Is it baseball?
A Yes, it is.

Task 3

Group Work Tell about a sport. Have your classmates try to guess the sport.

Task 4

🎧 Listen to three people talking about their favorite sports. Can you guess the sports? Which words helped you guess? Fill in the chart.

PERSON	SPORT	KEYWORDS
1		
2		
3		

94 Healthy Living

Task 5

a **Pair Work** Where do you think accidents happen? Write your guesses in the chart.

Example: "I think 50% of accidents happen in the home, for both men and women."

Where People Have Accidents

		OUR GUESS	NEWSPAPER INFORMATION
At Work	Men	%	%
	Women	%	%
Playing Sports	Men	%	%
	Women	%	%
At Home	Men	%	%
	Women	%	%
On the Road	Men	%	%
	Women	%	%

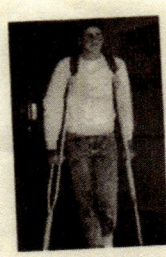

"We guessed that 20% of injuries to women happen at work. In the report, it says that 11.2% of injuries to women happen at work."

b **Pair Work** Now read the newspaper report and complete the chart. Compare your guesses with the newspaper information.

Americans are having more accidents these days. Between 1983 and 1990, the proportion of people injured in accidents rose from 7% to 13%. Over 2,800,000 accidents have been studied so far. Of these, 26.5% of men and 23.8% of women said they had an illness or injury attributable to an accident that occurred during sports, recreation, or exercise. Among men, 27.7% of accidents occurred at work, while for women the figure for accidents at work was 11.2%. Among women, 38.4% reported that their accidents occurred at their home or at the home of a friend or relative. For men, the figure for accidents at home was 30.5%. The final category included accidents that occurred on a sidewalk, road, or highway. Here the figure for men was 15.3%, compared with 26.06% for women.

Task 6

Pair Work Which of these headlines would you use for the article?

Women Are Healthier Than Men
Number of Accidents on the Rise
Get Less Exercise
Women Have Fewer Accidents Than Men

Healthy Living   95

📖 **Student text page 95**

Task 5. (a) Brainstorm with the class students' ideas about where most accidents happen. Read through the chart with the class, then have pairs cover the newspaper article and work together to fill in the "Our Guess" column. Change the pairs so that each student has a new partner. Have them tell their partner what they have written, using the model sentence from the book. Make sure this is a speaking practice task, not a reading task.

(b) Give students time to read the newspaper report individually and then, in pairs, complete the "Newspaper Information" column of the chart. Put pairs together into small groups and have students compare their predictions with the information in the report, using the quoted sentence in the left margin as a model. **Optional.** Discuss the statistics with the students. Are any of the percentages surprising? (Answers, newspaper information: at work—M 27.7%, F 11.2%; playing sports—M 26.5%, F 23.8%; at home—M 30.5%, F 38.4%; on the road—M 15.3%, F 26.06%)

Task 6. In pairs, have students read the newspaper report again and decide on the most appropriate headline.
(Answer: Number of Accidents on the Rise) **Optional.** Have students brainstorm other headlines that might be equally appropriate.

Healthy Living   95

Student text pages 96–97

Language Focus 1:
Present perfect and *Have you ever…?*

1. (a) 🎧 Have students listen to the tape and then role-play it. As they practice, circulate and check pronunciation. Then have them close their books and practice the conversation again.

(b) Have students substitute other sports for hang gliding. If they wish, they can choose sports from those on page 94.

2. In preparation for this task, put the following forms on the board:

Have you ever…?   Yes, I have.   No, I haven't.

Tell students that this is the present perfect tense form. Explain that one of its uses is to talk about past events when the particular time at which the event happened is unimportant. (In the Task 1 conversation, it does not matter when A went hang gliding; the important thing is that she had the experience and could talk about it.)

Now have the students make up and practice questions for the answers, using the present perfect tense. (Answers will vary, depending on activity chosen.)

3. Point out that most verbs have the form called past participle, and that this is used when we make the present perfect tense. In pairs, have students try to match the simple past verbs with their past participles. (Answers: was-been; came-come; did-done; drank-drunk; drove-driven; went-gone; got-gotten; had-had; knew-known; saw-seen; spoke-spoken; took-taken)
Alternative. If this is too difficult, do it as a whole class task, although you may want first to give pairs a little time to see how many forms they can match. (Probably they will be able to match items whose forms are closely related, for example "had-had," "came-come," "knew-known.")

4. (a) Give students time to add their own ideas to the survey list.

(b) Have students go around the room to collect names. Be sure this is a speaking exercise and that they

(Continued on page 97)

96 Healthy Living

Language Focus 1   Present perfect and *Have you ever…?*

1 a 🎧 **Pair Work** Listen. Then practice the conversation.

A: Have you ever been hang gliding?
B: No, I haven't. Have you?
A: Yes, I have.
B: What's it like?
A: It's great.
B: Have you ever had an accident?
A: Unfortunately, yes.

b Pair Work Now use information that is true for you.

2 Pair Work Make up questions for these answers and then practice them.

Questions	Answers
a ……………………………………?	No, she hasn't. It's too dangerous.
b ……………………………………?	No, I haven't. I don't have a license.
c ……………………………………?	No, he hasn't. He doesn't like high places.
d ……………………………………?	No, they haven't. They aren't old enough.
e ……………………………………?	No, we haven't. It's too expensive.

FIND SOMEONE WHO HAS…	NAME
driven a racing car	
been to a Grand Prix race	
played squash	
run a marathon	
had music lessons	
ridden a motorcycle	
flown an airplane	
been to a bullfight	
been scuba diving	
played tennis	

3 Pair Work Draw lines to match the verb tenses.

Simple Past	Past Participle
was	gone
came	taken
did	been
drank	gotten
drove	come
went	spoken
got	known
had	drunk
knew	seen
saw	done
spoke	driven
took	had

4 a Look at this survey chart above and add three activities to the list.

b Group Work Now go around the class and collect as many names as you can.

96 Healthy Living

Task Chain 2 Talking about habits

Task 1

What does the phrase *healthy living* mean to you? How many words can you add to these lists?

Healthy Living

EAT	DO	DRINK	AVOID
whole-grain bread	yoga	fresh fruit juice	tobacco

"I hate whole-grain bread."
"I love fresh fruit juice."
"I think yoga is boring."
"I have never used tobacco products."

Pair Work Now make statements using the words from the lists.

Task 2

You choose: Do **A** or **B**.

A **Group Work** Think about the last time you went grocery shopping. Make a list of all the things you bought. Compare this list with the lists of three or four other students. Whose list is the healthiest?

B **Group Work** Think about all the healthy things you did last week. Make a list. Compare this list with the lists of three or four other students. Who had the healthiest week?

Fitness Index

HABITS	POINTS	HABITS	POINTS
Eats red meat		**Walks**	
every day	1	every day	6
3–5 times a week	2	3–5 times a week	5
once a week	3	once a week	4
once a month	4	once a month	3
3–5 times a year	5	3–5 times a year	2
never	6	never	1
Eats vegetables		**Plays sports or does exercise**	
every day	6	every day	6
3–5 times a week	5	3–5 times a week	5
once a week	4	once a week	4
once a month	3	once a month	3
3–5 times a year	2	3–5 times a year	2
never	1	never	1
Drinks alcohol		**Smokes cigarettes or cigars**	
every day	1	every day	1
3–5 times a week	2	3–5 times a week	2
once a week	3	once a week	3
once a month	4	once a month	4
3–5 times a year	5	3–5 times a year	5
never	6	never	6

Fitness Index Scoring Key
30–36 points: *Excellent* You're in great shape.
13–29 points: *Average* You're in average shape, but you need to be careful.
6–12 points: *Poor* You should change your habits.

Healthy Living 97

📖 Student text pages 96–97 (cont.)

ask the questions in full and from memory. Be sure the questions are asked and answered orally, not read, and that students use the correct question forms. As well as gathering information the survey is a valuable task for practicing speaking.

Task Chain 2: Talking about habits

Task 1. Do this task as a whole class brainstorm activity. Write HEALTHY LIVING on the board and ask what students think of when they read or hear the words. Put responses on the board as they are given. Then put the chart headings on the board and ask students to give you words to add to those already on the chart. Write the responses under the appropriate headings. Expect arguments: what some students (and some cultures) consider healthy, others may not. Then raise the question of liking or disliking. Students may agree, for example, that whole-grain bread is good for them (i.e. "healthy") but may much prefer other kinds of bread. Organize the class into pairs and have them discuss how they feel about the listed items. They should model their statements on the quoted sentences in the left margin.

Task 2. Put students in small groups. Have each group choose either **A** or **B**. In **A** groups, each group member individually makes a list of what he or she bought. They then compare lists to see whose purchases were the healthiest. In **B** groups, each group member individually makes a list of the healthy things she or he has done in the past week. They then compare lists to see who had the healthiest week.

NOTE: The Fitness Index on this page is used in Tasks 3 and 4 on the following page.

Healthy Living 97

Student text page 98

Task 3. 🎧 Have students read the Fitness Index table at the bottom of page 97 before they listen to the conversations, and let them refer back to it as needed. They may want to use three different colored pencils or inks, or different symbols (check, X, circling) to record the health habits of the three people. **Variation.** Before they listen to the tape, have students work out their own fitness index. Give them at least five minutes for this; circulate as they write, monitoring understanding and performance. After they have completed their fitness index, they move to the tape and do the same for people 1, 2, and 3.

Task 4. (a) Pairs interview each other and figure out their fitness index.

(b) After pairs have discussed the Fitness Index table, open up a general discussion on the issue of health. (You may wish to point out recent research which claims that moderate alcohol consumption is beneficial.)

Task 5. Before they read the article, remind students that reading to understand does not mean that they have to understand every word. Remind them also that scanning means reading to find particular information. Explain that they are going to scan the article for things Gina did that were healthy and things that were unhealthy. Then have them read the article and discuss in small groups what healthy and unhealthy things Gina did. **Variation.** Divide the class into two groups and have one group scan for the healthy things Gina did and the other for the unhealthy ones. Then have each group report on what it found. (Suggested answers: Healthy: ate salad, did aerobics, had pasta meal, had sushi bar brunch, swam, played volleyball. Unhealthy: had three beers, had cocktails, stayed up till 4:00 A.M., had fast food meal)

Students are asked, "Is Gina basically a healthy person?" This task gives students an opportunity to make a general inference or deduction from specific information, an important cognitive skill. Have them decide individually on the answer and then, in their groups, discuss their opinions and give their reasons for them.

98 Healthy Living

Task 3

🎧 Listen to three people talking about their eating and exercise habits. Figure out their fitness indexes using the table on page 97. Record their scores and health ratings in this chart.

PERSON	SCORE	HEALTH RATING
1		
2		
3		

A How often do you eat red meat?
B Oh, once a week, I guess.

Task 4

a Pair Work Interview each other and figure out your fitness index.

b Pair Work Do you disagree with any of the scoring in the table?

Example: "I disagree that eating red meat every day is unhealthy. I eat red meat every day and look at me!"

Task 5

a Group Work Discussion. Read this section of a newspaper article. What did Gina do that was healthy? What was unhealthy? Is Gina basically a healthy person? Do you like weekends like Gina's? Why or why not?

The Single Life: Weekend Profiles

Gina Giorcelli is single and loves it. "I had a great time this weekend," she reports. Gina lives in San Diego, just 15 minutes from the beach. After a busy week, she was ready to relax on Friday night. The weekend started when she met friends for drinks at The Elephant Bar. "I'm not a big drinker, but I had three beers on Friday." They then went to B.J.'s Pizzeria where Giorcelli had a salad. She eats at B.J.'s about three times a month. Saturday morning she helped a friend move to a new house and then did the weekend shopping. In the afternoon she went to her weekly aerobics class. On Saturday evening, Giorcelli had cocktails at a friend's house and a pasta dinner at The Spot. Next she went to the Red Onion, where she danced until 4:00 a.m. She loves dancing and goes to a disco every Saturday night. On Sunday, she got up at 10 and went to a sushi bar for brunch. She spent Sunday afternoon at the beach swimming and playing volleyball, and then she had a fast-food meal. Finally, she walked down Seventh Street to the Mall for the San Diego Folk Festival. "How often do I have such a great weekend? Oh, every weekend."

98 Healthy Living

Language Focus 2
Time expressions and *How often...?*

1 a 🎧 **Pair Work** Listen. Then practice this conversation.

A: How often do you play sports, Pete?
B: Never.
A: And what about exercise? How often do you exercise?
B: Oh, about once or twice a year.
A: Once or twice a year?
B: Yeah. Usually once or twice during the summer I walk down to the park to watch a ball game.

b Pair Work Now use information that is true for you.

2 Pair Work Make questions and then practice them.

a You play tennis. — *Do you play tennis?* / *How often do you play tennis?*

b Tony plays tennis. ....

c Jean watches golf. ....

d They go to the ball game. ....

e She does aerobics. ....

f Pete and Dee hang-glide. ....

3 a Pair Work Student A: You know that your partner plays tennis, goes to the beach, exercises in a gym, goes jogging, gets a health check-up, and stays out late at night. Ask your partner questions using the words *How often*. Student B: Answer your partner's questions.

b Pair Work Now change roles.

4 Pair Work Role-play an interview.

Student A: You are a reporter. Use the information in the newspaper article on page 98 and interview Gina.

Student B: You are Gina. Use the information in the newspaper article on page 98 and answer the reporter's questions.

LEARNING STRATEGY

Role-playing = pretending to be someone else and using the right language for the situation you are in.

Healthy Living **99**

📖 Student text page 99

Language Focus 2:
Time expressions and *How often...?*

1. (a) 🎧 Play the tape and have students listen, then practice the conversation, exchange roles, and practice it again. As they practice, circulate and check pronunciation. **Optional.** Have them practice the conversation again from memory with books closed.
(b) Have students practice again, with speaker B substituting information that is true for him or her, then exchange roles.

2. Review the use of "does" with the third person singular when forming questions. In pairs, students make up questions, following the model for item a. The second question in each case should use the "how often..." structure. Give students time to make their questions and practice them. Circulate, checking accuracy. **Optional.** Working individually, students write out the questions, then practice in pairs.
(Answers: b. Does Tony play tennis? How often does Tony play tennis? c. Does Jean watch golf? How often does Jean watch golf? d. Do they go to the ball game? How often do they go to the ball game? e. Does she do aerobics? How often does she do aerobics? f. Do Pete and Dee hang-glide? How often do Pete and Dee hang-glide?)

3. (a) Have student A make up "How often..." questions, and have Student B answer them.
(Answers for Student A: How often do you play tennis? How often do you go to the beach? How often do you exercise in a gym? How often do you go jogging? How often do you get a health check-up? How often do you stay out late at night? Student B's answers will vary.)
(b) Have partners exchange roles and go through the questions and answers again.

4. Call attention to the Learning Strategy box. Explain that role-playing gives students the opportunity to practice language in a wide range of contexts. Have students role-play an interview with Gina Giorcelli. Review question forms that students might find useful in doing the task, circulate and check accuracy and pronunciation.

Healthy Living **99**

Student text page 100

Self-Check

Communication Challenge

Challenge 13 is on pages 125 and 127 of the student text. Suggestions for its use are on page 125 in this Teacher's Extended Edition.

1, 2, 3, 4, 5. Follow the procedures used in earlier Self-Checks. The first three tasks can be done outside of class. Task 4 should be discussed in class, and plans made for additional practice in areas in which students feel they need it.

- The key learning strategy in this unit is role-playing, that is, pretending to be someone in a particular situation and using language suitable for that situation. Discuss with students that the kind of language we use depends on who we are speaking to and the relationship between those involved in the conversation.

Present the class with four pairs of characters in the same situation: saying goodbye at an airport. The characters are:

1. a secretary saying goodbye to his/her boss
2. a grandmother or grandfather saying goodbye to a small grandchild
3. two teenage sweethearts saying goodbye
4. two adult friends saying goodbye

As a whole class, discuss how the language might be different in each case, for example, more or less formal. Explain that it would also differ in content—what the characters would say in addition to "goodbye."

Organize the class into pairs and have each pair choose three of the four role-plays. (Be sure that each of the four is represented in at least one pair's choices.) Give them time to discuss what they will say, and then have them practice the short conversations (not more than 3 or 4 exchanges). Encourage them to "ad lib" the conversations, that is, to do them without writing a formal script. Circulate and listen to the role-plays; choose one or more pairs to present their's to the class.

- Grammar summaries for this unit are on page 134.

100 **HEALTHY LIVING**

Self-Check

COMMUNICATION CHALLENGE

Pair Work Student A: Look at Challenge 13A on page 125. Student B: Look at Challenge 13B on page 127.

"I like role-playing because it gives me extra speaking practice."

"During class breaks, we talk about things we have done."

1 Write down five new words you learned in this unit.

2 Write down three new sentences or questions you learned.

3 Review the language skills you practiced in this unit. Check [√] your answers.

CAN YOU:

Talk about past experiences?	☐ yes	☐ a little	☐ not yet
Find or give an example:			
Talk about how often things happen?	☐ yes	☐ a little	☐ not yet
Find or give an example:			

4 What areas need more practice? How can you get more practice? Make a list.

5 Vocabulary check. Check [√] the words you know.

Adjectives	Nouns						Question	Verbs
☐ dangerous	☐ accidents	☐ cigarette	☐ indoors	☐ running	☐ swimming	☐ yoga	☐ how often	☐ eat
☐ healthy	☐ aerobics	☐ exercise	☐ meat	☐ skiing	☐ tennis			☐ smoke
☐ racing	☐ alcohol	☐ golf	☐ outdoors	☐ soccer	☐ tobacco			☐ stay up
☐ single	☐ baseball	☐ ice hockey	☐ recreation	☐ survey	☐ volleyball			

100 **HEALTHY LIVING**

14 A Day in the Life

Warm-Up

Unit Goals

In this unit you will:

Make comparisons
"The city is busier than the country."

Ask for and give advice
"I've missed the bus. What should I do?"
"You should take the subway."

Express obligation
"You have to be at school by 9:00."

"Well, I'd like to be a crime reporter."
"I'd like to meet movie stars."
"I'd like to be a political journalist and interview politicians."

---

1 a *Pair Work* Look at the pictures above. What is this woman's job? How do you know?

b *Group Work* Brainstorm. Make a list of all the things a journalist does.

c *Group Work* Compare your list with another group's list.

2 *Group Work* Discussion. Imagine you are a reporter. What would you like to do? Who would you like to interview?

3 a *Pair Work* You want some advice on the following list of topics. Take turns asking questions and answering questions using these models: "Should I . . . ?" "I think you should . . . ."

- visit parents or friends
- go to a movie or a concert
- study or watch TV
- take a bus or a train
- go away for the weekend or stay at home

b *Pair Work* Think of three more topics you would like advice on. Ask your partner.

A Day in the Life **101**

📖 Student text page 102

Task Chain 1:
But the city is more interesting

Task 1. Read the directions with the class, making sure that students understand that they are to answer by putting a check mark (√) in the appropriate column. Give pairs of students several minutes to decide which statements were made by city people and which by country people. When they have checked their answers, discuss the reasons for the choices.
(Suggested answers: a. country; b. city; c. country; d. city; e. city)

Task 2. (a) An aim of this task is to encourage students to contribute their own ideas. Have each group appoint someone to take notes, while the group decides on positive and negative aspects of city and country life. When the charts are complete, have each group compare its chart with another's.

(b) Have pairs of students talk to each other about differences between city and country living, using the dialogue in the left margin as a model. Be sure this is done as a true speaking exercise, not just a reading of the students' charts from part (a). Circulate and monitor accuracy of pronunciation and grammar.

Task 3. This vocabulary exercise deals with comparative adjectives. Have students draw lines to match words in column A with their opposites in column B.
(Answers: bigger-smaller; noisier-quieter; cheaper-more expensive; duller-more interesting; slower-faster)

Task 4. 🎧 Read the instructions with the students and play the tape. Be sure students understand they are to make their responses by circling the appropriate words in the two columns of Task 3.
(Answers: bigger, noisier, duller, more interesting, quieter)

102 A Day in the Life

Task Chain 1 But the city is more interesting

Task 1
Pair Work Carla is writing an article on differences between city and country living. She interviewed people in the city and the country; here are some things they said. Were these people in the city or the country? Check [√] your answers.

		City	Country
a	It's kind of quiet around here, but we like it.	☐	☐
b	They have to do something about the trash in the streets.	☐	☐
c	There's never anything to do in the evenings.	☐	☐
d	The traffic gets worse and worse every day.	☐	☐
e	The best way to get there is to take the subway.	☐	☐

A I love living in the city. There's so much to do.
B I love the country. It's much quieter.
A The city is more exciting.
B Yes, but there is much less crime in the country.

Task 2
a **Group Work** Discussion. Fill in the chart by writing good and bad things about living in the city and good and bad things about living in the country. Compare your chart with that of another group.

	POSITIVE	NEGATIVE
city life		
country life		

b **Pair Work** Talk about differences between city and country living.

Task 3
Pair Work Draw lines to match the words in column A with their opposites in column B.

Column A	Column B
bigger	faster
noisier	more interesting
cheaper	smaller
duller	quieter
slower	more expensive

Task 4
🎧 Listen. Carla is interviewing Angie and Michael. They are talking about city living versus country living. What are some of the words they use? Look again at the lists in Task 3 and circle the words you hear.

102 A Day in the Life

Task 5

🎧 Listen again. What are the positive and negative points Angie and Michael discuss?

	POSITIVE	NEGATIVE
city life		
country life		

LEARNING STRATEGY

Skimming = reading quickly to get a general idea of a text.

Task 6

a Pair Work Skim the following newspaper excerpt and make up a headline for it.

> Americans seem to be divided between those who enjoy city life and those who prefer living in the country. Angie Fatakis used to live in the country, but she now lives in the city. "It's so boring in the country," she says. "There are no nightclubs and few theaters." For Fatakis, cities are more entertaining and much livelier.
>
> Mike Boyd disagrees. He thinks that cities are noisier, more expensive, and more dangerous. Says Boyd, "The country is more relaxing—quieter, too. And the people are friendlier and more helpful."
>
> "And more intolerant," adds Fatakis.
>
> "Not so," responds Boyd. "My younger brother has just come out of prison, and he has moved back to the country to live with me. The people here are nicer to him than the city people who knew he'd been in trouble."

b Pair Work Read the article again. Which information is the same as the statements made in the interview in Task 5? Which information is different? What information has she left out? Complete the chart.

c Group Work Compare your chart with another pair's chart.

SAME AS TAPE

DIFFERENT FROM TAPE

MISSING INFORMATION

Task 7

Look back at your chart in Task 2. Can you add to it?

Task 8

You choose: Do **A** or **B**.

A Pair Work Use the chart in Task 2 for ideas. Talk about city life and country life in your country.

B Write your own article about city and country living. Use the chart in Task 2 for ideas.

A Day in the Life **103**

📖 Student text page 103

Task 5. 🎧 Play the tape again and have students note the positive and negative points raised. They can use more paper if necessary. **Variation.** This can be done as a cooperative task. Split the class into two groups with one noting the positive points and the other the negative ones—or with one group noting points pertaining to the city and the other, points pertaining to the country. Recombine the groups into pairs and have students share their information. (Answers: Positive, city: bigger, more exciting, more interesting; Positive, country: quieter, more peaceful, friendlier people. Negative, city: noisier, dirtier, more crowded. Negative, country: boring, no theater, few movies)

Task 6. (a) Tell students that Carla has written an article based on the interview they have just heard. Remind them that scanning is reading for specific information. Individually students scan Carla's article and mark key words or phrases about city or country life.

(b) Have students read the article more carefully to find out what information in it is the same as that in the tape, what is different, and what information in the tape was left out of the article. Have students complete the chart.
(Suggested answers: Same: country boring, quieter, people friendlier; city noisier. Different: country no nightclubs, no [instead of few] theaters, cities more entertaining and livelier [instead of much more interesting]. Missing: country more peaceful; cities bigger, more exciting, more crowded, dirtier)

(c) Have students compare charts.

Task 7. Have students look back at the charts for Task 2. Have the interview and article given them ideas to add to the chart? Have them add these to that chart.

Task 8. This should be a real task rather than a task of imagination. Students can choose to talk with a partner about city or country life (i) in their own original country or (ii) in the country they are now living in.

A Day in the Life **103**

📖 Student text page 104

Language Focus 1: Comparisons with adjectives

1. 🎧 Play the tape and have students practice the conversation, exchange roles, and practice it again. **Optional.** After they have practiced, have pairs close their books and role-play the conversation.

2. Work through the first two items with the class. Review the comparative structure using "than." Then have pairs of students do the remaining items. **Variation.** In small groups students write the comparative forms of the adverbs and adjectives used on this page. Have them do this under two headings, Comparative formed with -er, and Comparative formed with more. Groups can add as many other adverbs and adjectives as they can think of. Have groups mingle and compare lists. **Optional.** Have students do the task as a written exercise.
(Answers: a. The city is noisier than the country. b. Rock music is more popular than classical music. c. Los Angeles is bigger than San Francisco. d. Journalists are more interesting than actors. e. Work is more boring than leisure. f. Movies are more expensive than videos.

3. Have students fill in the blanks, then compare their responses with another student's. **Optional.** Have pairs practice the questions and answer, taking turns to ask and answer.
(Answers: Is, is, colder; Are, am, hungrier; Is, is, more interesting; Is, is, busier; Is, is, richer; Are, are, later)

4. Do this as a brainstorm activity. Explain that students need to choose and compare only two of the groups in each list.

104 A Day in the Life

Language Focus 1 Comparisons with adjectives

1 🎧 Pair Work Listen. Then practice this conversation with another student.

A: I really envy you, Carla.
B: Oh, yeah? Why's that?
A: As a journalist, you have such an interesting lifestyle—much more interesting than mine.
B: Sometimes I wish I had a quieter life.
A: Well, I wish my life were more exciting.

2 Pair Work Make sentences from these cues and then practice them.

Cues	Sentences
a city / noisy / country	*The city is noisier than the country.*
b rock music / popular / classical music	
c Los Angeles / big / San Francisco	
d journalists / interesting / actors	
e work / boring / leisure	
f movies / expensive / videos	

3 Fill in the blanks in the following questions and responses. Compare your answers with those of another student.

A: ...*Is*... it cold outside?
B: Yes, it ...*is*... . But it will be ...*colder*... later.

A: .... you hungry yet?
B: Yes, I .... But I'll be .... later.

A: .... Osaka interesting?
B: Yes, it .... But Tokyo is ....

A: .... Carla busy at the moment?
B: Yes, she .... But she'll be .... after lunch.

A: .... he rich?
B: Yes, he .... But his brother is ....

A: .... we late?
B: Yes, we .... But we'll be .... if we don't hurry.

4 Group Work Discussion. How many comparisons can you make between the members of these groups? Use your imagination, and give your own opinions.

a journalists, teachers, actors
b cities, towns, villages
c newspapers, magazines, books
d movies, plays, concerts

"Actors are more interesting than journalists."
"Journalists are more important than actors."
"Teachers are the most important."

104 A Day in the Life

Task Chain 2 Dear Deb

Task 1

Group Work Deborah Weissman writes a column called "Dear Deb." People write to her, and she gives them advice about their problems. What kind of advice do you think she gives? What kind of people do you think write to her? Are there advice columns in newspapers in your country?

Task 2

🎧 **Group Work** Listen. Four people are talking about their problems. Listen and identify the problems and the advice.

	PROBLEM	ADVICE
Conversation 1		
Conversation 2		
Conversation 3		
Conversation 4		

Task 3

a Here are some letters from the "Dear Deb" column. Match the letters to Deborah and the advice she gives by filling in the names of the writers in Deb's answers to them on page 106.

Dear Deb

Dear Deb,
I don't have a boyfriend, but I have been out with lots of different guys on a friendly basis. Last month I dated a guy I've known for a year and we had a great time, but he didn't ask me out again. I asked him out once but he didn't seem interested. I even wrote him a letter, but he said he forgot all about it. I know he is interested, because he told my friend Julio that he is. He seems very shy. Am I wasting my time with him, or is he just shy? What should I do?
Scorpio

Dear Deb,
I went out with my last boyfriend for two years, and then six months ago we broke up. I still miss him a lot, but he has a new girlfriend. He called me last week and said that he wants to see me again, but he also wants to stay with his new girlfriend. Do you think I am wasting my time?
Lou

Dear Deb,
My boyfriend and I have been together for six years. We have had some good times and some bad times, but recently my boyfriend started to spend a lot of time with his friends. I told him to choose me or his friends. He chose his friends and made me feel very unloved. Since we split up, he has been coming and going all the time. Now I am very unhappy and don't know what to do. Should I try and get back with him, or should I forget him and make a new life?
Confused

A Day in the Life **105**

📖 Student text page 106

(b) Give students an opportunity to agree or disagree with the advice and to offer suggestions of their own. What advice would they give Scorpio, Lou, and Confused? **Variation.** Have small groups each choose one of the three letters to Dear Deb. Decide in the group some different advice to give the writer. Then have the group do a rough draft of a letter of advice. Circulate and correct spelling, grammar and content, or have students exchange their letter with another group and offer and receive comments and corrections. In either case, have students write a second draft incorporating changes and corrections. Then exchange final drafts and read and discuss each other's advice.

Task 4. Have students read Worried Parents' letter individually. Clarify any vocabulary problems students may have, then put them in groups to discuss the letter and decide what advice to give. Have a representative from each group report his or her group's advice to the class.

Task 5 In pairs, have students decide on a problem for their letter to Deb and then write a first draft. As they write, circulate and correct errors in spelling and grammar. Have each pair exchange letters with another pair. Pair A reads the problem letter from Pair B and writes a reply; Pair B reads the problem letter from Pair A and writes a reply. Then each pair reads the reply that the other pair wrote. **Optional.** Put the two pairs together to discuss their reactions to the advice that was offered in the reply letter. This is a good chance for the students to clarify any problems they had in reading either the problem letter or the reply letter. Allow at least five minutes for this task.

106 A Day in the Life

"They could try talking to her."

"They have to make her see that she's making them unhappy."

"They could try giving her more freedom. It might help her grow up."

b Group Work Discussion. Do you agree with the advice?

Task 4

Group Work Discussion. What advice would you give to this person?

> Dear Deb,
> My husband and I are worried about our daughter. She refuses to do anything we tell her to do and is very rude to us. Also, she has become very friendly with a girl we don't like. We don't trust her anymore, because she is always lying to us. Are we pushing her away from us? We don't know what to do, and we're worried that she is going to get into serious trouble.
> *Worried Parents*

Task 5

Pair Work Write your own "Dear Deb" letter. Then exchange your letter with another pair and write an answer.

Language Focus 2 Modals: *have to, should, could*

1 🎧 **Pair Work** Listen. Then practice this conversation.

A: Tom and Tony have both asked me out. What should I do?
B: Who asked you first?
A: Tony.
B: Then you should go out with Tony, if you've already told him you would.
A: But I like Tom better.
B: Well, you could go out with Tom tomorrow.

2 Complete these statements with *have to*, *should*, and *could*.

a When you want to make a suggestion, you can use ....
b When you want to give advice, you can use ....
c When you want to express obligation, you can use ....

3 Fill in the blanks with *have to* or *could*. Then compare your answers with those of another student.

a How do I get a license? You .... take a test.
b Why are you staying home? I .... study for the exam on Monday.
c How will he recognize us? We .... wear name tags.
d How will you get there? We .... take a taxi or the subway.
e When will they study? They .... study tonight—the exam is tomorrow.

4 **Pair Work** In each situation, A asks B for advice. Read the conversations and decide what advice A is asking for. Give reasons.

A: What .... ?
B: Well, you don't have to wear a suit, but you do have to wear a jacket and tie.
A: I want to look really dressed up.
B: You could wear a flower in your buttonhole.

A: How .... ?
B: What time do you have to be there?
A: Eight o'clock.
B: It's 7:30 now, so you'll have to take a cab.

A: When .... ?
B: What time is the movie?
A: 8:30.
B: You have plenty of time, so you could walk.

A Day in the Life **107**

📖 Student text page 107

Language Focus 2: Modals: *have to, should, could*

1. 🎧 Play the tape and have students practice the conversation, change roles, and practice again. Circulate to check pronunciation. **Optional.** Discuss the situation with the class. Do they agree with speaker B's advice? Why or why not?

2. Remind students that "have to" signals compulsion, "should" is advice, and "could" is a suggestion or possibility. Have students complete the three sentences as a whole class exercise.
(Answers: a. could; b. should; c. have to)

3. Have the students work individually to fill in the blanks with "have to" or "could." Then in pairs or small groups, have them compare answers with others. Elicit responses from the class.
(Answers: a. have to; b. have to; c. could; d. could; e. have to) Accept alternative answers if students can justify them.

4. Have pairs of students study the situations and fill in the blanks. Accept alternative answers that carry the same meaning. When students have finished, elicit responses from around the class.
(Suggested answers: What should I wear? [He's going on a date/for a job interview]; How should I get there? [Needs to know how to get somewhere]; When should I leave? [Going to the movies and needs to know when to leave and how to get there])

A Day in the Life **107**

Student text page 108

Self-Check

Communication Challenge

Challenge 14 is on pages 126 and 128 of the student text, and suggestions for its use are on page 126 in this Teacher's Extended Edition.

1, 2. Have students do these in or outside of class and use the new words and sentences or questions in conversation with others.

3. Have students do this task in pairs or small groups. Circulate and be sure they can make comparisons. Then have them discuss and prepare to give advice to someone who is studying English on how to practice what she or he is learning. Write the following forms on the board and have them use them in the advice they give:

You should....	Make sure you....
You could....	Don't forget to....
You have to....	

Switch pairs and have students practice giving advice to each other. Circulate and monitor pronunciation and grammar. Be sure they understand the difference between "have to," "should," and "could."

4. Have students list the areas in which they believe they need more practice, and discuss with them how and where they can get this practice. Encourage them to listen to, speak, and read English whenever and wherever they can. English and American movies, radio and television programs are excellent ways to improve listening skills. Talking with native English speakers will help develop speaking skills. And encourage students to read as much English as they can—newspapers, magazines, novels, comic books—any and all sources of authentic written English.

5. As in earlier units, have students check the word list. Explain or have other students explain any words that particular students are unsure of. Encourage all students to keep vocabulary notebooks and refer to them regularly.

• Grammar summaries for this unit are on page 134.

108   A Day in the Life

Self-Check

COMMUNICATION CHALLENGE
Pair Work Student A: Look at Challenge 14A on page 126. Student B: Look at Challenge 14B on page 128.

"My friends and I ask each other for advice in English outside of class."

1 Write down five new words you learned in this unit.

2 Write down three new sentences or questions you learned.

3 Review the language skills you practiced in this unit. Check [√] your answers.

CAN YOU:

| Make comparisons? | ☐ yes | ☐ a little | ☐ not yet |

Find or give an example:

| Ask for and give advice? | ☐ yes | ☐ a little | ☐ not yet |

Find or give an example:

| Express obligation? | ☐ yes | ☐ a little | ☐ not yet |

Find or give an example:

4 What areas need more practice? How can you get more practice? Make a list.

5 Vocabulary check. Check [√] the words you know.

Adjectives
- ☐ bigger
- ☐ cheaper
- ☐ duller
- ☐ faster
- ☐ noisier
- ☐ political
- ☐ quieter
- ☐ slower
- ☐ smaller

Adverbs
- ☐ more
- ☐ most
- ☐ much

Nouns
- ☐ advice
- column
- ☐ city life
- ☐ comparison
- ☐ country life
- ☐ headline
- ☐ journalist
- ☐ lifestyle
- ☐ obligation
- ☐ reporter

Verbs
- ☐ could
- ☐ have to
- ☐ interview

108   A Day in the Life

15 Review

Task 1

Pair Work Match these newspaper headlines to the pictures.

.... **Thunderstorm Hits Atlanta**

.... *Light Plane Crashes in Mountains*

.... **Daring Art Gallery Robbery**

.... Fashion Show a Hit

.... *Explosion in Oil Refinery*

Task 2

a 🎧 Listen to the news broadcast and match the news items with the pictures at left.

b 🎧 Now listen again. Where did each of these events happen? Write each of the following places under the correct picture: *Boulder, New York, Cheyenne, San Francisco, Atlanta.*

Task 3

a Read these newspaper reports. Some of the information is different from the information in the radio reports. Can you find the differences? Fill in the chart on page 110.

Picture 1 ....

Picture 2 ....

Picture 3 ....

Picture 4 ....

Picture 5 ....

Denver, Colorado: Rescue workers are searching today for a helicopter. It was stolen by a person pretending to be a flying instructor. The thief ordered the pilot out of the helicopter at knifepoint and took off. Police believe that the thief flew to California.

San Francisco: The Second International Fashion Show is taking place at the Hilton Hotel in San Francisco this afternoon. Designers and models from over 30 countries have gathered for the show, which is one of the biggest in the world.

Austin, Texas: A huge explosion at an oil refinery injured eight workers today. Six of the workers are in the hospital, two of them with severe injuries. The explosion was caused by an oil leak.

New York City: Police are searching for a thief who stole some jewelry from the Blue Chip Diamond Store. The thief got into the store through the air conditioning system. Police say the person was lucky that the system was not turned on at the time.

Rochester, New York: A severe snowstorm caused many road accidents in Rochester yesterday. Police and rescue workers were busy into the night. Authorities expect the weather to improve tomorrow.

Review 109

Student text pages 109–110 (cont.)

Rochester, New York; radio, Atlanta, Georgia; paper, police and rescue worker were busy into the night; radio, residents are trying to clean up the damage; paper, weather to improve; radio, more rain expected tomorrow)

(b) Have students discuss the differences using the example sentence as a model.

Task 4. (a) This can be done individually or as a pair, group, or whole class task. If you do it as a whole class task, put the film review on the board or on an overhead and elicit responses from the students, underlining the words as they are given.
(Answers: is, is, has…sounded, include, start (fighting), has finished, is, haven't seen, go see, have seen, see)

(b) Have students write the verbs in the appropriate columns. As they work, circulate, check, and provide help if necessary (some students may have difficulty with "giving" and "go see").
(Answers: Simple present: is, is, include, start, is, go see, see; Present progressive: fighting; Simple past: (none); Present perfect: has…sounded, has finished, haven't seen, have seen) Note: "go see" is an imperative or command, which has no true tense but uses the simple present tense form and so is categorized as simple present.

Task 5. (a) and (b) 🎧 Have pairs listen to the tape and fill in the blanks in the conversation. Then have them practice the conversation, change roles and practice it again. Circulate and check, then ask for responses from the whole class and put them on the board.
(Answers: seen, have, did, see, week, was)

110 Review

	NEWSPAPER	RADIO
Story 1:	Denver	Boulder
Story 2:		
Story 3:		
Story 4:		
Story 5:		

b **Pair Work** Now discuss the differences with another student.

Example: "The newspaper said the aircraft theft was in Denver. The radio said it was in Boulder."

GIMME SHELTER (1970). This is a classic rock-'n'-roll concert movie, featuring the Rolling Stones at the Altamont Speedway in California. This is the best that Mick Jagger has ever sounded. Other groups and singers performing at the concert include Jefferson Airplane and Grace Slick. In the middle of the show, many people start fighting, and before the concert has finished, there is a murder. This movie has great music and great drama. If you haven't seen this movie before, go see it. If you *have* seen it before, it's time to see it again.

Task 4

a Read this film review and underline all the verbs.

b Write the verbs in the correct columns in the chart.

SIMPLE PRESENT	PRESENT PROGRESSIVE	SIMPLE PAST	PRESENT PERFECT

Task 5

a 🎧 **Pair Work** Listen. Then fill in the blanks and practice this conversation with another student.

A: Have you ……………… the new movie at the Odeon?
B: Yes, I ……………… .
A: Oh, really? When ……………… you ……………… it?
A: Last ……………… . I guess it ……………… Tuesday.

b **Pair Work** Change roles and practice the conversation again.

110 Review

Communication Challenges

Challenge 1

Task 1

🎧 **Group Work** Listen and take notes. Then form two groups. Group A: Listen again to Mike and Anna talking about people at a party and fill in columns 1 and 2. Group B: Listen again to Maggie and John talking about people at a party and fill in columns 3 and 4.

	1. YONGSUE	2. PAUL	3. MARIKA	4. PROF. TANAKA
From?				
Description?				
Job?				
Married?				

Task 2

Pair Work Look at the picture on page 9. Can you find these people?

📖 Student text page 111

Communication Challenge 1

The Communication Challenge tasks provide students with an opportunity to use the language they have been learning in a freer context.

Task 1. 🎧 Have the students listen to the tape and take notes. Then divide the class into two groups. Tell the groups that they will listen to the conversation again, but this time each group will listen for and record different information. Group A will listen to the first conversation and fill in columns 1 and 2. Group B will listen to the second conversation and fill in columns 3 and 4. You may wish to subdivide the two groups into smaller groups to record the information. Have both groups look at the chart. Elicit that "From?" means what country the person comes from; "Description?" means what the person looks like; "Job?" means what the person's occupation is, and "Married?" means whether the person is married or not.
(Answers: Column 1: Korea; small with dark hair; student; don't know. Column 2: Canada; brown hair and beard; businessman; yes. Column 3: Germany; tall blond; doctor; yes. Column 4. Japan; dark hair; professor; yes.)

Task 2. Have students look at the picture on page 9 and identify Yongsue, Paul, Marika, and Professor Tanaka.
(Answers: left to right, Professor Tanaka, Paul, Yongsue, Marika)

📖 Student text page 112

Communication Challenge 2

The aim of this task is to give students a further opportunity to describe families.

- Put students in small groups. Explain the task, or model it by pretending to be one of the people in one of the photographs and describing "your" family. Ask other students to guess who you are.
(NOTE: The example sentence is to illustrate the response form only. It does not correspond to any of the photographs.) Have each student individually choose one of the photographs and pretend to be one character in it. Have her or him describe the family from that person's point of view, while the other group members listen and guess which photograph is being described.

- As students do the task, circulate and monitor language use.

Communication Challenges

Challenge 2

Group Work Pick one of these families. Pretend to be one of the people in the photograph. Describe your family. Ask the other students to guess who you are.

Example: "I have a wife and five children. I have two sons and three daughters. I also have six grandchildren. Which person am I?"

Communication Challenges

Challenge 3A

Task 1

a **Pair Work** Here is a postcard about your partner's photographs. Read it carefully. Use it to answer your partner's questions.

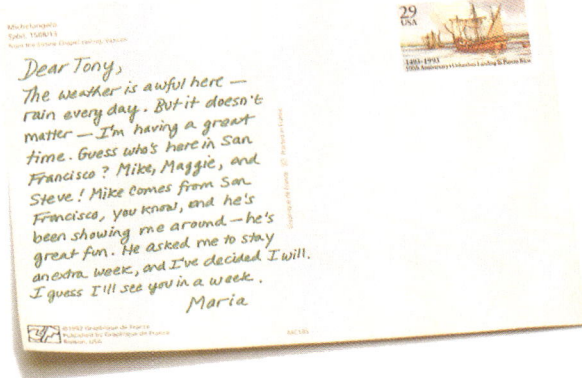

b **Pair Work** Tony is on vacation. These are his photographs. Show them to your partner and ask the following questions:

- Who is in the photograph?
- Where are they?
- Is Tony having a good time without Maria?

Task 2

Pair Work Write a reply to this postcard or your partner's.

Communication Challenges 113

Student text page 113

Communication Challenge 3A and 3B

Challenge 3A is on this page. Challenge 3B is on page 115. This can be done either as a pair activity, with one pair partner looking at Challenge 3A on this page and the other looking at Challenge 3B on page 115, or as a group activity, with one group looking at Challenge 3A and the other at Challenge 3B. Partners must not see each other's pages.

Task 1. (a) Have students read the postcard on their page carefully and be ready to answer their partner's questions on the basis of the postcard.
(b) Students show the photographs on their page to their partner (or to someone from the other group) and ask the questions. The partner or person from the other group answers them, based on the postcard on his or her page.
(Answers: Group A: Tony's family; Florida; No. Group B: Her friends Mike, Maggie and Steve; San Francisco; Yes)

Task 2. Have each student write a reply to either the postcard on his/her page or the one on the other page.

Communication Challenges 113

📖 Student text page 114

Communication Challenge 4A and 4B

Challenge 4A is on this page. Challenge 4B is on page 125. This can be done either as a pair activity, with one partner looking at Challenge 4A and the other at Challenge 4B, or as a group activity, with one group looking at 4A and the other at 4B. Partners must not see each other's pages.

- The 4A partner or group reads the four descriptions and uses them to answer the questions from the 4B partner or group. Then the 4B partner needs to identify the photographs on the basis of partner A's description.
(Answers: a. El Vez; b. George Thomas; c. Steve Peri; d. Don Jett. Photos: top, Don Jett; left, George Thomas; center Steve Peri; right, El Vez)

Communication Challenge 12A and 12B

Challenge 12A is on this page. Challenge 12B is on page 127. This activity may be done in pairs, with one partner looking at Challenge 12A and the other at Challenge 12B or in two groups, one looking at 12A and the other at 12B. Partners must not see each other's pages.

- Partner A compiles a list of activities he or she would like to do when visiting Partner B and talks about them with B. Partner B looks at the advertisements in 12B and makes suggestions about where they might do some of these things, following the model conversation.

114 Communication Challenges

Challenge 4A

Pair Work Read the following comments by singers who impersonate Elvis Presley. Then answer your partner's questions.

George Thomas: I play the young Elvis. He has a fresh face; he is young and slim. Just like me.

Don Jett: I play the older Elvis. He is at his peak, mature and solid. His voice is good. His personal appearance is good.

El Vez: I play the Mexican Elvis. I like the '50s Elvis. The older Elvis is too fat, so I couldn't play him.

Steve Peri: I play the '70s Elvis. He is a mature man. He is also heavy, just like me. He wears great clothes—flared pants and sequined jackets.

Challenge 12A

Pair Work You are visiting your partner for the weekend. Think of all the things you would like to do (for example, go out for a meal, go to the movies, go to a concert).

A What would you like to do this weekend?
B I'd like to eat out. And I want to hear some live music.
A Well, why don't we go to Lola's Hot Gospel Café and do both things at once?

114 Communication Challenges

Challenge 3B

Task 1

a Pair Work Here is a postcard about your partner's photographs. Read it carefully. Use it to answer your partner's questions.

Dear Maria,
Well, here I am in Florida with my family. The weather is great, but I'm having a terrible time without you. I miss you very much. Everyone else is having fun. My parents are enjoying themselves, and my sister is having a good time. She's going out with a guy she met just after we arrived. Hope you miss me too. See you next week.
Love,
Tony

b Pair Work Maria is on vacation. These are her photographs. Show them to your partner and ask the following questions:

- Who is in the photograph?
- Where are they?
- Is Maria having a good time without Tony?

Task 2

Pair Work Write a reply to this postcard or your partner's.

Student text page 115

Communication Challenge 3B

See page 113 for suggestions for using Challenge 3A and 3B.

Student text page 116

Communication Challenge 6A and 6B

Challenge 6A is on this page. Challenge 6B is on page 118. Divide the class into two groups. Group A looks at this page. Group B looks at page 118. They must not look at each other's pages.

Task 1. 🎧 Have group A listen to the tape. Be sure that group B cannot hear it. Group A students fill in Part A of the information form. Have group B fill in Part B of the form, using Teresa's letter on page 118 as a guide.

Task 2. Form pairs with one group A student paired with one group B student. Tell students not to look at each other's books. They must share their information to complete both parts of the form. Have the pairs look at the advertisements and find the most suitable place for Teresa.
(Answers will vary, but Tony's, at 555-1066 is probably the closest to what Teresa wants.)

Completed form:

Part A
Name: Teresa Marciano
Address: 34 Spring Street, Apartment 288
Occupation: Student
Married/Single: Single
Number of children: N/A
Type of Housing: Room
Shared/Alone: Alone
Price range (per month): $400–$500

Part B
Yes on furnished, near transportation, near shopping, with garden or yard

116   Communication Challenges

Challenge 6A

Room to rent in large apartment. Close to stores and transportation. Rooftop deck available. Fully furnished. $420/month. 555-2300.

Double attic room to rent. Perfect for young professional person. $550 per month. 555-3588.

Small apartment to let. Furnished or unfurnished. Close to stores. $500/month. 555-5089.

Furnished room to rent in small house with yard. Transportation available to city. Non-smoker only, please. $300/month. Call Tony at 555-1066.

Unfurnished room to rent. Close to stores and transportation. Good for student or single person. $380/month. Call 555-6429.

Task 1

Group Work Listen. Teresa is talking to a rental agent. Fill in Part A of the rental form.

Rental Agency Information Form

PART A
Name ....
Address ....
Occupation ....
Married / Single
Number of children ....
Type of housing: House / Apartment / Room
Shared / Alone
Price range (per month) $200–$300 $600–$700
                           $300–$400 $700–$800
                           $400–$500 $800–$900
                           $500–$600 $900–$1,000

PART B
Furnished / Unfurnished
Facilities
• near transportation   yes / no
• near stores   yes / no
• near school   yes / no
• near park   yes / no
• near health club   yes / no
• with garden or yard   yes / no

Task 2

Pair Work Now work with a student from Group B. Decide which of the places at left is best for Teresa.

116   Communication Challenges

Challenge 8

Task 1

🎧 Listen to the tour guide. Which places does the tour visit? Check [√] your answers.

	Yes	No
Lincoln Center	☐	☐
Dakota apartment building	☐	☐
New York Historical Society	☐	☐
American Museum of Natural History	☐	☐
Central Park Zoo	☐	☐
Metropolitan Museum of Art	☐	☐
Park Avenue	☐	☐
Bloomingdale's	☐	☐
Plaza Hotel	☐	☐

Task 2

🎧 Listen again. Look at the map and trace the route.

Task 3

a **Pair Work** Make up a tour of either your home community or the place where you are studying.

b **Group Work** Describe the tour to another pair.

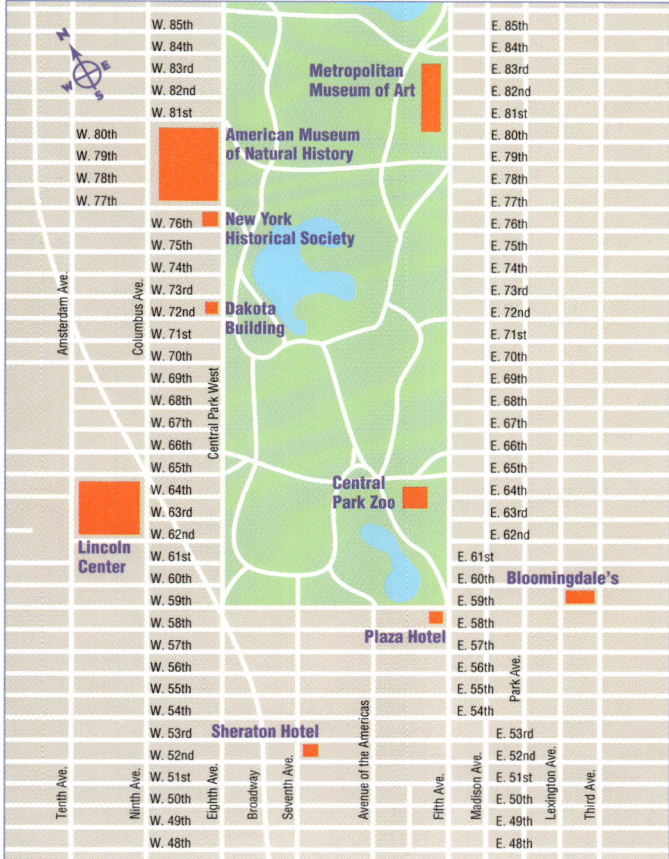

Communication Challenges 117

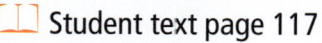 Student text page 117

Communication Challenge 8

Task 1. 🎧 Have students listen to the tape and check in the "yes" column for the places that the tour visits and in the "no" column for those it doesn't. (Answers: ["yes"] Lincoln Center, Dakota apartment building, American Museum of Natural History, Metropolitan Museum of Art. [All others are "no."])

Task 2. 🎧 Have students trace the route on the map. (Answers: See the map. Dakota Building and Natural History Museum are on Central Park West; tour would cross Central Park from West 81st Street to East 79th Street and up to the Metropolitan Museum, then down Fifth Avenue to 52nd Street and across to the Sheraton Hotel on Seventh Avenue. Most New York streets are one-way, so actual route may not be what looks like the most direct route.)

Task 3. (a) and (b) Have students use the recorded tour as a model for a tour of their home community or the one they are living in at present.

Communication Challenges 117

📖 Student text page 118

Communication Challenge 6B

See page 116 for suggestions for using Challenge 6A and 6B.

Challenge 6B

Task 1

Group Work Read the letter from Teresa to her friend Sandy and fill in Part B of the form.

Rental Agency Information Form

PART A
Name ....
Address ....
Occupation ....
Married / Single
Number of children ....
Type of housing: House / Apartment / Room
Shared / Alone
Price range (per month) $200–$300 $600–$700
                         $300–$400 $700–$800
                         $400–$500 $800–$900
                         $500–$600 $900–$1,000

PART B
Furnished / Unfurnished

Facilities
- near transportation   yes / no
- near stores   yes / no
- near school   yes / no
- near park   yes / no
- near health club   yes / no
- with garden or yard   yes / no

Dear Sandy,
This is my second week in Chicago, and I'm enjoying it very much. I'm staying with a friend of my brother's at the moment. However, I have to find somewhere of my own, a furnished place I can share. I need to share the house or apartment because housing is so expensive in Chicago, but I like privacy and I need to study, so I really need a room of my own. I'm looking for a place that's close to transportation and stores. It would also be nice to find a place with a yard or a garden.
I hope that I can find something by the time you come to Chicago! I'm really looking forward to seeing you.
Love, Teresa

Task 2

Pair Work Now work with a student from Group A. Decide which of these places is best for Teresa.

Double attic room to rent. Perfect for young professional person. $550 per month. 555-3588.

Furnished room to rent in small house with yard. Transportation available to city. Non-smoker only, please. $300/month. Call Tony at 555-1066.

Room to rent in large apartment. Close to stores and transportation. Rooftop deck available. Fully furnished. $420/month. 555-2300.

Unfurnished room to rent. Close to stores and transportation. Good for student or single person. $380/month. Call 555-6429.

Small apartment to let. Furnished or unfurnished. Close to stores. $500/month. 555-5089.

Challenge 9A

Task 1

Pair Work How much do you know about the Asian Pacific Rim region? Look at these places. Find the cities and countries and write them in the correct columns.

Ho Chi Minh City	Singapore	Taiwan	Bangkok
Kuala Lumpur	South Korea	Tokyo	Australia
Hong Kong colony	Philippines	Vientiane	Thailand
Republic of Singapore	Indonesia	Seoul	Japan
Hong Kong	Sydney	Taipei	Malaysia
Manila	Vietnam	Djakarta	Laos

Cities
Sydney
....
....
....
....
....
....
....
....
....
....

Countries
Vietnam
....
....
....
....
....
....
....
....
....
....

Task 2

Pair Work Now draw lines to match the cities and countries and make statements about them.

Example: "Sydney is in Australia."

Task 3

Pair Work You and your partner will each receive a set of clues about the same three mystery cities. Try to name the cities and then compare your clues and your answers with those of your partner. Student A: Look at Challenge 9B on page 122. Student B: Look at Challenge 9C on page 124.

Communication Challenges **119**

📖 Student text page 119

Communication Challenge 9A, 9B, and 9C

Challenge 9A is on this page. Challenge 9B is on page 122, and Challenge 9C is on page 124. Students work in pairs; both partners do Tasks 1 and 2 but partners work separately on Task 3, using Challenges 9B and 9C as clues.

Task 1. Have students sort the 24 place names into 12 cities and 12 countries and write these in the appropriate columns.

Task 2. Have the students draw lines to match each city with the country it is in and take turns telling their partners about each city, following the example. (Answers: Ho Chi Minh City, Vietnam; Kuala Lumpur, Malaysia; Hong Kong, Hong Kong Colony; Manila, Philippines; Singapore, Republic of Singapore; Sydney, Australia; Tokyo, Japan; Vientiane, Laos; Seoul, Korea; Taipei, Taiwan; Djakarta, Indonesia; Bangkok, Thailand)

Task 3. Have one partner look at Challenge 9B (page 122) and the other at Challenge 9C (page 124) and, using the clues, try to determine what the three mystery cities are. Partners must not look at each other's pages. (Answers: Singapore, Tokyo, Sydney)

Communication Challenges **119**

📖 Student text page 120

Communication Challenge 11A, 11B, and 11C

Challenge 11A is on this page. Challenge 11B is on page 122, and Challenge 11C is on page 124. Students work in 3 groups, group A with this page, group B with page 122, and group C with page 124. Students must not look at the other groups' pages.

Task 1. Group A students work together to discuss and number the activities in order from most to least popular, based on consensus opinion of the group members. Group B and C students read the excerpts from newspaper articles on their pages and underline the activities. Then recombine the students into groups of three, one from each of the original groups. Student A (from the original group A) checks and adjusts the list in the light of information from students B and C based on their reading of the articles.
(Answers, reading down: 10, 6, 2, 9, 8, 3, 4, 1, 5, 7)

Task 2. Reform the original groups and have students discuss and list the most and least popular weekend activities in their countries. **Optional.** This can be done as a whole class discussion.

120 Communication Challenges

Challenge 11A

Task 1

Group Work These were the five most popular and five least popular weekend activities in the United States on Independence Day (Fourth of July) weekend. Work with your partners to number them in order from most to least popular.

.... Going to the theater
.... Going dancing
.... Running errands
.... Going to a sporting event
.... Going fishing
.... Working out, jogging, walking, or biking
.... Working in yard
.... Visiting friends or relatives
.... Reading a book
.... Going to a museum or art gallery

Task 2

Make a list of how people spend time on the weekend in your country.

MOST POPULAR ACTIVITIES	LEAST POPULAR ACTIVITIES

120 Communication Challenges

Challenge 7A

Pair Work Ask your partner where the following places are and mark them on your map.

- the library
- the post office
- the bus station
- the school
- the hospital

Communication Challenge 7A and 7B

Challenge 7A is on this page. Challenge 7B is on page 123. Divide the class into pairs. Student A works with this page and student B with page 123. Students must not look at each other's pages.

• Each student has a map with five places listed on it; they are different places on the two maps. Have students A and B ask each other for the locations of the places on the other's map, and mark these places on their own map. They then compare their completed maps. (Answers: Compare the maps on pages 121 and 123. NOTE: Because there are two sides to each street, answers may differ and still be correct. For example, if student B says "The school is on Dover Street, between Jordan Avenue and Belmont Avenue," student A may place it correctly on either side of Dover Street.)

📖 Student text page 122

Communication Challenge 11B

See page 120 for suggestions for using Challenge 11A, 11B, and 11C.

Communication Challenge 9B

See page 119 for suggestions for using Challenge 9A, 9B, and 9C.

Challenge 11B

Task 1

Group Work Student A has a list of the five most popular and five least popular weekend activities in the United States on the Independence Day weekend. Student C has some information about the activities.

Share the following information to help Students A and C put the activities in order from most popular to least popular.

> Last July 4th weekend, 86% of Americans spent time with friends or relatives. 59% did some form of exercise such as jogging or biking, while only 4% watched sporting events. 5% went fishing. Only 3% of the population went to the theater.

Task 2

Make a list of how people spend time on the weekend in your country.

Challenge 9B

Mystery City 1
- is close to the equator
- is on a small island
- is always hot

Mystery City 2
- has a population of 27.7 million
- is very expensive
- has one of the tallest metal towers in the world

Mystery City 3
- has a population of 3.6 million
- has a famous opera house
- the main language is English, but you will often hear many other languages

Mystery City 1: ....
Mystery City 2: ....
Mystery City 3: ....

Challenge 7B

Pair Work Ask your partner where the following places are and mark them on your map.

- the department store
- the deli
- the police station
- the park
- the bank

📖 Student text page 124

Communication Challenge 11C

See page 120 for suggestions for using Challenge 11A, 11B, and 11C.

Communication Challenge 9C

See page 119 for suggestions for using Challenge 9A, 9B, and 9C.

Challenge 11C

Task 1

Group Work Student A has a list of the five most popular and five least popular weekend activities in the United States on the Independence Day weekend. Student B has some information about the activities.

Share the following information to help Students A and B put the activities in order from most popular to least popular.

> Last weekend, many people worked around the house: 64% ran errands, while 47% did chores in the yard. 44% relaxed with a book. 7% visited museums and art galleries, and 10% went dancing.

Task 2

Make a list of how people spend time on the weekend in your country.

Challenge 9C

Mystery City 1
- has a population of 3 million
- has four main languages: Chinese, English, Tamil, and Malay
- is a popular tourist destination

Mystery City 2
- is usually hot in summer and often cold in winter
- has a Disney theme park
- was nearly destroyed by an earthquake in 1923

Mystery City 3
- is usually warm in summer and cool in winter
- has a beautiful harbor
- has large immigrant population from over 130 different countries

Mystery City 1: ....
Mystery City 2: ....
Mystery City 3: ....

Challenge 13A

Task 1

Pair Work You are going to join a health club. Your partner is a trainer at the health club. Think about why you want to attend the club. Here are some possible reasons:

- to lose weight
- to gain weight
- to get into shape to go skiing
- to get into shape to play tennis

Talk to the health club trainer and answer his or her questions.

Task 2

Pair Work Now discuss what you need to do to get into shape.

Task 3

Pair Work Change roles and do the task again.

Challenge 4B

Pair Work Your task is to identify the singers. Find out this information from your partner.

a Who plays the Mexican Elvis? ....
b Who is young and slim? ....
c Who plays the '70s Elvis? ....
d Who plays the older Elvis? ....

Now match the descriptions and the photographs and write the artists' names under the photographs.

Communication Challenges **125**

Student text page 126

Communication Challenge 14A and 14B

Challenge 14A is on this page. Challenge 14B is on page 128. Divide the class into two groups. Group A looks at this page and group B looks at page 128.

Task 1. 🎧 Have both groups listen to Carla talking about her job. Each group listens for specific things, A for Carla's most interesting, most boring, and most dangerous assignments, and B for her funniest, most important, and most exciting tasks.

Task 2. Put the students into pairs, with one partner from group A and the other from group B. Have them work together to fill in the blanks.
(Answers: most interesting, covering Olympic Games; most boring, attending local flower show; most dangerous, reporting on Los Angeles street riots; funniest, interviewing Steve Martin; most important, covering trial of drug king; most exciting, going to Academy Awards)

Task 3. Have students look at pictures on page 101 and talk with partners about their choices.
(Answer will vary.)

Task 4. Reform the original groups and have them discuss the most interesting, boring, dangerous, important, exciting, and funniest things that have happened to them. **Variation.** Do this as a whole class task.

126 Communication Challenges

Challenge 14A

Task 1
🎧 Listen. Carla is talking about her job. Take notes about the most interesting, the most boring, and the most dangerous assignments.

Task 2
Pair Work Work with a student from the other group to complete the following. Student A: Fill in the first three blanks. Student B: Fill in the last three blanks.

Student A:
Most interesting: ....
Most boring: ....
Most dangerous: ....

Student B:
Funniest: ....
Most important: ....
Most exciting: ....

Task 3
Now look at the pictures on page 101. Which is the most interesting task, the most boring task, the most dangerous task?

Task 4
Group Work Talk about the most interesting, boring, dangerous, important, and exciting things and the funniest things that have ever happened to you.

126 Communication Challenges

Challenge 13B

HEALTH PROFILE

For .... Date ....

1. Weight ....
2. Height ....
3. Pulse rate ....
4. Past illnesses/injuries ....
5. Eating habits (usual foods) ....
6. Smoking habits ....
7. Drinking (alcohol) habits ....
8. Exercise habits ....
9. Reason for joining ....

Task 1

Pair Work You are a trainer at a health club. Your partner has come to you for advice. Ask him or her questions, and fill in the health profile at left.

Task 2

Pair Work Now discuss what your partner needs to do to get into shape.

Example: "You should eat more grains and fruits and vegetables, and you should cycle for 20 minutes every morning. You shouldn't eat so much junk food and you shouldn't smoke."

Task 3

Pair Work Change roles and do the task again.

Challenge 12B

Pair Work Your partner is visiting you for the weekend. Find out what your partner wants to do. Look at this guide and make suggestions.

- **A** What would you like to do this weekend?
- **B** I'd like to eat out. And I want to hear some live music.
- **A** Well, why don't we go to Lola's Hot Gospel Café and do both things at once?

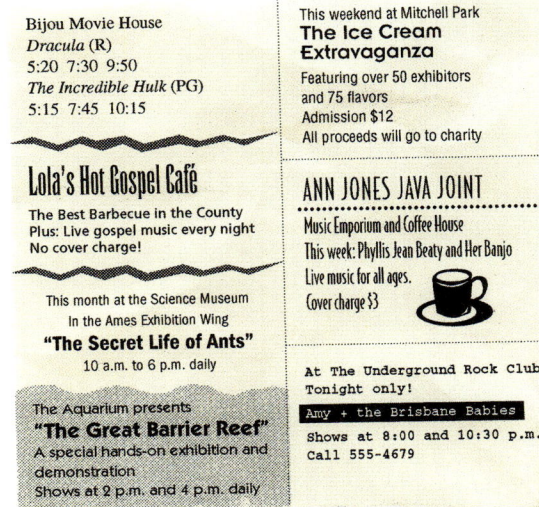

Student text page 127

Communication Challenge 13B

See page 125 for suggestions for using Challenge 13A and 13B.

Communication Challenge 12B

See page 114 for suggestions for using Challenge 12A and 12B.

Student text page 128

Communication Challenge 14B

See page 126 for suggestions for using Challenge 14A and 14B.

Challenge 14B

Task 1

🎧 Listen. Carla is talking about her job. Take notes about the funniest, the most important, and the most exciting tasks.

Task 2

Pair Work Work with a student from the other group to complete the following. Student A: Fill in the first three blanks. Student B: Fill in the last three blanks.

Student A:
Most interesting: ....
Most boring: ....
Most dangerous: ....

Student B:
Funniest: ....
Most important: ....
Most exciting: ....

Task 3

Now look at the pictures on page 101. Which is the funniest task, the most important task, the most exciting task?

Task 4

Group Work Talk about the most interesting, boring, dangerous, important, and exciting things and the funniest things that have ever happened to you.

Communication Challenges

Grammar Summaries

Unit 1

1 Pronouns

I	me	my		it	it	its
you	you	your		we	us	our
he	him	his		they	them	their
she	her	her				

2 Statements and yes/no questions with *to be*

I am late.	Am I late?	I'm (I am) not late.
You are early.	Are you early?	You're (you are) not early.
He is from Chile.	Is he from Chile?	He isn't (is not) from Chile.
She is from Boston.	Is she from Boston?	She isn't (is not) from Boston.
It is new.	Is it new?	It isn't (is not) new.
We are right.	Are we right?	We aren't (are not) right.
You are wrong.	Are you wrong?	You aren't (are not) wrong.
They are Japanese.	Are they Japanese?	They aren't (are not) Japanese.

3 *Wh* questions: *what* and *where* + *to be*

What's (what is) your name?	My name's (name is) Mike.
Where are you from?	I'm (I am) from Chicago.
What's (what is) his name?	His name's (name is) Kenji.
Where's (where is) he from?	He's (he is) from Tokyo.
What's (what is) her name?	Her name's (name is) Songporn.
Where's (where is) she from?	She's (she is) from Thailand.
What are your names?	Our names are Sylvia and Maria.
Where are you from?	We're (we are) from Mexico.
What are their names?	Their names are Tomoko and Yumi.
Where are they from?	They're (they are) from Japan.

Unit 2

1 Singular and plural nouns

Regular
boy, boys
girl, girls
husband, husbands
daughter, daughters
son, sons

aunt, aunts
uncle, uncles
cousin, cousins
family, families

Irregular
child, children
man, men
woman, women
wife, wives

2 Statements and yes/no questions with *do/does*

Do I sit here?	Yes, you do.	No, you don't.
Do you have a brother?	Yes, I do.	No, I don't.
Does he go to school?	Yes, he does.	No, he doesn't.
Does she have a father?	Yes, she does.	No, she doesn't.
Does it leave soon?	Yes, it does.	No, it doesn't.
Do we wait here?	Yes, we do.	No, we don't.
Do you have sisters?	Yes, I do.	No, I don't.
Do they have cousins?	Yes, they do.	No, they don't.

3 *Wh* questions with *do/does*

What do I need?	You need a work permit.
What do you do?	I'm a teacher.
Where does he work?	He works in a bank.
Where does she live?	She lives in California.
Where do you go to school?	We go to Boston University.
What do they do?	They're students.

Unit 3

1 Present-tense questions with *do/does*: a review

Do I need a student card?	Yes, you do. No, you don't.
What do you do on the weekend?	I study, play tennis, and go to the movies.
Do you like talking about friendships?	Yes, I do. No, I don't.
What does your best friend do?	She's a teacher.
Does she have a close friend?	Yes, she does. No, she doesn't.
Where does he go to school?	He goes to Davis College.
Do we need a ticket?	Yes, you do. No, you don't.
Do they have girlfriends?	Yes, they do. No, they don't.

2 *Wh* questions: *who* + *do/does*

Who do I look like?	You look like my brother.
Who do you study with?	I study with my best friend.
Who does he like?	He likes Maria.
Who does she talk to?	She talks to her friends.
Who do they work with?	They work with Tony and Steve.
Who do you live with?	We live with our parents.

Unit 4

1 Simple present with *like*

Do you like classical music?	Yes, I do.	No, I don't.
Does she like rock music?	Yes, she does.	No, she doesn't.
Does he like jazz?	Yes, he does.	No, he doesn't.
Do you like theater?	Yes, we do.	No, we don't.
Do they like modern art?	Yes, they do.	No, they don't.

2 Adjectives

Am I disorganized?	Yes, you are. You're a really disorganized person.
Are you busy?	Of course I am. I'm a really busy person.
Is he good-looking?	Yes, he is. He's a really good-looking guy.
Is she intelligent?	Yes, she's a very intelligent woman.
Is it interesting?	Yes, it is. It's a rather interesting painting.
Are we good?	Yes, you are. You're very good students.
Are they funny?	Yes, they are. They're a very funny group.

Unit 6

1 Modal: *can*

Can I speak to Bill?	Yes, you can.	No, you can't.
Can you call Mary?	Yes, I can.	No, I can't.
Can Tony see the movie?	Yes, he can.	No, he can't.
Can she use your office?	Yes, she can.	No, she can't.
Can we visit you?	Yes, you can.	No, you can't.
Can they miss school today?	Yes, they can.	No, they can't.

2 *How much? How many?*

How many rooms do you need?	I need only one room.
How much is the rent?	Eight hundred dollars a month.
How many rooms does it have?	It has six main rooms.
How much do they pay?	Over a thousand dollars a month.
How many friends does he have?	He has dozens of friends.
How many bedrooms do we need?	We need three.

Grammar Summaries

Unit 7

1 Prepositions: *on, next to, near*

Where is the art gallery?	It's on Miller Street.
Where are the deli and the bank?	They're on Fourth Avenue.
Where is the gym?	It's next to the park.
Where is the hotel?	It's near the subway.

2 Present progressive for actions in progress

Am I studying enough?	Yes, you are studying enough.
Are you working?	No, I'm not working. I'm taking a break.
Is Tony enjoying the party?	No, he isn't enjoying the party much.
Is she watching TV?	Yes, she is. She's watching the news.
Are we working tonight?	Yes, we are. We're working till 9 o'clock.
Are they staying home?	No, they aren't. They're going out.

Unit 8

1 Making suggestions with *Why don't you . . . ?*

Why don't I call a cab?	Why doesn't she visit the museum?
Why don't you go to a movie?	Why don't they go home?
Why doesn't he get a guidebook?	Why don't we go to a restaurant?

2 *There is/there are* and *one, any, some*

Is there a shoe store near here?	Yes, there is. There's one near the subway.
Is there a park around here?	No, there isn't. But there's one a few blocks down there.
Are there any restaurants nearby?	Yes, there are. There are some right by the hotel.
Are there any museums near here?	No, there aren't. But there are some on Fifth Avenue.

Unit 9

1 Adverbs of frequency

Does it always rain in Rio?	Yes, it does. No, it doesn't.
Do you ever go abroad?	Yes, I do. No, I don't.
Does he often come here?	Yes, he does. No, he doesn't.
Does she sometimes take a vacation?	Yes, she does. No, she doesn't.

2 Modal: *should*

When should I go to Thailand?	You shouldn't go in summer or the wet season.
	You should go in December.
What should my cousin do in Japan?	She shouldn't miss the Imperial Palace.
	She should visit Kyoto.
What should we take to Europe?	You shouldn't take much luggage.
	You should take lots of money.

Unit 11

1 Simple past: statements and yes/no questions

Did you play golf Saturday?	Yes, I did.
Where did she go last night?	She went to the movies.
Did he go home?	No, he didn't.
How was your weekend?	It was great. I went to the beach and relaxed.
When did they get home?	They got home at midnight.
Where did you leave the car?	We left it in the parking lot.

2 Simple past: connecting words and *wh* questions

I had a great time on Saturday. First, I went shopping and bought myself some new clothes. Next, I had lunch with my best friend. After that, I went to a show. Then I danced until midnight. Finally, I went out for a late-night supper.

Unit 12

1 Present progressive for planned future

What are you doing next New Year's Eve?	I'm going to bed at nine o'clock.
Where are you going on your next vacation?	I'm going to Mexico.
When are you next driving to Maine?	I'm driving to Maine this weekend.
Who are you seeing tomorrow?	I'm seeing José and Carl.
What are you buying next time you go shopping?	I'm buying things for the party.

2 Intensifiers: *too, fairly, pretty, very*

Is that an interesting book?	Yes, it's very interesting.
Is that a good play?	No, it isn't. It's a fairly boring play.
Is the new Tom Cruise movie worth seeing?	Yes, it is. It's pretty entertaining.
Are those TV movies worth seeing?	No, they're not. They're too dull.

Unit 13

1 Present perfect and *Have you ever . . . ?*

Have I ever made you angry?	Yes, you have.	No, you haven't.
Have you ever played golf?	Yes, I have.	No, I haven't.
Has she ever watched a Grand Prix race on TV?	Yes, she has.	No, she hasn't.
Has it ever rained during the match?	Yes, it has.	No, it hasn't.
Have we ever forgotten the tickets?	Yes, you have.	No, you haven't.
Have you ever seen a ball game?	Yes, we have.	No, we haven't.
Have they ever been late?	Yes, they have.	No, they haven't.

2 Time expressions and *How often . . . ?*

How often do you play tennis?	I play tennis about once a week.
How often does she swim?	She swims every day.
How often does he exercise?	He exercises about three times a month.
How often do they play golf?	They play golf about five times a year.

Unit 14

1 Comparisons with adjectives

Are you hungry yet?	Yes, I am. But I'll be hungrier later.
Is Osaka interesting?	Yes, it is. But Kyoto is more interesting.
Is Carla busy at the moment?	Yes, she is. But she'll be even busier after lunch.
Is he rich?	Yes, he is. But his brother is richer.
Are we late?	Yes, we are. But we'll be even later if we don't hurry.

2 Modals: *have to, should, could*

Why are you staying home?	I have to study for the exam on Monday.
When will she be here?	She should be here by eight o'clock.
How will he recognize us?	We have to wear a carnation in our buttonholes.
How do you get there?	We have to take a taxi or the subway.
When will they study?	They'll have to study tonight—the exam is tomorrow.
Where shall we go tonight?	We could try the new movie at the Odeon.
How do I get to the post office?	You could go down First Ave. and turn right. Or you could go left at the subway and turn left again onto Market Street.

Grammar Summaries

Credits

Photographs

Cover Sextant, Courtesy Peabody Essex Museum, Salem, MA. Photo by Mark Sexton; FLORIDA ROADMAP © 1993. Used by permission of the publisher, H. M. Gousha/A Division of Simon & Schuster; © Replogle Globes, Inc. (r); **9** Tracey Wheeler (tr); © Ancil Nance/AllStock (t); © Jun Kishimoto/Photonica (tl); **10** Tracey Wheeler (all); **11** Tracey Wheeler (t); **12** Tracey Wheeler (all); **14** Tracey Wheeler; **15** Tracey Wheeler; **17** © Terry Wild (t); Tracey Wheeler (tl); **22** Tracey Wheeler; **23** Tracey Wheeler; **25** Tracey Wheeler (all); **26** © Kindra Clineff/AllStock (tl); © Robert Holmes/AllStock (bl); © Mark E. Gibson (tr); © Charles Gupton/Tony Stone Images, Inc. (bcr); © Lawrence Migdale/Tony Stone Images, Inc. (br); **27** Tracey Wheeler; **29** © Terry Wild; **31** Tracey Wheeler (all); **33** © Superstock (r); © SCALA/Art Resource (c); © Superstock (l); © Ken Fisher/Tony Stone Images, Inc. (t); Tracey Wheeler (tl); **35** Tracey Wheeler; **36** © Telegraph Colour Library/FPG, Int.; **38** © Bennett-Spooner/Gamma-Liaison; **39** Tracey Wheeler (all); **43** © Chad Ehlers/Tony Stone Images, Inc. (r); © Jane Lewis/Tony Stone Images, Inc. (l); © E. Alan McGee/FPG, Int. (br); © Tony Freeman/PhotoEdit (bl); © S. S. Yamamoto/Photonica (t); Tracey Wheeler (tl); **44** Tracey Wheeler; **45** Tracey Wheeler; **46** Tracey Wheeler (all); **49** Tracey Wheeler (all); **51** © S. S. Yamamoto/Photonica (t); © Richard B. Levine (tl); **54** Tracey Wheeler; **59** Tracey Wheeler (r); © Kazuya Shimizu/Photonica (t); © Yagi/Superstock (tl); **62** © Joseph Pobereskin/Tony Stone Images, Inc.; **64** Tracey Wheeler; **65** Tracey Wheeler; **67** © John Lamb/Tony Stone Images, Inc. (br); © Tony Stone Images, Inc. (bc); © Hugh Sitton/Tony Stone Images, Inc. (r); © Joe Cornish/Tony Stone Images, Inc. (c); © Ed Pritchard/Tony Stone Images, Inc. (bl); © Haroldo Castro/FPG, Int. (l); © Mike McQueen/Tony Stone Images, Inc. (t); **69** Tracey Wheeler; **72** Tracey Wheeler; **73** © Telegraph Colour Library/FPG, Int.; **75** Tracey Wheeler (all); **76** Tracey Wheeler; **77** © Tony Freeman/PhotoEdit (tr); © Tony Freeman/PhotoEdit (l); © Kevin Morris/AllStock (c); © Anthony Neste Photos (r); © Elena Rooraid/PhotoEdit (bl); © David R. Austin/Stock Boston (bc); © David Young-Wolff/ PhotoEdit (br); © Chris Noble/AllStock (t); **79** Tracey Wheeler; **80** © Raymond Gendreau/AllStock (l); © Billy Barnes/PhotoEdit (r); **82** Tracey Wheeler; **83** © Mark Junak/Tony Stone Images, Inc.; **85** © Marc Pokempner/Tony Stone Images, Inc. (tc); © Cathlyn Melloan/Tony Stone Images, Inc. (tr); **85** © Robert E. Daemmrich/Tony Stone Images, Inc. (bl); © Robert Frerck/Tony Stone Images, Inc. (bcl); © David Young-Wolff/Tony Stone Images, Inc. (bcr); © Lawrence Migdale/Tony Stone Images, Inc. (br); © Telegraph Colour Library/FPG, Int. (t); Tracey Wheeler (tl); **86** Tracey Wheeler (bl); Courtesy of Heinle & Heinle (br); Tracey Wheeler (bc); **87** Courtesy of John Steczynski (br); Tracey Wheeler (bl); Tracey Wheeler (bc); **88** Tracey Wheeler; **90** © Al Green/Archive Photos; **91** Tracey Wheeler; **93** Tracey Wheeler (r); Tracey Wheeler (br); © M. Yamazaki/Photonica (t); Tracey Wheeler (tl); **95** © Mary Kate Denny/PhotoEdit; **96** © Eugen Gebhardt/FPG, Int.; **98** © Vic Bider/PhotoEdit; **99** Tracey Wheeler; **101** © William Thompson/Photonica (t); Tracey Wheeler (tl); **106** Tracey Wheeler; **107** Tracey Wheeler; **109** © Scott Dietrich/Tony Stone Images, Inc. (tc); © John Warden/Tony Stone Images, Inc. (c); UPI/Bettmann (bc); © Daniel Simon/Gamma-Liaison (b); UPI/Bettmann (t); **112** © Andy Sacks/Tony Stone Images, Inc. (c); © Frank Siteman/Tony Stone Images, Inc. (tl); © RSI/AllStock (tc); © David Young-Wolff/PhotoEdit (bl); © L. Powers/AllStock (tr); © David Young-Wolff/PhotoEdit (br); **113** Tracey Wheeler (t); **115** Tracey Wheeler (t); **120** © AllStock (tl); © Eugen Gebhardt/FPG, Int. (bl); © Bob Daemmrich/Stock Boston (r); **125** © Schwartz/Gamma-Liaison (bl); © Schwartz/Gamma-Liaison (bc); © Victoria Brynner/Gamma-Liaison (br); © Richard B. Levine (tl).

Illustrations

Mark Kaufman, pages **17, 20, 21, 41, 81**; Bill Thomson, pages **11, 18, 37, 48, 51, 57, 101, 104, 113, 115**

Irregular Verb Chart

SIMPLE FORM	PAST FORM	PAST PARTICIPLE	SIMPLE FORM	PAST FORM	PAST PARTICIPLE
arise	arose	arisen	let	let	let
be	was	been	light	lit	lit
begin	began	begun	lose	lost	lost
bite	bit	bitten	make	made	made
blow	blew	blown	mean	meant	meant
break	broke	broken	meet	met	met
bring	brought	brought	pay	paid	paid
build	built	built	put	put	put
buy	bought	bought	read	read	read
catch	caught	caught	ride	rode	ridden
choose	chose	chosen	ring	rang	rung
cost	cost	cost	run	ran	run
cut	cut	cut	say	said	said
do	did	done	see	saw	seen
draw	drew	drawn	sell	sold	sold
drink	drank	drunk	send	sent	sent
drive	drove	driven	shoot	shot	shot
eat	ate	eaten	show	showed	shown
fall	fell	fallen	shut	shut	shut
feed	fed	fed	sing	sang	sung
feel	felt	felt	sink	sank	sunk
fight	fought	fought	sit	sat	sat
find	found	found	sleep	slept	slept
fly	flew	flown	speak	spoke	spoken
forget	forgot	forgotten	stand	stood	stood
get	got	gotten	swim	swam	swum
give	gave	given	take	took	taken
go	went	gone	teach	taught	taught
grow	grew	grown	tell	told	told
have	had	had	think	thought	thought
hear	heard	heard	throw	threw	thrown
hold	held	held	understand	understood	understood
keep	kept	kept	wake	woke	woken
know	knew	known	wear	wore	worn
learn	learned	learned	win	won	won
leave	left	left	write	wrote	written

Student Tapescript

Unit 1 New People

Task 3, page 9

A: Hello, my name's Mike.
B: Pleased to meet you, Mike. I'm Yoko. This is Noriko.
C: Nice to meet you, Mike.
A: Nice to meet you, Noriko.

Task 1, Conversation 1, page 10

Officer: Can I help you, sir? Is something wrong?
Mike: Yes. I lost my bag.
Officer: Where?
Mike: I don't know!
Officer: What was in it?
Mike: My passport, money, plane ticket, credit cards, driver's license—everything.

Conversation 2, page 10

Officer: All right, now I'd just like to ask you some questions.
Mike: Certainly, officer.
Officer: Last name?
Mike: Frota.
Officer: How do you spell that?
Mike: F-R-O-T-A.

Conversation 3, page 10

Officer: Are you Mike Frota?
Mike: That's right.
Officer: Good news, Mr. Frota. We've got your bag back for you.
Mike: Where did you find it?
Officer: You left it in the men's room.

Tasks 2 and 3, page 10

Officer: All right, now I'd just like to get some information.
Mike: Certainly, officer.
Officer: What's the date today? March 5th, isn't it?
Mike: That's right.
Officer: OK, then, last name?
Mike: Frota.
Officer: How do you spell that?
Mike: F-R-O-T-A.
Officer: First name?
Mike: Mike.
Officer: What's your address, Mr. Frota?
Mike: I'm staying at the Harbor Hotel, 24 Smith Street, North Beach.
Officer: Telephone?
Mike: Let's see—555-3847
Officer: Thanks. And what's your date of birth?
Mike: November 11, 1975.
Officer: OK. And what's your occupation?
Mike: I'm a student.
Officer: A student. Right. Now, you lost a bag.
Mike: Yes, a black travel bag.

Task 1, page 12

A: So I'll meet you at Gate 11 at 9:30. Now, what do you look like?
B: Well, I'm twenty-one. I'm of average height and weight. I have dark curly hair and brown eyes.
A: OK.
B: And I'm with my girlfriend. She's nineteen. She's tall, and she has blond hair and blue eyes. You can't miss us!

Tasks 1 and 2, page 13

Mike: Hello. Are you John? Sorry I'm late.
John: That's OK. I'm John.
Mike: Nice to meet you, John.
John: And this is Anna.
Mike: Hello, Anna—good to meet you.
Anna: Hi!
John: And this is Maggie.
Mike: Pleased to meet you, Maggie.
Maggie: Hi, Mike—come and have a drink and tell us what happened to you.
Mike: Well, I lost my bag at the airport....

Task 1, page 15

A: Hi! I'm Yongsue. What's your name?
B: Vera.
A: Where are you from?
B: Chicago. What about you?
A: I'm from Seoul, Korea. What do you do?
B: I'm a student. What do you do?
A: I'm a student, too.

Communication Challenge page 111

Anna: Do you know everyone?
Mike: No, I don't. Who is the small woman over there?
Anna: The one with the dark hair?
Mike: Yes.
Anna: That's Yongsue. She's a student from Korea.
Mike: And what about the guy with the brown hair and beard?
Anna: Oh, that's Paul. He's Marika's husband. He's a businessman from Canada. Come and I'll introduce you.

John: Do you know everyone here?
Maggie: No, I don't. Who is the tall, blond woman over there?
John: That's Paul's wife Marika. She's a doctor.
Maggie: Is she from here?
John: No, she isn't. She's from Germany, but she and her husband are moving to the States soon.
Maggie: And what about the guy with the dark hair, over by the door?
John: Oh, that's Professor Tanaka. He's a professor of Japanese Studies, and he's visiting the college from Tokyo. Come and meet him and his wife.

Unit 2 Meet the Family

Tasks 2 and 3, page 18

Friend: Is that your family, Vera?
Vera: Yes, it is. It's my grandfather's eightieth birthday. That's me, my Grandfather, and that's my brother, Jose, on the other side.
Friend: Who's that next to you?
Vera: That's my mom.
Friend: And who are those cute kids in front?
Vera: Oh, they're the twins—my nephew, Juan and my niece, Cristina.
Friend: And that's your sister, right?
Vera: Yeah, that's Sandra.

Task 2, page 20

A: Do you have any brothers or sisters, Helen?
B: Yes I do. I have two brothers and three sisters. I also have six aunts and eight uncles and 25 cousins.
A: Do you have any nieces and nephews?
B: Yes, I do—my sisters' kids. They live with us.

Tasks 1 and 2, page 21

Host: Welcome to *Game, Set and Match!* Tell me a little about yourselves.
Eva: Hi! I'm Eva. I'm twenty-one years old. I'm

American, but my family comes from Costa Rica. I speak Spanish and English. I have three sisters and four brothers.
Host: And what about you?
Sylvia: I'm Sylvia. I'm nineteen. I live in Los Angeles. I study languages at UCLA, and I speak Mandarin, Japanese, and English. I'm an only child.
Host: Great! And finally, we have . . .
Pete: Pete. I'm twenty-six, and I'm a salesperson. I have a brother and a sister.

Task 3, page 22

Host: Hello. Welcome to our show, *Know Your In-Laws*. Our contestants are all married couples. Husbands and wives compete against each other to see who knows the most about the other's family. Our first couple is Mary and James Garcia.
Mary: Hello.
James: Hi.
Host: So. How well do you know your in-laws? We'll soon find out. Are you ready?
Mary: Guess so.
James: Sure.
Host: OK. First question. Does your sister-in-law have any children? Mary?
Mary: Yes, she does. Three girls.
Host: What about you, James? Does your sister-in-law have any children?
James: No, she doesn't.
Host: OK, no problems there. Next question. Mary. Where does your father-in-law work?
Mary: At a hospital, he's a doctor.
Host: James? What about your father-in-law? Where does he work?
James: He doesn't work.
Host: Doesn't work?
James: He's retired.
Host: Good. Mary, where does your brother-in-law go to school?

Mary: He goes to San Francisco State University.
Host: And James. Where does your brother-in-law go to school?
James: He doesn't go to school. He works in a bank.
Host: OK. Mary, where does your mother-in-law work?
Mary: In a publishing house.
Host: And James? Where does your mother-in-law work?
James: Sorry, I can't remember—I think she changed jobs recently.
Host: You don't know?
James: Sorry.
Host: So, we have a winner.

Task 1, page 23

A: Who's that?
B: That's my brother.
A: Great-looking guy. What's his name?
B: Joe.
A: And what does he do?
B: He goes to school.
A: Oh, where does he go?
B: He goes to McGill University in Montreal.

Unit 3 Old Friends

Task 2, page 25

Maria: Here is a picture of some of my school friends in class. That's Tom, and that's Eric. This is Tomoko—she's an exchange student from Japan. Then there's Nina and Nina's new boyfriend—I can't remember his name, and Sally. Now here's my favorite picture. These are my very best friends, we are all going to a party together. That's Pamela on the left—she's a student, like me. Then there's Maggie and her boyfriend,

Steve, and then my boyfriend, Tony and me—you know Tony, don't you?

Task 2, page 26

Victor: Tony, I'm doing a survey. Can I ask you some questions?
Tony: Sure, Victor.
Victor: First of all, I want to ask about your friends.
Tony: Sure.
Victor: Do you have many good friends?
Tony: Good friends—yes, a few. I guess I have four really good friends.
Victor: What do they do?
Tony: Well, first of all, there's Maria—she's my girlfriend, as you know.
Victor: Does she work?
Tony: Well, kind of—she's a student.
Victor: Mmm.
Tony: Then there's Pamela, one of my housemates—she's a student too.
Victor: Right.
Tony: My other good friends are Maggie and her boyfriend, Steve. Maggie's a secretary, but she really wants to be a singer. Steve works with me at the hospital.
Victor: Oh, he's a nurse too?
Tony: That's right.

Task 1, page 28

A: Do you have a best friend?
B: Yes, Tomoko.
A: What does she do?
B: She's a student.
A: What do you do together?
B: Oh, we study together. Sometimes we go to the movies.

Task 1, page 29

A: Hi Jenny. How is school?
B: Fine.
A: Must be lonely in a new city.
B: It is a little. But I have some new friends.
A: That's nice.
B: And I see my classmates every day.

Tasks 2 and 3, page 29

Victor: Now, Tony, I'd like to ask you about other people you know.
Tony: OK, Victor.
Victor: First of all, who do you talk to every day?
Tony: Every day? Well, let's see. There's Maria.
Victor: Mmm, your girlfriend, Maria. OK.
Tony: And the people I work with, of course.
Victor: Who are they?
Tony: Steve, Sophie, Karen, and Agnes.
Victor: Mmm.
Tony: Who else? Let me see—my parents, and Uncle Carlos.
Victor: Is that all?
Tony: Well, there's my boss, Ms. Mills.
Victor: Your boss—right.
Tony: And Sam the bus driver.
Victor: The bus driver, uh-huh.
Tony: Mmm, and I guess I talk to my landlady, Mrs. Williams.

Task 1, page 31

A: Excuse me. I'm doing a survey for *People* magazine. Can I ask you some questions?
B: Sure.
A: First of all, what do you do?
B: I work in a bank. I'm a teller.
A: Uh-huh. And who do you spend most of your time with?
B: My friends and family.
A: Who is your best friend?
B: My husband, I guess.
A: OK. And who do you talk to every day.
B: Well, now let's see. My husband, my children, the people I work with, and the bank customers.

Student Tapescript

Unit 4 Interesting People

Tasks 2, 3, and 4, page 34

A: What do you think of that one?
B: I don't like it much. Do you?
A: Yes, I do. I like it a lot. I think the woman looks really interesting.
B: But she don't even look like a woman.
A: Yes, she does—you can see her face. And that's a musical instrument. Anyway, I like it because of the colors and the shapes. What about you? Which one do you like?
B: I like that one because they look like real people.
A: Yes, I like that one too—the women are beautiful.

Task 1, page 36

A: Do you like modern art?
B: No, I don't like it very much. Do you like it?
A: Yes, I do. What about music?
B: I like rock music and jazz.
A: So do I. I like classical music, too.
B: What kind of movies do you like?
A: I like thrillers.

Tasks 3 and 4, page 37

Host: I'm talking to an interesting person. His name is Gary Smith. Gary, welcome to the program.
Gary: Thanks.
Host: I understand that you have an unusual occupation, Gary. What do you do?
Gary: I'm an impersonator. I pretend to be someone else.
Host: Why?
Gary: People pay me a lot of money to do it.
Host: Really? Who do you pretend to be?
Gary: Elvis Presley.
Host: Do you play him as a young man or a middle-aged man?
Gary: As a young man.
Host: Oh. The young Elvis.
Gary: That's right.
Host: And how much do you earn?
Gary: Oh, about $400,000 a year.
Host: Wow, that's a lot of money!
Gary: Yes, it's a lot more than I used to earn.
Host: Oh, really? What was your job before?
Gary: I was a university professor.

Task 1, page 39

A: Sandy, would you like to go on a date with my brother?
B: What's he like? Is he interesting?
A: Oh, yeah. He's an artist.
B: Is he good-looking?
A: Yes—very.
B: And is he nice?
A: Of course.
B: He sounds too good to be true!

Unit 5 Review Unit

Task 3, page 41

Chuck: Good morning. My name's Chuck Wilson and I'm your teacher. I'm from Toronto, Canada although I've been living here for six years. Now, I'd like you to tell me your name, where you're from, and what you do.

Chuck: You're a new student, aren't you?
Tomoko: Yes.
Chuck: What's your name?
Tomoko: Tomoko Furikawa.
Chuck: And you're from Japan, right?
Tomoko: That's right.

George: Hi. New student?
Anita: That's right.

Student Tapescript

George: So am I. My name's George. What's yours?
Anita: Anita.
George: Where are you from?
Anita: France.
George: Oh, really?
Anita: What about you?
George: I'm from Argentina.

Interviewer: OK. I'll just take your details. Name?
Cynthia: Cynthia Lee.
Interviewer: Where are you from?
Cynthia: Taiwan.
Interviewer: And what do you do?
Cynthia: I'm a doctor.

Task 4, page 41

Interviewer: What's your last name, Carmen?
Carmen: Costas. That's C-O-S-T-A-S.
Interviewer: Where are you from?
Carmen: Argentina.
Interviewer: And what do you do?
Carmen: I'm a flight attendant with Aerolineas Argentinas.
Interviewer: Any qualifications?
Carmen: I have a high school diploma.
Interviewer: OK. What's your local address?
Carmen: 39 Silver Street, Apartment 4.
Interviewer: And why do you want to study English?
Carmen: Well, I want to understand English native speakers. And I want to be able to talk to the passengers I have to deal with. I'd also like to practice filling in forms, understanding TV, and buying things in shops.
Interviewer: Fine.

Unit 6 A Place to Stay

Task 2, Message 1, page 44

Lisa Martinez: Pacific Holdings. Lisa Martinez speaking. Can I help you?
Mary Sellers: Can I speak to Bill Jennings, please?
Lisa Martinez: I'm sorry, but Mr. Jennings is out right now. Can I take a message?
Mary Sellers: Yes, please. Can you tell him Mary called, and did he get my fax?
Lisa Martinez: Did . . . he . . . get . . . fax.
Mary Sellers: And, er, tell him I'll see him in LA.
Lisa Martinez: OK. I'll see he gets the message.

Message 2, page 44

Receptionist: Pacific Holdings. Hold the line, please. Sorry about that. Can I help you?
Mary Sellers: This is Mary Sellers from Eastern Holdings in Boston. Can I speak to Bill Jennings, please?
Receptionist: I'm sorry, but Mr. Jennings isn't in right now. Can I take a message?
Mary Sellers: Yes. Can you tell him that Mary Sellers from Eastern Holdings called.
Receptionist: . . . Mary . . . Sellers . . . Eastern . . . Holdings. And the message is?
Mary Sellers: Can he call me back? It's rather urgent.
Receptionist: Sure. And what's your number, please?
Mary Sellers: 617-555-1819.
Receptionist: 617-555-1819. OK, I'll ask him to call you right away.

Message 3, page 44

Phil Cross: Pacific Holdings. Phil Cross speaking. Can I help you?
June Matthews: Oh, hi. This is June Matthews, from Eastern Holdings in Boston. Is Mr. Jennings there?
Phil Cross: Sorry, he's out at the moment.
June Matthews: Oh, well,—can you ask him to call Mary in Los Angeles?
Phil Cross: Sure. No problem. Does he have the number?

June Matthews: I think so. She's at the Beverly Hills office.

Message 4, page 44

Receptionist: Pacific Holdings.
June Matthews: This is June from Eastern Holdings in Boston again.
Receptionist: Oh, you're after Bill Jennings, aren't you?
June Matthews: That's right.
Receptionist: He's not in, I'm afraid. I think he may have left for the airport already.
June Matthews: Well, I have a really urgent message for him from Mary Sellers.
Receptionist: Let me have it, and if he calls in from the airport I'll give it to him.
June Matthews: Tell him the Beverly Inn is full, and can he please meet Mary at the Beverly Hills Ritz?
Receptionist: OK, I'll tell him.

Task 3, page 45

Bill Jennings: Hello, Lisa?
Lisa Martinez: Speaking.
Bill Jennings: This is Bill Jennings. I'm calling from the airport. I'm just about to leave for Los Angeles. Are there any messages for me?
Lisa Martinez: Yes, there are. One of them is urgent. It's from June in Boston.
Bill Jennings: Yes.
Lisa Martinez: There's a change in your hotel reservation in Los Angeles.
Bill Jennings: Really?
Lisa Martinez: Yes, the Beverly Inn is full, so she's booked a room for you at the Beverly Hills Ritz. Can you meet Mary there?
Bill Jennings: The Beverly Hills Ritz.
Lisa Martinez: That's right.
Bill Jennings: Any address or telephone number?
Lisa Martinez: No, not on the message. All I have is the name of the hotel.
Bill Jennings: OK. I guess I can find it.

Task 4, page 45

Cab Driver: Where can I take you?
Bill Jennings: Beverly Hills, please.
Cab Driver: Sure.
Cab Driver: Where do you want to go in Beverly Hills?
Bill Jennings: The Ritz.
Cab Driver: The what?
Bill Jennings: The Beverly Hills Ritz.
Cab Driver: Sorry, man, there's no such hotel.
Bill Jennings: What?
Cab Driver: There's no hotel called the Beverly Hills Ritz.
Bill Jennings: But there must be. I have an important meeting there.

Task 1, page 46

A: Can I speak to Terry, please?
B: Sure. Who's calling?
A: Sally.
B: OK. Wait a minute—I'll get her.
A: Thanks.
C: Terry here.
A: Hi! This is Sally.
C: Hi, Sally!
A: Can I come over and visit?
C: Sure.

Task 2, page 47

Respondent 1: Well, I have a family, so I'd like to live in the suburbs in a large house with my family. I guess I'd have to pay at least $1000 a month. I'd like to be near a park where the kids could play.
Respondent 2: I'd like a room in the center of the city, because I like to go out at night and have fun. I'd like to live alone. I can

only afford to spend $400 a month. I'd like it if there were a fitness club nearby, so I could exercise.

Respondent 3: I'm a visitor from Brazil. I'd like to have a room with a family in a small town, so I can find out about how people in this country live. I could pay $500 a month, and I'd like it if there were a library nearby because I'm a student.

Task 3 b, page 48

A: Hello, I'm calling about the room you have for rent.
B: Yes.
A: Can you tell me about it, please.
B: Sure. It's a regular type of bedroom. It has a bed and a chest of drawers.
A: Uh-huh. What about a desk? I'm a student, so I need a desk.
B: No, it doesn't have a desk, I'm afraid, but it does have a table and chair. You could use the table as a desk, I guess.
A: Yes, that sounds fine. And how much is the rent?
B: Well, it's $250 a week.
A: How much?
B: $250 a week. What's the problem?
A: That's far too expensive for me, I'm afraid.
B: Well, I could let you have it for $230 a week.
A: No, that's still too expensive.

Task 1, Page 49

A: I'm calling about the apartment you have for rent.
B: Yes?
A: How many rooms does it have?
B: Five.
A: OK. How many bedrooms does it have?
B: Two.
A: Oh, I want a three-bedroom apartment. How much is the rent?
B: $800 a month.
A: Oh, I'm sorry, that's too much.

Communication Challenge, page 116

Rental Agent: Name?
Teresa: Teresa Marciano.
Rental Agent: Address?
Teresa: 34 Spring Street, Apartment 288.
Rental Agent: What do you do?
Teresa: I'm a student.
Rental Agent: Married?
Teresa: No, single.
Rental Agent: And what kind of accommodation are you looking for, Ms. Marciano?
Teresa: A room.
Rental Agent: Are you willing to share a room?
Teresa: No, I want my own room.
Rental Agent: And how much are you prepared to pay?
Teresa: Not more than $500 a month.

Unit 7 In My Neighborhood

Task 3 a, page 52

Friend: Are you still looking for somewhere to live, Silvia?
Silvia: Yes, I am.
Friend: And, you're not having any luck, right?
Silvia: Right. I can't even find the right neighborhood.
Friend: So what kind of neighborhood are you looking for?
Silvia: Well, I want somewhere with good facilities. It's got to be close to the center of the city, or it has to have transportation—a subway or bus stop or something. And I'd like somewhere that has a bank, a post office, shops, and a church.

Friend: You don't want much, do you?
Silvia: Oh, and I'd like a park, or somewhere nice where I can go jogging.
Friend: Is there anything you don't want?
Silvia: Well, I hate noise, so if there's a freeway nearby it's no good. Bars and nightclubs are noisy, too, so I don't want any of those in the neighborhood.
Friend: Why don't you call my cousin Charlie. He knows the city well, so he might be able to help you.

Task 3 c, Page 52

Silvia: Hello. Is that Charlie?
Charlie: Yes, it is.
Silvia: My name's Silvia. I'm a friend of Teresa. She suggested that I call you for information about where to live.
Charlie: Sure. I've lived all over this town, so I should be able to help. The three most interesting neighborhoods are Barker Street, Beaker Hill, and Kellyville.
Silvia: Can you tell me about them?
Charlie: Well, Barker Street and Beaker Hill are near the center of the city. Kellyville is farther out. Barker Street is good because you can walk to the city. Do you work in the city center?
Silvia: Yes, I do.
Charlie: Well, Barker Street would be good. There are lots of shops, banks, etc.
Silvia: Is it noisy?
Charlie: Hmm—no, not too bad.
Silvia: What about parks?
Charlie: No, there's no park anywhere near, I'm afraid.
Silvia: OK. And what about Beaker Hill?
Charlie: Well, it's on the other side of the city center, but it's almost as close. It's in the old part of town, but there are plenty of shops and things. There's also a park close by.
Silvia: Sounds good. The only problem is that inner-city neighborhoods can be noisy.
Charlie: Yes, there are lots of bars on Beaker Hill—that could be a problem. Now Kellyville is quiet. It's pretty far out of town, though, and the public transportation's not very good. But there are parks, shopping malls, and other stuff. So maybe you should think about moving out of town a ways.
Silvia: Yes, I'll think about it. Thanks for your help.
Charlie: You're welcome. Give my regards to Teresa when you see her.

Task 1, page 54

A: Excuse me.
B: Yes?
A: Where's the nearest subway entrance?
B: It's on High Street.
A: And is there a post office anywhere near here?
B: Yes, there's a post office next to the museum.

A: Where's the bank, please?
B: It's on Third Avenue.
A: Thank you.
B: You're welcome.

Task 2, page 55

Mike: What's the best thing about your neighborhood, Jerry?
Jerry: Hmm, the best thing about my neighborhood. . . . Well, there's not much crime—in fact, it's a really safe place to be. How about yours?
Mike: Well, the good thing about my neighborhood is that we have lots of stores and restaurants. It's exciting and fun. The problem is that we have a lot of crime as well. Why is your neighborhood so safe, do you think?

Student Tapescript

Mike: Probably because the neighbors are all friends and watch out for each other.
Jerry: So it's a pretty good place to live.
Mike: Well, it's not perfect.
Jerry: Why? What's wrong?
Mike: Oh, it's kind of boring. There's nothing to do. What about your neighborhood, Helen?
Helen: I guess no neighborhood is perfect. I live near the center of the city, so the architecture's interesting, and there's good shopping. Unfortunately, it's also really crowded, and there's nowhere to park.

Task 1, page 57

Mike: Hi, Helen. What are you doing?
Helen: We're having a neighborhood cleanup.
Mike: Really? Sounds interesting. What does it involve?
Helen: Well, we're picking up all the trash, and the kids are painting a mural on that wall, and we're planting some trees along the sidewalk.
Mike: That's great. Can I help?
Helen: Sure. You can help Tina. She's emptying that trash can over there.

Unit 8 New York, New York

Tasks 5 and 6, page 60

Ron: What'll we do today?
Pauline: Well, there's an interesting exhibition at the Metropolitan Museum. Let's go there.
Ron: No, I'm tired of looking at art.
Pauline: What about some shopping? There are some sales this week.
Ron: No, the stores are crowded and noisy.
Pauline: Well, let's walk through Central Park—it's an interesting park.
Ron: It's also very busy at lunchtime.
Pauline: I know—let's go to a nice restaurant.
Ron: Nah, the restaurants are expensive.
Pauline: Well, there's only one thing left for us to do.
Ron: What's that?
Pauline: Stay here.

Task 1, page 62

A: What are you planning to do today?
B: What do you suggest?
A: Why don't you go on the boat trip around Manhattan?
B: No, it's too cold today.
A: Well, why don't you go to a museum or gallery?
B: That's a good idea.

Task 3, page 63

Friend: How was your trip to New York?
Ron: Terrible.
Friend: What happened?
Ron: Well, first of all, there was a mix-up over our hotel, and we didn't have reservations. So we had to spend the first day trying to find accommodations.
Friend: That's no good. What else happened?
Ron: Well, we wanted to visit some museums and galleries, so the next day we went to the Museum of Modern Art.
Friend: How was that?
Ron: We don't know.
Friend: You don't know?
Ron: No, we went on a Wednesday, and it was closed.
Friend: Oh, dear!
Ron: Then, on Thursday, we decided to go shopping. We went to Macy's and got lots of nice things—they had a sale on.
Friend: That sounds OK.

Student Tapescript

Ron: Except that when I went to pay I found I'd lost my wallet.
Friend: Oh, no!
Ron: So, by Friday, we were looking forward to getting home. Unfortunately, there was a problem with our flight, and we were stuck at the airport for eight hours.
Friend: So much for New York!
Ron: Yeah, so much for New York!

Task 1, page 65

A: Is there a bookstore around here?
B: No, there isn't. But there's one near the subway. Why?
A: I want to get a guidebook.
B: Oh, there are some guidebooks on the shelf—help yourself.
A: Thanks a lot.

Communication Challenge, page 117

Nina: Good morning, ladies and gentlemen, welcome to the half-day tour of fabulous New York. My name's Nina, and I am your tour guide today. There are lots of great things to see and do in New York, and we're going to see some of them today. This tour is called "Something for Everyone." The tour leaves from Lincoln Center. We travel up Central Park West to West 71st Street, past the famous Dakota apartment building where John Lennon was murdered, to the American Museum of Natural History. From there, we'll travel through Central Park and to the Metropolitan Museum of Art. Finally, we'll take a ride down to the Sheraton Hotel for lunch.

Unit 9 Going Places

Task 3, page 67

Tony: Boy, it's cold today. I heard on the radio that it's only 28°.
Fabio: Hmm, that must be about minus two.
Tony: Oh, do you think in terms of Celsius?
Fabio: Yeah. We use Celsius to measure temperature in my country.
Tony: So what do you do here in the United States?
Fabio: I convert the temperatures.
Tony: How do you do that?
Fabio: Well, I subtract 32, multiply by 5, and divide by 9.
Tony: Wow, you must have a good memory to remember that so easily!

Task 5, page 69

Forecaster # 1: That's the news at this hour. Now for the weather. It will continue partly sunny, with showers at night, and a high tomorrow of 82. Outside now, it's 81.
Forecaster # 2: Now for the weather. It will continue sunny with a high of 81. A mild night tonight, followed by a partly sunny day tomorrow with a high of 84.
Forecaster # 3: After a sunny start to the day, it will be partly cloudy this afternoon with a high of 74. Not so good tomorrow, with a chance of rain in the afternoon and a high of 68.

Task 1, page 70

A: What's the weather like where you come from?
B: Well, it's always hot in summer—usually over 40° Celsius.
A: Wow, that's hot. What about winter?

Student Tapescript

B: It's usually warm in winter. And it hardly ever rains in summer or winter.

Task 3 b, page 71

Doctor: Let's see now, when you travel in foreign countries, there are a few things you should keep in mind. First of all, you should take medicine with you—especially for stomach problems. You should also find out about common local diseases before you go. When you are in the country, you shouldn't drink untreated water because a lot of diseases are transmitted through the water supply. You also shouldn't eat uncooked food. You should have medical insurance, and you should carry a card with your name and medical history.

Task 1, page 73

A: Where should we go for our vacation?
B: Why don't we go to Mexico?
A: No, we went there last year.
B: You're right. I guess we should go somewhere new.
A: And somewhere interesting.
B: Why don't we go somewhere really different, like Thailand?
A: That's a good idea.

Unit 10 Review Unit

Task 4, page 76

A: Hi, Maria. What are you doing?
B: Nothing much—just watching TV.
A: I'm not doing anything special either. Why don't we go to a movie.
B: No, not tonight. I'm tired.
A: Oh, that's what you always say.
B: Yes, I'm always tired when you call.

Unit 11 Time Out

Tasks 4 and 5, pages 78 and 79

Friend: What did you do on the weekend, Sophie?
Sophie: Well, I got up late on Saturday and went jogging. Then I had breakfast and took my nephew to the park where he flew his model plane. After that, I had lunch, and in the afternoon I went whale watching.
Friend: Whale watching!
Sophie: Yeah, it's great fun.
Friend: Sounds a little dull to me!

Friend: What about you, Teresa? What did you do this weekend?
Teresa: Well, I had a very quiet Saturday. I did some chores in the morning—shopping, laundry, that sort of thing, and in the afternoon I helped my mother with her garden.
Friend: Uh-huh. And what about Sunday?
Teresa: Sunday was rather busy. I went to an antique market in the morning and then had lunch with a friend. After that, I went for a long walk. In the evening, I cooked some Chinese food for a few friends, and then we went to the movies.

Friend: Ken, how was your weekend? What did you do?
Ken: Let me see. Well, I spent most of the weekend taking care of my little brother. It was fun. We did all sorts of things I hadn't done in years.
Friend: Like what?
Ken: Like, um, well, we stayed indoors and played chess Sunday morning because it was raining. We went out for pizza for lunch, and then we went shopping. I bought him a new album for his stamp collection and a

model boat kit. Sunday evening I treated myself to the movies—alone.

Task 1, page 80

A: What did you do over the weekend, Pete?
B: Well, on Saturday, I played golf and then I went shopping. After that, I worked in the yard. On Sunday, I ran a marathon. What about you?
A: Well, on Saturday, I read a book. After that I took a nap. On Sunday, I watched videos and listened to music.

Tasks 2 and 3, page 81

A: I had a wild time yesterday.
B: Really? What happened?
A: Well, first of all I won $5000.
B: You won five grand?
A: I did. You know "*PM Today*" has a production called "*Call and Win*"?
B: "*Call and Win*"? Never heard of it.
A: Well, there's this crazy rock station and every day during their afternoon show they invite people to call it. They take the tenth person to call. If you can identify the songs that they play for you, you'll win $5000.
B: And you did.
A: And I did.
B: So, what happened then?
A: Well, I took Jerry and Kay out to dinner to celebrate. That got rid of a few hundred. Then we went to the theater. That took a few hundred more. After that we went to that new disco on Broadway and danced all night. Then I took a limo home.
B: A limo. And then what?
A: Well, I crashed into bed, and the next morning I discovered I had no money.
B: Oh, no! So what did you do then? Did you call the police?
A: No, I didn't. I went back to bed and slept most of the day.
B: Why didn't you call the police?
A: Well, I figured that we must have spent it all the night before. Either that or I left it in the limo.
B: What a sad story.
A: Oh, I don't know—easy come, easy go!

Task 1, page 83

A: What did you do on your vacation, Sandra?
B: Oh, I had a great time. I did lots of different things.
A: Where did you go?
B: Well, first I went hiking in Nepal, and then I went scuba diving in Australia. Finally, I went skiing in Switzerland.
A: Wow, sounds like you had a great time.

Unit 12 That's Entertainment

Task 2 b, page 87

John: Hi. I have good news and bad news. The good news is that you've reached John and Michael's place. The bad news is we're not in right now. Why don't you make our day and leave a message.

Harvey: This is Harvey. I just wanted to let John know that I've got the tickets for the opera tonight. John, can you call me when you get in?

Kiti: You have reached 555-6978. I'm not in at the moment, but if you leave your name and number I'll call you back.

David: Hi, Kiti, this is David. Sorry you weren't in when I called. I've got some great tickets for a show tonight, so if you're free, give me a call.

Lorraine: This is 555-7394. We're out right now, but we'll call you back as soon as we get in. Just leave your name and number.
Eva: Hi, Lorraine. Eva here. If you're not doing anything tonight, give me a call.

Task 3 b, page 87

Harvey: Hello. Harvey speaking.
John: Hi, Harvey. This is John. I just got in and got your message.
Harvey: Well, I wondered if you want to come with me to the opera tonight. I know how you love Mozart, so I've asked them to hold a second ticket for me—but don't feel that you have to say yes.
John: I'd love to come. Thanks for thinking of me.
Harvey: Great. I'm leaving home about 7:00, so I could come by your place and pick you up around 7:30.
Harvey: I'll be ready.

David: Hello.
Kiti: Hello, David. This is Kiti.
David: Hi, Kiti. I'm so glad you called. Do you like modern dance?
Kiti: Yes, I do. Why?
David: I've got some tickets to a performance by the Sydney Dance Company. They're one of the best modern dance groups in the world, and they're on at the Astra. What do you say?
Kiti: Sounds great.

Eva: Hello, Lorraine?
Lorraine: Speaking.
Eva: It's Eva.
Lorraine: Oh, Eva, hi. Are you free tonight?
Eva: Yes, I am. Why?
Lorraine: How would you like to go to a concert. I won two free tickets to the Tina Turner show at Radio City.
Eva: Oh, I love Tina Turner.
Lorraine: Great. I can meet you in the front bar of the Sheraton Manhattan at 7:00. It's just around the corner from Radio City. Does that sound OK?
Eva: Fine. I'll see you there.

Task 1, page 88

A: Hi, Artie. What are you doing tonight?
B: I'm going to the movies.
A: What are you seeing?
B: *Blade Runner*.
A: But that came out years ago. Haven't you seen it yet?
B: Yes, I've seen it five times before. I love it.

Task 4, page 90.

A: Well, what did you think?
B: It was OK, I guess. But you're asking someone who never really grew up. What did you think?
A: I liked it, although I thought it was about 30 minutes too long.
B: Yes, I know what you mean. There are only so many ways to be attacked by cartoon characters.

A: Wow! What an experience!
B: It was terrifying. When he grabbed her by the throat, the hairs on the back of my neck stood on end.
A: And I really thought he was going to get away with it.
B: So did I. He was almost clever enough, but not quite.
A: I wouldn't mind seeing it again.
B: Yeah, I think I'll take my sister when she comes to visit. She loves thrillers.

A: Oh boy! What an awful movie!
B: I guess we should have known better.
A: Yeah, but I like those two actors. Guess it goes to show that the actors are only as good as the director and the script.
B: Still, parts of it were well filmed.
A: True. Those action scenes in the desert were good. But the rest was pretty boring.

A: Well, I thought that was a really good movie.
B: Yeah! I must admit that I wasn't looking forward to it all that much. In fact, I thought it was going to be pretty boring.
A: But it got good reviews.
B: I know, but usually I don't agree with reviews. I must say, it was a very interesting film.

Task 1, page 91

A: Where do you want to go?
B: Well, it's too cold to stay outdoors.
A: Why don't we go to the movies? There's one at the Showcase that sounds pretty interesting.
B: What is it?
A: *Wild Horses*
B: Oh, with Kurt Russell. He's a very good actor. OK, let's go.

Unit 13 Healthy Living

Task 4, page 94

A: I guess I've played it most of my life. I got my first racquet when I was six. When I was ten, we moved to the country, and there was a court next to our house, so I played every day. I like to play singles, but I sometimes play doubles.

B: My first race was when I was eighteen, but I was so careful I came in last. I've won lots of races since then. My parents don't like me to do it. My mother never comes to the racetrack. When I'm away from the track, I'm very careful, and I've never gotten a speeding ticket.

C: I started playing because I love ball games and because it's the most popular team sport in my country. I've played for my country many times now. I first got onto the national team for the World Cup competition in 1994. That was a great thrill. We didn't get into the finals, but I scored a goal against Germany.

Task 1, page 96

A: Have you ever been hang gliding?
B: No, I haven't. Have you?
A: Yes, I have.
B: What's it like?
A: It's great.
B: Have you ever had an accident?
A: Unfortunately, yes.

Task 3, page 98

A: Excuse me, sir.
B: Yes?
A: We're conducting a survey of people's health habits. Can I ask you some questions?
B: Sure.
A: How often do you play sports?
B: Let's see . . . I guess about three times a year—yeah, I play tennis about once every four months.
A: OK. And what about other kinds of exercise, like walking to work or to the stores.
B: No, I never walk anywhere—I always drive.
A: What about your diet? What sort of food do you eat?
B: Well, regular-type food. I eat burgers and fries about four times a week.

A: What about vegetables?
B: Oh, I guess I eat vegetables about once a week.
A: Do you drink?
B: Oh yeah, I drink a six-pack of beer every day.
A: Drinks . . . everyday. . . . What about smoking?
B: Yep—every day.

A: Tricia?
B: Yes?
A: Why do you always look so healthy?
B: Well, I guess it's because I work hard to keep in shape.
A: You mean you get a lot of exercise?
B: Yeah. I swim or work out in the gym four or five times a week. I walk to work or to the stores every day. I don't smoke.
A: What about alcohol?
B: I have a glass of wine three or four times a week. It's good for you in moderation, you know.
A: What do you eat?
B: I live mainly on fruit and vegetables—I eat them every day. And I eat meat only about once a week.

A: Would you call yourself a healthy person Steve?
Steve: I guess so. I don't drink much—maybe three times a week I'll have a few beers on the way home.
B: Do you smoke?
A: Sometimes, I have a cigar on Saturday night.
B: How often do you exercise?
A: Well, I go to the gym a few times a month.
B: What about walking?
A: I walk to the supermarket about once a week.
B: What about your eating habits?
A: I eat beef or chicken and vegetables four or five times a week—maybe pizza or pasta the other days.

Task 1, page 99

A: How often do you play sports, Pete?
B: Never.
A: And what about exercise? How often do you exercise?
B: Oh, about once or twice a year.
A: Once or twice a year?
B: Yeah. Usually once or twice during the summer I walk down to the park to watch a ball game.

Unit 14 A Day in the Life

Tasks 4 and 5, pages 102 and 103

Carla: What do you like about living in the city, Angie?
Angie: Well, I lived in a country town once, and it was kind of boring. Nothing ever seemed to happen. The city is much bigger and more exciting.
Carla: What do you think, Michael?
Michael: Well, it's true that the city is bigger and more exciting. But it's also noisier, dirtier, and more crowded.
Angie: The other thing I don't like about the country is that it's so much duller than the city—there are no theaters and very few movies. The city is much more interesting.
Michael: Well, I agree that the country is quieter, but that's good. It's also more peaceful, and the people are friendlier.

Task 1, page 104

A: I really envy you, Carla.
B: Oh, yeah? Why's that?

Student Tapescript

A: As a journalist, you have such an interesting lifestyle—much more interesting than mine.
B: Sometimes I wish I had a quieter life.
A: Well, I wish my life were more exciting.

Task 2, Conversation 1, page 105

A: What's the matter?
B: I've just seen my girlfriend with another guy.
A: Are you sure?
B: Of course I'm sure. What should I do?
A: You'll have to ask her what's going on.

Conversation 2, page 105

A: You look upset.
B: I am. Tony and I have money problems.
A: What's wrong?
B: Tony lost his job recently, and we can't live on my income—I just don't earn enough. What do you think I should do?
A: Well, you could write to "Dear Deb."
B: Hey, cut it out—this is serious!
A: I *am* (stress) serious. She gives really good advice.

Conversation 3, page 105

A: What's up?
B: Anita wants to get married.
A: Hey, that's great!
B: No, it isn't. She wants to marry that guy from Toronto—Steve.
A: I guess, you'll have to find another girlfriend.

Conversation 4, page 105

A: Is anything the matter?
B: It's Bill—he wants to borrow my car.
A: So?
B: So last time he borrowed it, he had an accident.
A: Why don't you tell him that it's in the garage for repairs?

Task 1, page 107

A: Tom and Tony have both asked me out. What should I do?
B: Who asked you first?
A: Tony.
B: Then you should go out with Tony, if you've already told him you would.
A: But I like Tom better.
B: Well, you could go out with Tom tomorrow.

Communication Challenge, page 128

Interviewer: Tell us about your work as a journalist, Carla.
Carla: Sure, what do you want to know?
Interviewer: What's the most interesting story you have ever covered?
Carla: The most interesting—I guess the most interesting for me was covering the Olympic Games and meeting people from all over the world. Of course, journalism is not all excitement. The most boring story I ever did was at the beginning of my career, when I had to cover the local flower show.
Interviewer: Why was that so bad?
Carla: I hate gardening and I know nothing about flowers.
Interviewer: I see. What about the most dangerous story?
Carla: I guess the most dangerous story I ever did was the L.A. street riots in 1992.
Interviewer: I guess you've had plenty of funny things happen to you.
Carla: Sure. The funniest interview I ever did was with the comedian Steve Martin. You know, lots of comedians aren't that funny in real life, but Martin's a very funny guy.
Interviewer: What would you say was your most important story?
Carla: My story on the trial of Carlos Mendoza, the drug lord.

Student Tapescript

Interviewer: And the most exciting?
Carla: The most exciting was going to the Academy Awards in Hollywood last year.

Unit 15 Review Unit

Task 2, page 109

(Newscast)

Boulder, Colorado: Rescue workers are searching today for a small plane hijacked by a person pretending to be a flying student. The hijacker ordered the pilot out of the plane at gun point and took off. Police fear that the place crashed in the rugged mountains not far from the city.

New York City: Police are searching for a daring thief who stole several works of art from the Landscape Gallery. The thief got into the gallery through the air conditioning system. Police say he or she was lucky that the system was not turned on at the time.

Cheyenne, Wyoming: A huge explosion at an oil refinery injured six workers today, four of them critically. The cause of the blast is not yet known.

San Francisco: The Third International Fashion Show will take place in the St. Francis Hotel in San Francisco this evening. Designers and models from more than 20 countries have gathered for the show, which is the largest in the world.

Atlanta, Georgia: A severe thunderstorm today caused many road accidents and minor flooding. Residents are trying to clean up the damage. More rain is expected tomorrow.

Task 5, page 110

A: Have you seen the new movie at the Odeon?
B: Yes, I have.
A: Oh, really? When did you see it?
A: Last week. I guess it was Tuesday.

Atlas Workbook 2 Answers

Unit 1 New People

1.A) 🎧

Sam Crane: Julia's son. Teenager. Curly blond hair.
Carlos Rivera: Sam's friend. Student. 18, good-looking, tall, thin. Short, dark hair. From Puerto Rico.
Tanya Malova: sexy cabaret singer, about 28, tall, dark brown eyes, long black hair. From an Eastern European country.
Sergeant Miller: police officer. Short, heavy, middle-aged. Beard. Hair is gray. Intelligent eyes.
Jack Stewart: Julia's neighbor. Elderly man, about 75. White hair. Friendly eyes.

1.B)
Top row: Carlos, Tanya, Julia
Bottom row: Jack, Sergeant Miller, Sam

1.C) Carlos Rivera

2. Koala bear
1. dark
2. police
3. tall
4. twelve
5. what
6. big
7. eyes
8. want
9. elderly

3. A)
1) smart
2) ugly
3) meat
4) toaster
5) peas

3.B)

heavy	dark	ankle	green	thirty
large	fair	eyes	mauve	teenager
tiny	curly	chin	blue	toddler

4.
eighteen/not very/I'm slim/long, dark/brown/twenty-one/average height/heavy/short, *(curly blond)*/green eyes.

5.
1. Pleased to meet you.
2. Yes, we are.
3. From New York.
4. Yes, you are.
5. I'm a student.
6. Yes, they are.
7. Yes, it is.
8. Sally.
9. No, she isn't.

6. (Answers may vary but should make sense in the context.)
What's your last name?
you spell
what's your first name?
What's your address?
(what's) your phone number?
color
Are

7.
Scarface Mick
About 27
He is tall and thin. He has a very large nose. He has red hair and a dark red beard.
He wears old blue jeans and a leather jacket. He has a tattoo of the Mona Lisa on his left arm.

8. Answers will vary.

Atlas Workbook 2: Answers   155

Unit 2 Meet the Family

1.
1. daughter
2. children
3. aunt
4. uncle
5. dad
6. family
7. in-laws
8. brother
9. nephew
10. niece
11. divorced

2.B)
1. Yes, they do.
2. Yes, she does.
3. Yes, they are.
4. No, they don't.
5. Yes, she does.
6. No, she doesn't.
7. Yes, he is.
8. Yes, they do.
9. No, he doesn't.
10. No, he isn't.

2.C)
what do you
Do you
Is it
Are you.
What does your husband
Do you
Does
Does she
Do

3.A) 🎧
Grade: 7th
Age: 13
Family: single parent
Lives with; her dad, one brother, and her grandmother.
Other relatives: a brother, a niece, an uncle, two aunts.

3.B) Example. Alternatives are possible:
Cheryl Wilson is in the 7th grade. She comes from a single-parent family. She lives with her father, her brother Jack, and her grandmother. Her brother Denny is married. He has a daughter. Her mother's parents are not alive. She has an uncle and two aunts. She doesn't have any cousins.

4. Answers will vary.

5. parrot, kitten, turtle, goldfish, rabbit, hamster, dog.

6. Answers will vary.

Unit 3 Old Friends

1.

1. together
2. dancing
3. usually
4. nurse
5. play/movies
6. talk
7. phone
8. close
9. kind/outgoing
10. serious

2. 🎧 walk in the park/watch TV/talk.

3.
BANK: account, checkbook, security guard, investment
HOME: bedroom, sofa, slippers
COFFEE SHOP: pastry, menu, waitress, sandwich

SCHOOL: blackboard, recess, library, examination

4.
1. do you talk
2. cooks
3. cleans
4. Do you have
5. do you do
6. do you play
7. do you play
8. do you go
9. is
10. What does she do?
11. does she come
12. does she look

5. Answers will vary.

6. Answers will vary.

7. Answers will vary.

Unit 4 Interesting People

1.A)

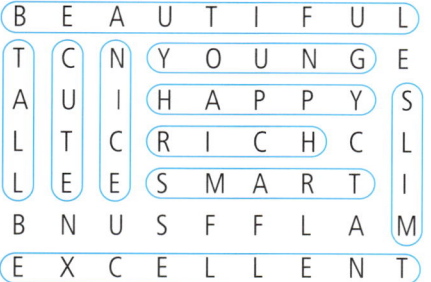

1.B) beautiful/young/rich/cute/happy/slim/excellent

2.A) Alaska: bottom center; Skiing vacation: middle right; Paris: bottom right; Coruna River: top right; Camera safaris: bottom left; Dance: middle left; Beach vacation: top center.

2.B) Answers will vary.

2.C) Answers will vary.

3.A) bellhop, receptionist, security, operator, waitress, waiter, housekeeper, laundry service, room service

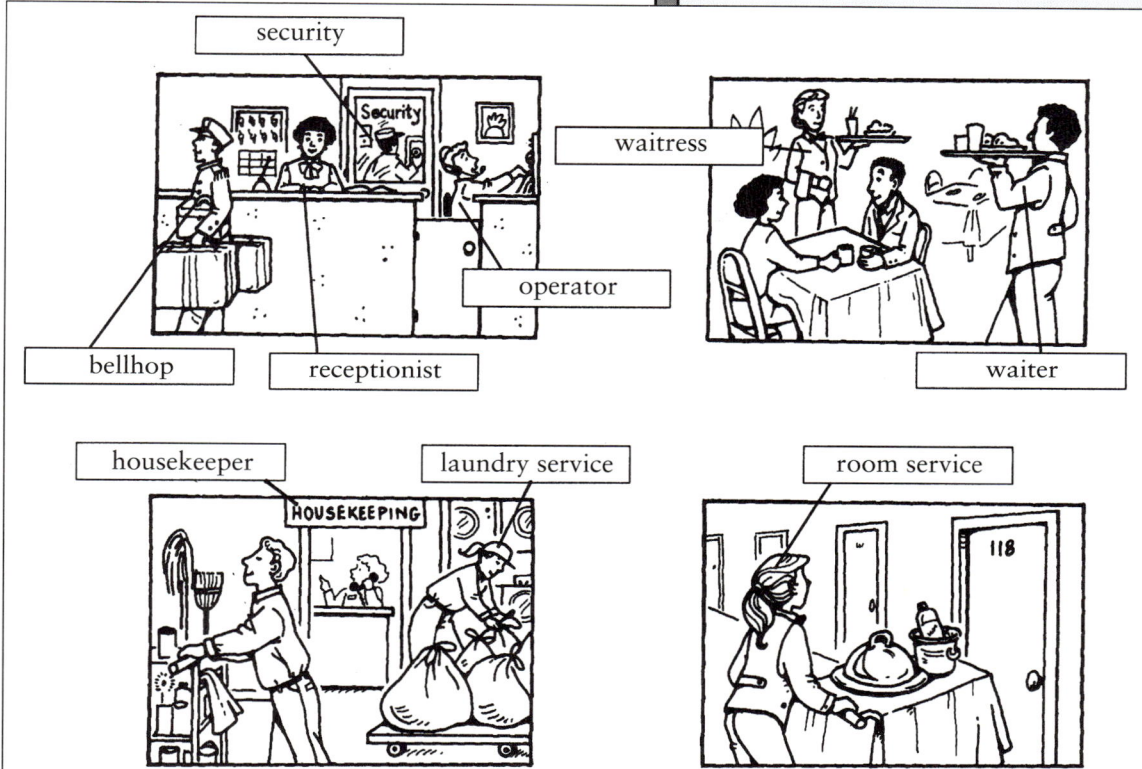

3.B) receptionist/bellhop/security/operator/room service/waiter/laundry service/waitress/housekeeper

3.C)
1. Because there is a wonderful view of the ocean.
2. No, she doesn't.
3. Because she wants a sandwich and a glass of soda.
4. She gives him a generous tip.
5. Because she doesn't like dirty or crumpled clothes.

Atlas Workbook 2: Answers 157

6. She is old.
7. Because she doesn't like large, modern hotels.
8. It's comfortable and she likes the people./
It's a small family hotel.
9. Every year (or year after year).

4.
1. I don't like rap very much.
2. That movie is very interesting.
3. I like modern art a lot.
4. Who is your favorite pop star?
5. Bill has an interesting new job.
6. They have a beautiful new baby.
7. Tony is a very energetic young man.
8. I don't like winter sports very much.
9. Do you like horror movies?
10. What kind of dancing do you like?

5.A) 🎧
NATIONALITY: Canadian
PLACE OF WORK: Wyatt Hotel
JOB: Pastry cook
LIKES: his job
DISLIKES: sweet things/the heat
FAVORITE FOOD: hamburgers

5.B) Answers will vary. Example: Pierre LeMonde comes from Canada. He is a pastry cook and he works in the Wyatt Hotel. He likes his job, but he doesn't like the heat in the kitchen, and he doesn't like sweet things. His favorite food is hamburgers.

6.A) Answers will vary.

6.B) Answers will vary.

Unit 5 Review

1.
is	Buenos Aires
delayed	interesting
bored	name
coffee	show
plane	husband
two	prepare
first	

2. (Suggested answers, accept reasonable alternatives.)
1. Are you from France/Korea/Mexico?
2. Who does he like?
3. What are your names?
4. Who do you live with/Where do you live?
5. Where do you work?
6. Does he have any brothers/sisters?
7. Does she like pop music/rap music/jazz?
8. Are they intelligent?

3. (14, 12, 1, 4, 5, 8, 2, 3, 6, 7, 9, 13, 10, 11)
Hi! What's your name?
Peter.
Where are you from Peter?
Australia.
Do you live in Sydney?
Yes, I do.
And who do you live with?
With my wife, Mary, and our son, Jeff.
Does Mary work?
Yes, she does.
What does she do?
She's an architect.
And you? Are you an architect, too?
No, I'm a student.

4. Answers will vary.

5.
1. receptionist
2. three
3. favorite
4. niece
5. dentist
6. like
7. architect
8. westerns
9. neighbor
10. smart
11. from
12. handsome

Answer to puzzle: Practice hard

Unit 6 A Place to Stay

1.A)
1. chair
2. bath
3. armchair
4. television
5. table
6. shower
7. toilet
8. bed
9. sink
10. closet
11. refrigerator
12. sofa

1.B)
television   chairs
armchairs/chairs   bath
sofa   shower
tables   toilets

Suggestions:
Maybe she can/divorce her husband/call her lawyer
I guess she can/drink some herbal tea/take a swim and plan her revenge.

3. 🎧
From: Jennifer Mitchell
To: Dave Hanson
Message: Can you come over Sunday, about 8PM? Can you bring some CDs?

2.A) below

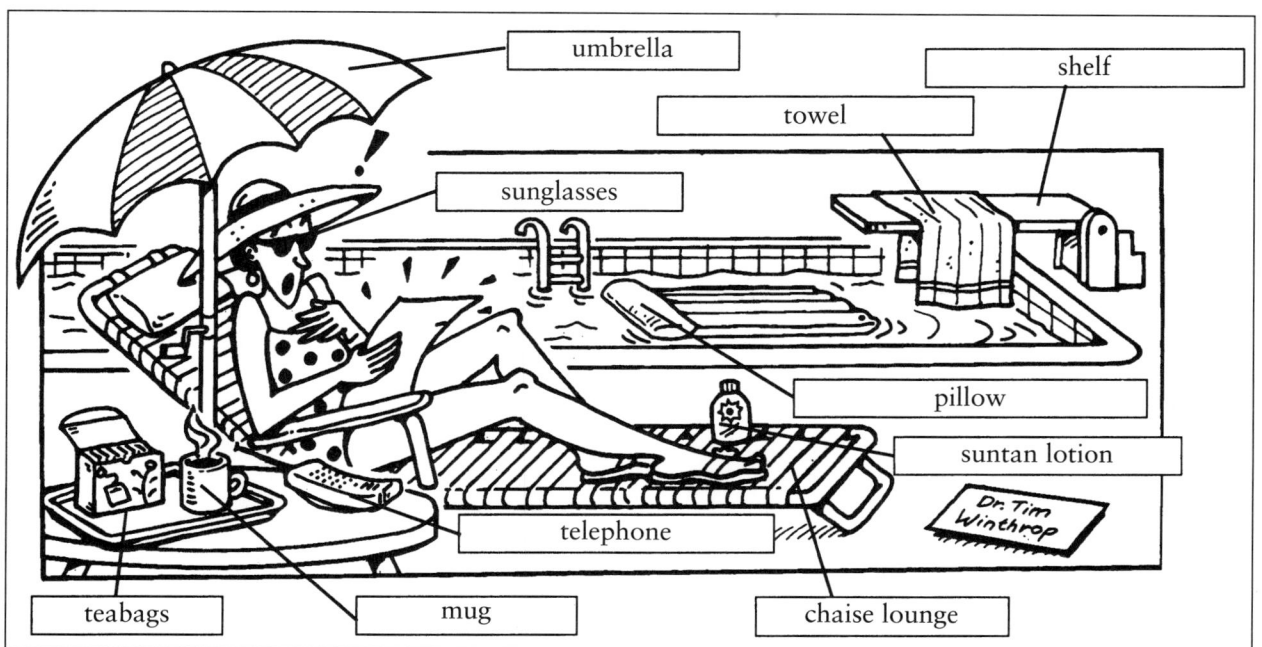

4.

1. Can … can't
2. How many
3. can't
4. How much
5. phoning/calling
6. How many
7. can't
8. can
9. How much
10. like/hate/love

5. Answers will vary.

6. Answers will vary.

Unit 7 In My Neighborhood

1. pizza parlor, post office, video store, bank, disco, bus stop, gym, library, fast food restaurant, museum, swimming pool, supermarket, beach

2.
florist: roses, carnations
stationery store: birthday card, envelopes
hardware store: hammer, nails
bakery: rolls, bagels
beauty salon: pedicure, haircut
butcher: sausages, steak
drugstore: aspirin, bandages
grocery store: can of soup, box of rice

3.A) 🎧
The video store is on corner of 6th avenue and Main Avenue, next to Post Office. The theater is next to the park. The deli is on the corner of 5th and Main. The library is next to the Sports Center.

3.B) Answers will vary.

3.C) Answers will vary.

4.
1. 904–1540
2. 7:15 AM
3. Yes
4. 8 PM
5. Mexican
6. Mornings
7. 387 North Street
8. Shirley Long
9. Corner of 8th and Main

5. Answers will vary. **Examples:** The elderly man with grey hair is sweeping the sidewalk. A man with a beard is painting a bench. A young woman and a boy are picking up trash. A young man with dark hair is sitting under a tree. Two elderly women are talking.

6.
1. next to
2. are
3. going
4. on
5. Where
6. having
7. is
8. buy
9. am
10. playing

7. Answers will vary.

Unit 8 New York, New York

1. Across
1. IS
5. GIFT
7. SIGHTSEEING
9. UGLY
11. ARE
12. CROWDED
13. THERE
14. BUSY
15. SOME
16. ONE
17. DIRTY
18. TOUR

Down
2. SUGGEST
3. POSTCARD
4. QUIET
6. WHY
8. GUIDEBOOK
10. NOISY
11. ANY
13. TOO

2.A) Answers will vary. **Example answer:**
Either Central Park or the Statue of Liberty can be chosen.
PLACE: Statue of Liberty
REASONS: The trip on the ferry is fun for children. It's a famous place.
There's a wonderful view of the city from the top of the statue.
The museum is interesting for the children.

2.B)
The Statue of Liberty is a good place to visit on Sunday. The ferry leaves every half hour in the summer. There's a museum in the statue. It's open on Sundays. I know the children love history so they will like it. It's the Museum of Immigration. You can take the elevator up 10 stories and then you walk to the top—168 steps! It's good exercise and the view from the top is wonderful. Take your camera!

3. (Suggested answers. Accept reasonable alternatives.)
1. How are you (doing)?
2. What
3. Excuse me?/Sorry?
4. do you suggest?
5. Why don't you
6. (for example) it's too cold today.
7. (for example) I don't like museums.
8. idea
9. Is there
10. one

4. 🎧
Restaurants: Try the Greek restaurant on 15th Street.
Transportation: Take a cab./Don't take the subway./ Don't rent a car.
Shopping: Go to the "Child Center."

5.

dirty	filthy	spotless
exciting	thrilling	dull
crowded	packed	empty
expensive	costly	cheap
small	tiny	huge

6. Answers will vary.

7. Answers will vary.

Unit 9 Going Places

1.
1. showers
2. sunny
3. breeze
4. storm
5. hot
6. wet
7. cold
8. cloudy

2.
A) sun hat, Bermuda shorts, insect repellent, sandals
B) fur-lined boots, wool scarf, ski pants, parka
C) waterproof boots, lightweight sweatsuit, guidebook, raincoat

3. Many answers are possible. Some examples:
A) Call the embassy./Explain the mistake./Find an English–speaking person.
B) Try to run away./Panic.
C) Take photos./Call his business contacts./Go sightseeing.

D) "This is not my suitcase."/"I'd like to call the American Embassy."
E) "Can you help me?"/"Where can I buy some warm clothes?"
F) "Why do you have a gun?"/"Why is there a bikini in your case?"

4. 🎧
Money: should: carry most of your money in traveler's checks. shouldn't: carry too much cash.
Going places after dark: should: only visit crowded places.
OR: shouldn't: go places where there aren't many people.
Transportation at night: should: take a taxi shouldn't: ride the subway

5.
1. Visitors to big cities should never walk alone at night in lonely places.
2. It rarely rains in Mexico in winter.
3. Young people usually like pop music.
4. They sometimes take winter vacations.
5. The Jimenez family always go to the beach on vacation.
6. There are often snow storms in the mountains in winter.
7. He never takes an Easter vacation.
8. Travelers to the United States always have to go through customs.
9. Don't go there in the winter because it's often cold.
10. College students in the United States usually go home at Thanksgiving.

6. Answers will vary.

7. Answers will vary.

Unit 10 Review

1. Answers may vary. Suggested answers: p. 44, top left 4, top right 5, bottom right 3, p. 45, top left 6, middle left 8, bottom left 7, top right 2, bottom right 9. Accept other numbering if student can justify it.

2. Answers will vary.
Example questions:
1. Is there a book store near here?
2. Where's the bank?
3. Why don't you take a cab?
4. How many bedrooms does the apartment have?
5. Do you often go to the movies?
6. Are there any restaurants near here?
7. What's the weather like in Italy?
8. Is Peter enjoying the vacation?
9. How much does it cost?
10. What's she doing?
11. Can you speak Russian?
12. How many do you have?

3. Answers will vary.
Example answers:
The weather: cloudy, wet, storm, cool, sunny, rainy
Buildings/places in town: post office, bank, subway, theater, museum, restaurant
Positive ways to describe a place: wonderful, interesting, beautiful, exciting, inviting, welcoming
Negative ways to describe a place: horrible, ugly, awful, terrible, depressing, filthy
Furniture: sofa, table, armchair, bookcase, desk, bed

4.

can	did
Is there	shouldn't
one	storm
How many	should
on	morning
next to	weather
you	usually
Where	sunny
any	How much

5. Answers will vary.

Unit 11 Time Out

1.

S	C	U	B	A	D	I	V	I	N	G	T
K	P	R	R	T	R	N	T	O	O	K	Y
I	H	O	B	B	Y	S	Z	P	T	R	P
I	Q	S	V	O	U	T	D	O	O	R	S
N	S	E	F	O	W	R	C	O	O	K	V
G	X	S	I	K	N	U	M	K	P	T	A
W	R	T	N	Y	D	C	A	R	D	S	C
D	F	G	A	H	K	T	L	P	Z	X	A
I	H	N	L	B	X	I	Z	W	S	W	T
D	A	K	L	P	M	O	D	E	L	R	I
W	D	W	Y	B	X	N	C	N	C	C	O
N	P	N	E	X	T	S	W	T	Q	Q	N

1. did
2. scuba diving
3. skiing
4. hobby
5. outdoors
6. cook
7. roses
8. went
9. cards
10. model
11. book/took
12. had/next/finally
13. vacation
14. instructions

2.
Cooking: oil, saucepan, apron
Playing chess: knight, queen, pawn
Gardening: lawn mower, fertilizer, spade
Reading: comic, novel, biography

3.
D, A, C, F, B, E

4.

1. listened
2. did ... play
3. did ... stay
4. visited
5. work
6. did ... do
7. ran
8. went
9. watch
10. see

5. 🎧
(blanks, in order
down, left column)   (right column)

31%	watching TV 21%
3.5%	playing/hobbies
jobs	sports
reading	friends and relations
eating	
4.5%	

6.
(2, 1, 6, 4, 3, 5, 9, 7, 8)
Last night Fred and Susie went out.
It was their second wedding anniversary.
Susie loves dancing.
So first they went to the Decibel Discotheque on the corner of 43rd Street and 9th Avenue.
Next they went to Danielo's where you can get really great Italian food at reasonable prices.
After that they stopped at Benjie's Ice Cream Parlor for a banana split.
Then it was time to go home.
It was a really warm night, so they walked across the park to their house.

That was when they noticed they didn't have a key. . . .
Ending: Answers will vary.

7. Answers will vary.

8. Answers will vary.

Unit 12 That's Entertainment

1.
1. movie
2. rink
3. theater
4. festival
5. concert
6. television
7. star
8. singer
9. dancing/singing
10. musicals
11. opera
12. restaurant
13. ballets

2. Answers will vary.

3. 🎧
Don/concert/jazz/Arts Center/8:30/7:00

4.A) (Answers will vary in wording. Accept reasonable answers.)
1. Where are you going in the summer?
2. Who are you going with?
3. What are you going to do?
4. When are you going?
5. When are you coming back?

4.B)
1. It was a very exciting movie.
2. I think she is a really good actress.
3. The movie has some pretty funny lines in it too.
4. It is a fairly long movie.
5. But it isn't too long because it's so interesting.

5.A) Answers will vary depending on dictionary used.

5.B) Answers will vary.

5.C)
Positive: tender, sensational
Negative: mysterious, disturbing, weird, frightening, desperate, frightened, anxious, strangely

5.D)
Many alternatives are possible:
1. A student meets a mysterious young man in Greece.
2. They develop a disturbing relationship.
3. The girl can think of no one else and disappears.
4. Deperate family members contact Interpol.
5. Interpol returns the girl to her family, but the family notice disturbing changes.
6. Years later a middle–aged Greek comes to find her.

6. Answers will vary.

7. Answers will vary.

Unit 13 Healthy Living

1.
Mystery word: thermometer
1. doctor
2. unhealthy
3. headache
4. dangerous
5. smoke
6. alcohol
7. meat
8. check-up
9. eaten
10. accident
11. exercise

2. first aid kit: bandage, cotton balls, aspirin, antiseptic ointment, scissors
sewing kit: pin, tape measure, thread, button, scissors

3. 🎧
Exercise: every day, 1 hour weekdays, 2 hours Saturday and Sunday
Food: No junk food, no red meat, for breakfast glass of fresh fruit juice and half a banana

4.
1. 3.7 million.
2. 6.8 million.
3. Small stores and gas stations.
4. No.
5. 12–16.
6. About once a week.

5.
How often do you
How often do you eat
Do you eat/How often do you eat
how often do you eat
Have you ever had
have you ever
How often do you
How often do you get
Have you ever been
On the corner

6.

column 1	column 2
knew	gone
was/were	spoken
had	come
	taken
	driven

7. Answers will vary.

8. Answers will vary.

Unit 14 A Day in the Life

1.A)

U	N	U	S	U	A	L	X	B	A	I
O	S	B	U	N	L	N	K	E	A	N
E	M	I	P	C	F	O	V	X	M	T
D	J	G	F	T	A	I	T	P	Q	E
C	H	E	A	P	S	S	A	E	W	R
E	P	T	L	N	T	Y	G	N	I	E
G	Z	D	E	B	R	L	Z	S	P	S
C	J	P	O	S	A	Q	U	I	E	T
B	U	S	Y	L	N	F	C	V	S	I
E	S	W	O	O	G	A	J	E	H	N
I	T	G	R	W	E	V	L	A	H	G
R	E	L	A	X	I	N	G	B	P	D

ER Than
quieter
busier
slower
stranger
cheaper
bigger
noisier

More Than
more unusual
more interesting
more expensive

1.B)
Answers will vary. Example answers:
A bike is slower than a car.
My street is noisier than yours.
A big pizza is more expensive than a small one.

2.
The country: seeds, tractor, crop, harvest
The town: underpass, smog, escalator, sewers

3. Answers will vary.

4.
1. have to
2. have to
3. could
4. should
5. could
6. have to
7. should
8. could
9. could
10. have to

5. Many answers are possible.
Here is an example:

Dear Cathy,
I'm going to University in England in September, and there are lots of things I'm worried about because I'm sure life in England is very different from life here in San Diego. For example, I suppose I have to look for a room in the town. Perhaps I should share. Will it be very expensive to have a room on my own? ... etc.

6. 🎧
a) tomorrow
b) nervous
c) more exciting
d) airport
e) Continental
f) quarter after eleven

7. Answers will vary.

Unit 15 Review

1. Answers will vary, but should be based on the article and conversation.

2.
1. Has Mr. Inami ever been to Darwin?
2. What can you do in Darwin?/What is there to do in Darwin?
3. Has Mr. Inami's friend (ever) been to Darwin?
4. When did he/they go?
5. Where did he/they stay?
6. How many pools does the Motel have?
7. What's the weather like?
8. How often is the market open?

3.
1. bigger
2. doing
3. noisier
4. meet
5. more expensive
6. played
7. went
8. more popular
9. eating
10. ridden

4.
1. have to
2. could
3. should
4. could
5. have to
6. should

5.
1. down = journalism

1. junk
2. too
3. fun
4. worse
5. country
6. really
7. usually
8. advice
9. shower
10. comedy

166 Atlas Workbook 2: Answers

Atlas Workbook 2 Tapescript

Unit 1 New People

Task 1A, page 1

A: Julia Crane is a mother of four. She is 53, but looks young for her age. She is average height, and has blue eyes and short, blond hair.

B: Sam Crane is Julia's son. He's a teenager, with curly blond hair.

A: Carlos Rivera is Sam's friend. He's a student, 18 years old, good looking, tall and thin with short dark hair. He's from Puerto Rico.

B: Tanya Malova is a sexy cabaret singer of about 28. She is tall and she has dark brown eyes and long black hair. She is from an Eastern European country.

A: Sergeant Miller is a police officer. He is a short, heavyset, middle-aged man with a beard. His hair is grey and he has intelligent eyes.

B: Jack Stewart is Julia's neighbor. He's an elderly man, about 75, with white hair and friendly eyes.

Task 1C, page 1

Miller: Good afternoon, I'm Sergeant Miller from the San Francisco Police Department. I'm looking for a Mr. Sam Crane.

Sam: Oh, I'm Sam Crane. Nice to meet you officer. How can I help you?

Miller: We're looking for a woman. The one in this photograph. Do you know her?

Sam: Er ... yes.

Miller: Is she a friend of yours?

Sam: Yes, and she's here now. Please come in, Officer. This is Tanya.

Tanya: Pleased to meet you, Officer.

Miller: Hello ... Tanya ...? What is your last name?

Tanya: Malova.

Miller: How do you spell that?

Tanya: M-a-l-o-v-a.

Miller: You work at the Silver Moon cabaret. Am I right?

Tanya: Yes, you are, Officer.

Miller: You're not from around here, are you? Where are you from?

Sam: I'll get it. Ah, mom! And Mr. Stewart! Mom, this is Sergeant Miller. Sergeant Miller, this is my mother.

Mrs. Crane: Pleased to meet you, Sergeant. Oh, and this is our neighbor, Mr. Stewart. He lives next door.

Mr. Stewart: Good afternoon, Officer.

Miller: Mrs. Crane, I was just asking your son and Miss Malova some questions....

Unit 2 Meet the Family

Task 3A, page 8

Alma Gonzalez: Come in and sit down.

Cheryl: Thank you.

Alma Gonzalez: O.K., Cheryl. Let's talk. How old are you?

Cheryl: I'm 13.

Alma Gonzalez: Thirteen.

Cheryl: Nearly 14.

Alma Gonzalez: Thirteen, nearly 14. O.K. Tell me about your family, Cheryl.

Cheryl: What do you want to know?
Alma Gonzalez: Well, do you have a large family, or a small family?
Cheryl: Small, I guess.
Alma Gonzalez: Do you live with your mom and dad?
Cheryl: With my dad.
Alma Gonzalez: And your mom?
Cheryl: I don't know where she is. My mom and dad are divorced.
Alma Gonzalez: Divorced. Go on.
Cheryl: I have two brothers.
Alma Gonzalez: Do they live with you and your dad?
Cheryl: Jack does. Denny's married.
Alma Gonzalez: Ah. Do you have any nephews or nieces?
Cheryl: Yeah. One niece. But they don't live near here, so I don't know her.
Alma Gonzalez: That's too bad. Grandparents? Do you have any grandparents?
Cheryl: Yes. My dad's mom. She lives with us.
Alma: And your mom's parents? Are they alive?
Cheryl: No.
Alma: And uncles and aunts? Do you have any uncles and aunts?
Cheryl: I have one uncle. He lives in Cleveland. I don't ever see him. And I have two aunts. One lives in Florida, and one lives near here. That's my Aunt Christie. I don't see her often. She doesn't get along with my dad.
Alma: Do you have any cousins?
Cheryl: No, I don't.

Unit 3 Old Friends

Task 2, page 11

Friend: Do you ever get lonely, Mr. Baker?
Mr. Baker: Not me.
Friend: But you live alone, don't you?
Mr. Baker: Yes, I do.
Friend: Do you have many visitors?
Mr. Baker: Not many.
Friend: Do your children visit you?
Mr. Baker: My daughter does sometimes, but she lives a long way away, you know, so she doesn't come often.
Friend: But you don't get lonely?
Mr. Baker: No, no.
Friend: So you have lots of friends, do you?
Mr. Baker: Not a lot. . . . I have one. My best friend. He's always with me.
Friend: What do you do together?
Mr. Baker: Oh, almost everything. We go for walks in the park. We watch TV together. He's good company, and he's smart, you know. We talk for hours . . . well, I talk and he listens to me. Here he comes. Good boy!

Unit 4 Interesting People

Task 5A, page 19

Interviewer: I'm in the Wyatt Hotel and I'm talking to Pierre LeMonde. Hi, Pierre.
Pierre: Hi.
Interviewer: Now, you're French, Pierre, aren't you?
Pierre: No! I speak French, but I come from Canada.
Interviewer: Oh, I see. What's your job here at the hotel?
Pierre: I'm the pastry cook.
Interviewer: Oh! That's interesting. And do you like your job?
Pierre: Sure I do—most of the time.
Interviewer: What don't you like about your work here?
Pierre: Well, it's very hot in the kitchen. I don't

like the heat at all! But anyway, I love the work I do.
Interviewer: Mmmm! So you're the pastry cook. That means you make all these delicious-looking cakes and pies and things, I suppose.
Pierre: That's right.
Interviewer: So I guess you like cakes a lot?
Pierre: Well, it's very strange, but I don't like sweet things at all, as a matter of fact. Being a pastry cook is just the work I do!
Interviewer: So, what's your favorite food?
Pierre: Well, actually . . . I just love hamburgers!

Unit 6 A Place to Stay

Task 3, page 27

Phil: Philip Hollingdale speaking. Can I help you?
Jennifer: Can I speak to Dave Hanson, please?
Phil: I'm sorry, but Dave isn't here right now. Can I take a message?
Jennifer: Oh . . . yes . . . thanks! Can you tell him Jennifer Mitchell called?
Phil: Is that Jennifer with a "J"?
Jennifer: Yes, and two "n"s and Mitchell is M-i-t-c-h-e-l-l.
Phil: O.K. Any message?
Jennifer: Yes, can he come over Sunday?
Phil: Can . . . he . . . come . . . over . . . Sunday. Got it! What time Sunday?
Jennifer: About 8 o'clock.
Phil: AM or PM?
Jennifer: Er...PM. And can he bring some CDs?
Phil: O.K. I'll make sure he gets the message.

Unit 7 In My Neighborhood

Task 3A, page 30

A: Who's asking the questions first?
B: You.
A: How many questions can I ask?
B: Twelve. You have to guess the location of the places in 12 questions.
A: O.K. I'm looking for the video store, the deli, the library, and the …
B: The theater.
A: Right. Let's start. I'm looking for the theater. Is it on Fifth Avenue?
B: No, it isn't.
A: Is it on Main Avenue?
B: No, it isn't.
A: Is it on South Street?
B: Yes, it is.
A: Is it next to the park?
B: Yes, it is.
A: How many questions is that?
B: Four. Eight to go.
A: I'm looking for the deli. Is it on Fifth Avenue?
B: Yes, it is!
A: Is it next to the church?
B: No, it isn't.
A: Is it on the corner of Fifth and Main?
B: Yes, it is.
A: Right . . . I'm looking for the library. Is the library next to the hotel?
B: Next to the hotel? Emmmm, no, it isn't.
A: The library isn't next to the hotel. Is it next to the Sports Center?

B: Yes, it is! Three questions left.
A: The video store. Is it on 5th Avenue?
B: No, it isn't.
A: Is it on 6th avenue?
B: Yes, it is.
A: Is it on the corner of 6th and South?
B: No, it isn't!
A: Where is it?
B: It's next to the post office, on the corner of Main Avenue.
A: Oh.

Unit 8 New York, New York

Task 4, page 37

Sandy: How long are you staying in New York, Mrs. Ghali?
Mrs. Ghali: We only have two days, Sandy.
Sandy: And what do you plan to do?
Mrs. Ghali: Well . . . perhaps you could give us some advice.
Sandy: Emm, well, the museums are wonderful . . .
Mrs. Ghali: Yes, but we don't want to visit museums, or art galleries this trip. We'd like to get a general idea of the city, and then maybe on our next trip. . . .
Sandy: O.K. Then what you need is a city tour. There are two or three good ones. There's a morning tour that leaves from Eighth Avenue at 53rd Street . . . No, wait a minute! The helicopter tour! Of course! There's a helicopter tour. It lasts about 40 minutes and they take you all over . . . to the Statue of Liberty, over Central Park, over Wall Street . . . You get wonderful views of the city.
Mrs. Ghali: Yes, that sounds very exciting, Sandy. Now, we are thinking of renting a car. . . .
Sandy: No, no! Don't do that! There isn't any parking! And the traffic is horrible! And don't go on the subway either. It's quick, but its crowded and of course you won't see the city! No, the only way to travel in New York is by cab. You can just sit back and relax and let the cab driver worry about the traffic.
Mrs. Ghali: Oh yes, you're right! Now, my husband wants to know where we should eat. Are there any good French restaurants in town?
Sandy: Of course. There are lots! But, why don't you try the wonderful Greek restaurant on 15th Street? It's very famous. I can't remember its name, but the cab driver will know. It's next to the library. . . . It's very expensive, but it's very good.
Mrs. Ghali: Oh! And I'd like to go shopping and buy some gifts for my kids. Where do you suggest?
Sandy: Well, there's only one place to go and that's the Child Center on Fifth Avenue. They have a wonderful selection of all the best toys. I'm sure you'll find something there.
Mrs. Ghali: Well, thank you Sandy. You've been very helpful.
Sandy: You're welcome.

Unit 9 Going Places

Task 4, page 41

Travel Agent: Well, here are your tickets. Oh, just a few words of advice.
Rosemary: Yes?
Travel Agent: You shouldn't carry too much cash with you.
Rosemary: Oh?
Travel Agent: No, you should carry most of

your money in traveler's checks.
Rosemary: Travelers checks . . . right.
Travel Agent: And after dark, you shouldn't go places where there aren't many people. That could be dangerous.
Rosemary: You mean like Central Park?
Travel Agent: That's right. You should only visit crowded places at night.
Rosemary: Crowded places . . . got it.
Travel Agent: And be careful about riding the subway after 11:00 at night. You shouldn't do it.
Rosemary: But . . .
Travel Agent: No! The subway at night can be dangerous. You should take a taxi when it's late.
Rosemary: Taxi when it's late . . . right.
Travel Agent: These are just normal precautions, you know. You should be careful in any big city. I think that's all. Have a good trip!
Rosemary: Thanks . . . I will!

Unit 11 Time Out

Task 5, page 51

Interviewer: Dr. Emily Quinn, thank you for being with us tonight on Spotlight News. Tell us about this new survey on how kids spend their days.
Quinn: Well, the survey shows us that kids in the United States have a lot of free time, and most of that time is unsupervised. That is to say their mothers and fathers are out of the home, working, and they do not know what their children are doing. For over five hours a day, our young people have nothing particular to do—and this is a matter for concern.
Interviewer: I see. Can you give us some details of the study?
Quinn: Yes. The study shows that 37 percent of the adolescents' day is spent being productive. That is to say that children are at school 31 percent of their day. Then they spend 3.5 percent of the day studying—doing their homework, for example. The survey shows that 1.5 percent of the time is spent on jobs, and they only spend 1 percent of their time reading. The next category is maintaining themselves—21 percent of the day is spent on this. Eating takes up 10 percent. Personal care takes up 6.5 percent.
Interviewer: Personal care?
Quinn: Yes, you know, washing, brushing your teeth, combing your hair … that kind of thing. Then 4.5 percent is spent doing jobs in the house and running errands.
Interviewer: And the rest of the time is free time?
Quinn: Yes. That's right. We see that 42 percent of the day is for free time, for doing what they want to do, and usually their parents are not around.
Interviewer: Forty-two percent—that's almost half the day!
Quinn: That's right.
Interviewer: And what DO they do in this spare time?
Quinn: Well, they spend 21 percent of it watching TV. Nine percent is spent on playing, hobbies, and art activities. Sports and outdoor activities account for 7 percent of the time. They spend 2.5 percent going to church, and another 2.5 percent on visiting friends or relatives.
Interviewer: What are the conclusions of the study?
Quinn: That we, as a society, do not provide enough structured activities in the afternoons for our young people. We need to think seriously about providing more community programs and after-school activities.
Interviewer: Thank you, Dr. Quinn.

Unit 12 That's Entertainment

Task 3, page 55

Don: Hi, Tricia.
Tricia: Oh hello, Don.
Don: What are you doing this evening?
Tricia: Well, I don't know. Nothing special, I guess!
Don: I have two tickets for the Gold Gang concert. What about coming with me?
Tricia: Well. . . .
Don: You like jazz, don't you?
Tricia: Yes. Yes, I do. O.K. That's great! I'd love to go to the concert with you. Where is the concert?
Don: At the Arts Center.
Tricia: Fine.
Don: It's at 8:30. I'll pick you up at 7:00.
Tricia: O.K. I'll be ready.
Don: See you later, then.
Tricia: Right . . . at seven. Thanks, Don.

Unit 13 Healthy Living

Task 3, Page 59

Interviewer: Here we are at the White Bridge Bungee Jumping Park, and we are talking to Angela Frink, who is 90 years old today. Hello, Mrs. Frink. Happy birthday. What are you doing here?
Frink: I'm going to bungee jump.
Interviewer: Have you ever done it before?
Frink: No, I haven't. I have wanted to for the last 10 years, but today is my first jump.
Interviewer: Well, bungee jumping is . . . er . . . dangerous. Aren't you worried?
Frink: Worried? Oh no! I'm in very good physical condition!
Interviewer: Yes, you look healthy. How do you keep in such good shape?
Frink: Exercise . . . a lot of exercise.
Interviewer: How often do you exercise?
Frink: Every day. That's the trick. One hour a day during the week and two hours on Saturdays and Sundays.
Interviewer: Have you ever smoked?
Frink: No, I haven't. And I've never eaten junk food, and I've never eaten red meat. But the secret is breakfast. I always have one glass of fresh fruit juice and half a banana. Every morning! You should try it! Well, it's time to jump.
Interviewer: Good luck, Mrs. Frink! We're up here on the bridge. It's a hundred meters above the ground. Now Mrs. Frink is tying the cords around her ankles. Her children Henry, 70, and Charles, 68, are waiting anxiously down below. She's ready to jump! She's off! She's falling! . . Oh . . . down she goes . . . She's done it! Over to my colleague, Dan Lather, on the ground.
Lather: Thank you, Bob. Mrs. Frink! Mrs. Frink, how do you feel?
Frink: I've never felt better! Wonderful experience!
Lather: Are you going to jump again today?
Frink: Well, not now, no.

Unit 14 A Day in the Life

Task 6, page 66

Hilton: Hello.
Anna: Hi, Hilton?
Hilton: Oh hi, Anna. What's the matter? You sound upset.
Anna: I'm calling all my friends to say goodbye. I'm going to England tomorrow.
Hilton: But that sounds great!

Anna: Well, I know . . . but I'm nervous!
Hilton: You shouldn't be nervous! I wish I were going! I wish my life were more exciting!
Anna: Hilton, could you come to the airport?
Hilton: Nothing easier! Sure, I will. What time are you leaving?
Anna: At a quarter after eleven. And I'm flying Continental.
Hilton: I'll be there.
Anna: Good. Look . . . I have to go. I still have to pack. See you tomorrow.
Hilton: And good luck with the packing!
Anna: Thanks. Good-bye.